SPECIAL CATALOGUING

SPECIAL CATALOGUING

with particular reference to

MUSIC, FILMS, MAPS, SERIALS and

the MULTI-MEDIA COMPUTERISED CATALOGUE

by

John Leonard *Horner*

BA FLA ALAA

LINNET BOOKS & CLIVE BINGLEY

Library of Congress Cataloging in Publication Data

Horner, John Leonard, 1926–
Special cataloging.

Bibliography: p.
1. Cataloging of special collections in libraries. I. Title.
Z693.H67 025.3'4 73-8787
ISBN 0-208-01189-7

FIRST PUBLISHED 1973 BY CLIVE BINGLEY LTD
THIS EDITION SIMULTANEOUSLY PUBLISHED IN THE USA BY
LINNET BOOKS, AN IMPRINT OF SHOE STRING PRESS INC,
995 SHERMAN AVENUE, HAMDEN, CONNECTICUT 06514
PRINTED IN GREAT BRITAIN

Contents

List of illustrations

Figure

Abbreviations

AA 1908	LIBRARY ASSOCIATION *Cataloguing rules . . .* 1908
AACR	ANGLO-AMERICAN CATALOGUING RULES 1967
ALA 1941	AMERICAN LIBRARY ASSOCIATION *ALA catalog rules, preliminary American edition* 1941
ALA 1949	AMERICAN LIBRARY ASSOCIATION *ALA cataloging rules for author and title entries,* second edition 1949
ASLIB	ASLIB *Film cataloguing rules*
BCM	*British catalogue of music*
BFI	British Film Institute
BM	BRITISH MUSEUM *Rules for compiling the catalogue of printed books, maps and music*
BNB	*British national bibliography*
BNFC	*British national film catalogue*
BTI	*British technology index*
CCR	LUBETZKY, Seymour *Code of cataloging rules . . .* 1960
CUTTER	CUTTER, C A *Rules for a dictionary catalog,* fourth edition 1904
DC	*Decimal classification* (Dewey)
HMSO	Her Majesty's Stationery Office
IAML	International Association of Music Libraries
ICCP	INTERNATIONAL CONFERENCE ON CATALOGUING PRINCIPLES, *Paris,* 1961
LC	Library of Congress
LCRDC	LIBRARY OF CONGRESS *Rules for descriptive cataloging,* 1949
MLA	Music Library Association
MARC	MAchine Readable Cataloguing
MASS	MARC-based Automated Serials System
MEDLARS	MEDical Literature Analysis and Retrieval System
MESH	MEdical Subject Headings
NBM	Non-Book Materials
NLL	National Lending Library for Science and Technology (England)
PI	The PRUSSIAN instructions
PRECIS	PREserved Context Indexing System
UDC	Universal Decimal Classification . . .
UNESCO	UNESCO *International rules for the cataloguing of educational scientific and cultural films and filmstrips . . .*

Acknowledgements

Appreciation is expressed to the following publishers for their permission to reproduce illustrations from their works:

International Association of Music Libraries—Music code; Unesco—Film code; British Film Institute—Film code; Aslib—Film code; Library Association—*Anglo-American cataloguing rules* and the Cutter Code; Special Libraries Association—Boggs' *Classification and cataloging of maps and atlases;* National Council for Educational Technology—Gilbert's *Non-book materials*.

Thanks are due to Miss Robin South of the Western Australian Institute of Technology Library for her special efforts in obtaining so many loan or facsimile copies of codes and articles used in writing this book, and to Mrs Rita Evans for her meticulous typing of the text.

Introduction

IN STATING the purpose of this book, it may be useful to start with what it specifically is not. It is not intended to be comprehensive and detailed in respect of all special materials. It is not intended to be a working manual: in effect a set of codes to which cataloguers can refer in their day-to-day work. Rather it sets out to examine academically the problems of special materials as a group in cataloguing and indexing, and to use certain materials as concentration points to point up the application and effects of problems as they affect these selected materials. The relevant materials selected for detailed treatment embrace, we feel, most of the problems likely to be encountered in special cataloguing. However, if a need is manifested, any future edition of this book which is called for can be extended to include other materials.

We feel, meanwhile, that many materials can be covered by general or representative principles and rules. The content of this book can be viewed as of two types. Firstly, the first and last chapters deal with special materials in general, the former dealing with basic cataloguing principles and problems, and the latter with the ultimate application of such principles as manifested by the concept of the multi-media catalogue and as aided by the computer. Secondly, in between come chapters dealing with individual categories of materials in detail. Each category receives two types of treatment. First, the problems of both approaches and description are examined as they apply to the particular medium. Second, the solutions put forward by representative codes are summarised and commented upon. The latter aspect may possibly be criticised as being academic in the 'possibly interesting but useless' sense. However, we suggest that in some respects the wheel is repeatedly re-invented by some librarians who approach a problem pragmatically and rush into print along the lines of 'how I done it good in my library', but without reference to what has already been put forward in basic codes and by past workers with similar problems. For this reason, some authors may feel that their contributions to various topics have been neglected. However, we have tried to select, and to detail, contributions in the literature which are original in the obvious sense of having been published first, or which are practically representative of how problems are being tackled in a creative or thought-provoking manner. A survey of the literature relating to special materials is embarrassing in the number of contributions, but —we cannot help saying—in many respects the literature is repetitious and tedious. At the risk of 'acting God', we have tried to select, cite, or examine in detail, contributions which may prove of value to both lecturers and students to whom special cataloguing is but part of a basic course in retrieval processes. We hope that practitioners may derive some value, even if indirectly, from the flood of published information which we have selected from, and distilled, in producing this book. So, although this book is not intended as a working manual, it may provide some guidelines which practitioners may find useful— if only in contradiction of the suggestions made. In support of this hope, it may be mentioned that the basic manual *Cataloguing*, published in 1970, although written as a textbook for students and lecturers, seems to have proved useful for answering some day-to-day enquiries and in inservice training in practical situations.

Bibliographic references are indicated by quoting the principal author of a book or article in capitals, in parentheses, in the text. Full bibliographic citations may be found, by those who are interested, by referring to the Bibliography at the end of the book. In addition, a list of relevant documents is given in abbreviated form at the end of each chapter.

CHAPTER ONE

Special cataloguing: problems and criteria

ANY TYPE of material other than ' normal ' full-size mainly verbal monographic works could conceivably be regarded as ' special ' depending on local circumstances. One example, of many, is that a report from a government department might receive ' normal ' cataloguing in the average public library yet be given ' special ' treatment in a research library or in a special department of, say, a tertiary education library.

One very important—but not the only—category of ' special ' material is that of audio-visual documents. Currently, there seems to be a ' band-wagon ' craze for such materials, often in an educational context. While not wholly subscribing to the current fashion, we admit that such materials usually do call for ' special ' treatment, even if only in description detail. The categories in this area are quite ably enumerated in GILBERT (see Bibliography), and the reader may wish at this stage to scan GILBERT'S listing as reproduced on pages 291-293 of this work.

It is suggested here that further categories could be included as possibly needing ' special ' cataloguing, since their requirements may go beyond those of ' normal ' monographic materials, as mentioned above. The types of material in the following list are taken from the present author's general work *Cataloguing*. This list, and that summarising problems which may arise in cataloguing special materials, which follows it, are the only instances in which the earlier work is drawn upon consciously to any substantial extent, and it is hoped that the two works may prove complementary.

POSSIBLE FORMS OF MATERIALS

(From Horner's *Cataloguing*, p 206 ff)

1. Manuscripts
2. Printed letterpress
   - (i) Pamphlets
   - (ii) Government publications
   - (iii) Research reports
   - (iv) Incunabula
   - (v) Sets (multiple copies)
   - (vi) Serials
3. Graphic materials
   - (i) Atlases, maps
   - (ii) Art works
   - (iii) Other fugitive material
4. Music scores
5. Reprographic reproductions
6. Local history
7. Audio-visual materials
   - (i) Moving films
   - (ii) Film strips
   - (iii) Slides
   - (iv) Opaque illustrations
   - (v) Sound recordings
     - (a) Music
     - (b) Spoken
     - (c) Sound effects

Also: Subject collections, *eg* Medicine

And: Types of libraries

SPECIAL CATALOGUING: POSSIBLE PROBLEMS

1. Machinery may be needed to use the documents.

2. The materials may be more fragile, rare and expensive than normal book-form materials.

3. Special subject knowledge may be needed to catalogue the materials thoroughly and quickly.

4. Special knowledge and experience of the physical form may be needed.

5. Special cataloguing tools, *eg* codes and thesauri, may be needed.

6. Hence: it may be necessary to compile one's own aids because of the rarity of the type of material.

7. Information may be harder to obtain from the documents to be catalogued than with normal monographic materials, *eg* lack of title page or adequate title-page substitute.

8. The information obtained from one source in the document may conflict with that obtained from another source in the document.

9. External sources of information, *eg* bibliographies, may have to be used, in which case there may be difficulty in thoroughly identifying documents in hand with corresponding entries in the external sources.

10. Scope of externally compiled indexes and abstracts may not correspond economically with the stock; therefore, extra internally executed indexing and abstracting may be necessary.

11. The type of material may not be covered by central cataloguing and similar services.

12. It may be harder to reach cataloguing decisions than is the case with normal monographic materials, *eg* intellectual responsibility may be more diffuse and it may be harder to find an author equivalent.

13. More variable degrees of limited cataloguing may be necessary.

14. The bibliographic unit may be less easily defined, ranging from mere collocation to the incidence of separately issued excerpts and the need for more analysis of individual physical units.

15. A single document may include a mixture of different forms of material, *eg* audio-visual and printed.

16. If the collection is part of a larger system, there may be a conflict between the case for separate catalogues for the various materials and that for incorporating entries for them into the library's general catalogue.

17. Some materials are confidential, *eg* some research data in private industry. This can militate against the whole concept of library science, which implies mutual sharing of information and materials.

18. In some forms of material, forgery or inadvertent misinterpretation of the information content is more likely to be encountered than with printed book form materials.

19. Some materials are more international and so a knowledge of foreign languages may be more necessary than in dealing with more routine forms of material.

Overlapping the problem of what is special in the physical sense is that of the types of problem encountered in special cataloguing. As happens with many 'normal' materials, we suggest that in general there are six main areas, although the manifestation of each problem may well vary with special as compared with normal materials. These are: (a) Heading, usually author/title; (b) Added entries of an author/title type; (c) Uniform title, usually as a sub-head under (a) or (b) but sometimes as a manifestation of either; (d) Description; (e) Location, physically, irrespective of location or approaches in a catalogue or index; and (f) Subject/Form approach or approaches.

Most of these problems, particularly (a), (b) and (c), may seem to be answered by the *Anglo-American cataloguing rules 1967* (AACR), whether one uses the North American or British text. There is only occasional difference between the two texts in relation to special materials, since the content of each is substantially derived from the *Library of Congress rules for descriptive cataloging* of 1949 (LCRDC). This fact may be an advantage in that it can help to ensure continuity with existing practices, especially for those many libraries which follow LC in their cataloguing of the more conventional modern media such as motion pictures and phonorecords, to use the LC terms. However, it may be a disadvantage, because adherence to rules evolved (and we use the term advisedly) over twenty years ago may sidestep advances derived from more recent thought on the needs and convenience of users. Whether or not this is the case, there seems to have been a steady volume of criticism of, and comment on, AACR since it was issued. AACR maintains that it is intended to cater for the integration of entries for all types of medium into one catalogue, in effect the realisation of the multi-media catalogue; which is the current, and we suggest justifiable, trend in cataloguing special materials. Comment on AACR's treatment of selected special materials is incorporated into the various sections dealing with those materials, and the reader may wish to make up his own mind, possibly taking into account the comment which we offer, in conjunction with the summaries of our interpretations of the code's emergent attitude towards these materials. However, we feel we are justified in making some comment on various aspects of AACR's decisions on special materials in general.

Two types of comment may be crystallised at the outset: (a) the type of catalogue, and use made of it, envisaged by AACR; and (b) approaches not intended to be covered by AACR, namely subject and form, whether in verbal or coded (classification scheme notation) form.

(a) will be commented upon at some length as the occasion arises throughout this book, but we feel that no apology is needed for introducing it at this point. Concerning (b), it may be pleaded that we cannot criticise AACR for not doing what it did not set out to do.

However, whatever AACR does, the fact remains that the subject and physical form approaches obviously must be catered for, that in some instances they are far more relevant to information retrieval than authors and titles, and that there is sometimes an inextricable connection between author and subject/form approaches.

As to (a), as we suggest throughout this book, very roughly two types of catalogue are likely to be needed. The first is the bibliographic-oriented catalogue, whose great contribution is minute bibliographic description of documents, it being more or less assumed that the relevant work is known of, and that the seeker is looking for further detail on the work itself to help identify it, or that the seeker is trying to identify a particular edition or rendering of a work. The second type of catalogue is what we dub the retrieval-oriented catalogue. Usually, the user is aware of a subject, however specific or generic, and possibly an author or author-equivalent, and he is seeking individual works which will support his needs in the area contemplated, and very likely in a variety of physical forms.

AACR, we suggest, is definitely bibliographic-oriented. It aims at collocation according to intellectual responsibility, and it attempts to give minute physical description for documents under a collocating author-type heading. As a further means towards bibliographic collocation, it often uses a uniform title, interposed between the primary filing heading, usually author-type, and the title of a specific document as given in the document itself. This latter can be of value for retrieval-oriented use, say, in collocating a textual representation of a play by Shakespeare and a disc recording of the same play, although as it happens its basic purpose appears to be the collocation of entries of various textual versions of such a play. To this extent, then, the objects of the two types of catalogue, as we have them in mind, overlap. On the other hand, a film of a Shakespeare play would be entered under title, while a textual version goes under the author. This does not matter too much as long as added entries are given, under author and title respectively. However, there may be occasions when a check list has to be prepared, in a library, for a particular purpose, which has only one entry for each work. In such a case, there is obviously a need for reconciling the types of entry used for various media. Yet AACR purports to make possible the integration of entries for all forms of material. Perhaps we need to introduce for films a distinction between those which stand on their own, as films, and those which rely, in their value to potential users, on a basic author.

A similar principle applies in sound recordings, which AACR would usually enter under author. A form of cross classification, and contradiction in solution, happens in the case of a sound recording taken from the sound track of a film. A retrieval-oriented catalogue would integrate all representations of a certain conception, whether it were *Lawrence of Arabia,* known basically as a film, or Shakespeare's *King Lear,* known basically as a play. Such a conception of a catalogue cuts across principles of intellectual responsibility, we admit, but it would attempt to cater for immediate demand. A similar type of problem emerges in the average motion picture as compared with the filmstrip. It may well be that many motion pictures are best entered under titles. However, some, at least, filmstrips may be best entered under author, quite often a lecturer or other teacher who worked out the content of the filmstrip, who wrote projected, or accompanying, text whether in printed or in sound-recorded form, or generally in effect 'directed' the production. Incidentally, viewed this way, one can sympathise with those who wish to enter motion pictures under director (GELLER, p 250).

The above confirms that there may well be confusion between the bibliographic-oriented catalogue and the retrieval-oriented catalogue. Also, it may confirm that there may be confusion as to what constitutes the retrieval-oriented catalogue, at least from the author/title point of view.

In attempting to crystallise the practical difference between our conception of the two types of catalogue one can say that the bibliographic catalogue concentrates on minute detail, but not necessarily with a great variety of entries, while the retrieval-oriented catalogue concentrates on a great variety of entries, or approaches, whether author, title, subject, or form, but with a minimum of bibliographic data at each entry. The bibliographic-oriented catalogue would include as much information as may be needed for most users, and it should include in this information whatever may be needed for the basis of the variety of approaches needed in a retrieval-oriented catalogue. One might imagine that the bibliographic-oriented catalogue might include the data for a document stored at a national bibliographic centre, which may be drawn upon as required by local libraries and resource centres depending on the needs of their users. We shall take up this aspect in the last chapter of this work, on the multi-media catalogue and the computer.

At this point, we wish to emphasise that, in our opinion, most libraries are likely to need the multiple-approach short-entry type of catalogue. Further, we suggest that few libraries are likely to need the type of catalogue which caters for the minutest type of detail. The average research library is not likely to need the ultimate in bibliographic data; we try to substantiate this throughout the present work. The situation is pinpointed in the literature by comparisons between the type of library apparently catered for by AACR and, say, the needs of the average school library. The latter type is usually cited, but we should like to add that the average local public library has a similar need which is becoming more and more apparent as public libraries progress beyond just gramophone record collections to a variety of media.

In general, catalogues have three types of approach: the main entry, the added entry, and the reference. As we state elsewhere, we maintain that the concept of the main entry still has relevance, even in a unit entry catalogue. It is usually the final identifying factor for shelving or filing of documents 'within' a class number, although an exception is when, say, films or records are shelved by accession or other arbitrary unique numbers. It is usually the sole entry for documents in selective reading lists, check lists and many union catalogues. And it is the ultimate choice of entry when a strict limited cataloguing policy dictates only one author-type entry per document. As we know, references are traditionally used to redirect a catalogue user from a sought but unused entry point into a catalogue to a used heading. An important precedent has recently been set in a catalogue which abbreviates entries to such an extent that references can be dispensed with and turned into actual entries. The principle used in this, the Bath University 'mini-catalogue', is summed up succinctly (like the catalogue itself) as 'minimal data, maximal access' (BRYANT, P, p 3). Each entry has the following data: surname and initials for personal authors; short title; date; class number; book number (similar in structure to BNB numbers, *eg* 68-01234). Up to four author entries, and two title entries, are catered for; a second title may be, say, a series or 'popular' title. An example of the use of actual entries for various forms of an author's name is that works by Sidney Webb are entered as both WEBB, S and PASSFIELD (BRYANT, P, p 11). Similarly compound names are entered under both components, and prefixed names under the first and final components. A somewhat similar practice is applied to some corporate names, *eg* actual entries appear under both U. N. ECONOMIC COMMISSION FOR EUROPE and ECONOMIC COMMISSION FOR EUROPE (BRYANT, P, p 13). This catalogue deserves more attention in itself than it can receive here, but it is cited as an example of a new look at cataloguing to support our thesis of many short entries rather than few long ones, especially as this need applies to special materials.

The Bath mini-catalogue achieves one further objective which can apply particularly to special materials, in that it could give headings according to AACR as well as according to what are estimated to be local needs. Therefore, such a catalogue can be MARC-compatible, a quality which has obvious advantages if a library is to have access to any future machine-readable data for special materials, compiled at such centres as BNB or LC.

One can see readily how the Bath mini-catalogue principle could be used in special cataloguing, *eg* a film could be entered under, say, title, director, producer, and composer of music in a concise yet helpful way. For entry under, say, director, just the latter's name, title of film, and location could be given.

Notwithstanding a possible value of the Bath mini-catalogue principle in reconciling AACR to some extent with its critics, the remedy as advocated at present is a rewriting of its rules for special materials. There are, currently, such activities in progress in both Britain and the US. The British effort had not reached fruition at the time of writing (mid-1972) but it was hoped that a code would be published in mid-1973. The project is being worked upon by the British Non-Book Media Cataloguing Rules Committee. This body is deliberately separate from the basic Cataloguing Rules Committee which coordinates revision of AACR as a whole, to ensure that nonbook media problems are not prejudiced by those of ' normal ' books (BRADFORD). Despite Miss Bradford's reasoning, we suggest that there is a risk in having two disparate committees, because of the risk of conclusions being reached which could undermine an avowed objective of AACR, that of facilitating the integration of entries for all types of materials whether traditional or modern.

The American effort seems to be more diffuse than that represented by the single British committee, although to date some conclusions have been produced. There are, in effect, three committees at work, details of which are given in the article by GELLER. The work of the three-part committee is incorporating and partly revising the Canadian Library Association's *Non-book materials: the organization of integrated collections* of 1970 (RIDDLE). The British and American committees are collaborating, one manifestation—and a fundamental one

—being attempts to reconcile terminology for the media being dealt with.

Problems which appear to be crystallising—and we write at the moment fairly tentatively—may be said to fall into four main areas: (a) headings decisions; (b) description detail; (c) terminology; (d) separate in relation to integrated catalogues. We would also add: (e) subject approach; and (f) form approach. These problems are dealt with in varying degrees throughout this work, but certain items are selected for treatment here.

Basically, we view sceptically the assumption in much of the literature that AACR is inaccurate, useless, or wrongly oriented in relation to special materials. One example of what we regard as a rash assumption is 'One thing is clear—the new rules of cataloging give no more help than did the old and should not be followed' (DAILY, p 288). We suggest that such statements are ill-conceived and unsubstantiated, and should be used and acted upon with discretion by students. Although many of the 'special' elements of AACR are derived from LC practice and codification of over twenty years ago, this does not mean they are worthless. So, while we recommended considering such rules carefully, we do not advocate rejecting them entirely, or eggs may be broken and we shall be left, not with an omelette, but just a chaotic mess.

Throughout this work, we tend to emphasise the differences between 'book' and 'special' materials, but this does not mean that they have nothing in common. If anything, AACR occasionally makes too much distinction between the two types of document, as we shall mention below. DAILY (p 283) says, presumably in relation to AACR, that nonbook materials are treated as 'sub-books', for cataloguing purposes. Such an assertion seems to deny the existence of any common ground between the two types of forms.

We applaud AACR's attempts to establish a basic philosophy or set of principles, even though we do not always agree with the results of such principles whether applied to books or to other materials. We do not agree with critics who assert that special materials are treated as, in effect, second-class citizens.

Let us look at AACR in relation to the six basic problems mentioned above. As to (e) and (f), we cannot criticise AACR for not dealing directly with the subject and form approaches, since it avowedly does not cover these topics. Overall, we may regret this, but it does not constitute grounds for accusing AACR of ignoring important aspects of special materials as such. On the other hand, we admit, the subject of some special materials often transpires to be more important than the author/title approach, examples being maps and slides. Therefore AACR is of less value to special cataloguers than it is to book cataloguers, but by the accident of certain special materials rather than through misunderstanding on the part of the compilers of the code.

Now to take the relevant items in order. Concerning (a) headings, AACR is probably at fault in not applying its basic 'intellectual responsibility' principle strictly enough. In some cases—GELLER quotes possibly 25%—filmstrips may have an author in the code's broad interpretation of the term, yet the code rules for entry under title as with motion pictures. AACR, then, should have treated these as it does normal printed book materials, and so prescribed author-type entry unless authorship were so diffuse as to become unsought. Emerging from this, we would suggest that, as far as possible, special materials should be entered under author. In cases where authorship is so diffuse and multifarious as to become intellectually meaningless and practically unsought, entry should be under title. Serials, a letterpress special material, provide a practical precedent in the code itself. We are not suggesting that the 'intellectual responsibility' principle can be applied to all forms. A film, written and manufactured as such, may well qualify for title entry. On the other hand, a film derived from a literary work might qualify for entry under the author of the original work, as already suggested. We admit that decisions like these might be regarded as inconsistent. But a most important factor to remember is that AACR is based on principles of authorship and not category of work. If an encyclopedia is treated not as such but according to the principles of intellectual responsibility in relation to title as a sought label, and if AACR really sets out to guide the construction of headings according to a basic philosophy, then films should be subjected to the same treatment. Of course, we are not suggesting that all films should be entered under director as maintained by some French authorities; this would again ignore the basic philosophy of the code.

We feel that (b) description need not detain us long. We suggest that too much fuss is made by some critics about, say, the interpretation of collation as either number of pages for a book or number of slides for a phonodisc—or gramophone record if the reader wishes. A lot of descriptive detail is, we suggest, a matter of commonsense, and AACR provides an acceptable basis on which to build up physical description of a document. Surely, a qualified and sensible cataloguer should not expect to turn to a rule book in deciding on every point of detail. In any case, if he needs to do this, AACR gives more than enough detail. As we say later in relation to our selected categories of special materials, there is doubt about whether such detail is necessary. We feel, then, that AACR is not likely to be improved upon as to detail, but only expanded upon—and pedantic detail does not necessarily betoken quality. There is a limit to the infinite capacity for taking pains! In any case, as we expand upon in our final section, those who want minute detail may in the future be able to call upon the data accumulated at a machine-stored centre.

We said earlier, and we shall reiterate later, that the concept of the uniform title is particularly relevant to special materials. One reason is the self-evident one that many special materials are international by their very nature, being often pictorial or possibly musical. Yet we find the allegation that 'The peculiar rule which insists that music have a uniform title and that such an entry [!] be made even if it is not supplied is of little service in music and of even less in phonorecordings' (DAILY, p 286). The author of this sweeping assertion does not substantiate his statement. At this point we shall not pursue the matter, as we feel we deal adequately with it later in our treatment of selected types of special materials. We shall content ourselves with asking what the author of the statement would do when confronted by actual live users of a library who ask for musical works in the various forms of titles by which many works are known. Need we say that this type of thoughtless and unconstructive comment on AACR is the type of statement which makes one appreciate how valuable the code can be as a basis for helpful cataloguing?

On the other hand, (c) terminology can cause a real problem. This is particularly so since documents may be retrieved by their form, in addition to the more conventional author/title or subject approaches. We are accustomed by now to the concept of naming the physical form at the end of the title or uniform title. AACR does not always prescribe this. It does so for, say, motion pictures, filmstrips and various forms of sound recording, but not for still reproductions. This of course is a cause for criticism, particularly since AACR is intended to cater for an integrated catalogue. It is not enough to name the physical form in the collation, which is low in the entry and therefore may not be reached by the user before he ends his scanning of an entry. Naturally, this problem does not arise when a single-medium catalogue is involved, as recommended by some authorities. Experiments have been tried or advocated using coloured cards or coloured edging or stripes across cards. In such cases, a key must be provided on the catalogue indicating the meanings of colours and patterns, and these may be ignored by catalogue users with resultant frustration when it is finally realised that the document required transpires to be in an inconvenient form for a user. We suggest that the physical form should be named prominently at the top of the entry, verbally, and if possible in distinctive typography.

The next problem in terminology is its structure, which brings in semantics. A basic decision is to whether to give, say at the end of the uniform title, generic or specific terms: whether to give, say, 'sound recording' or 'phonodisc', 'phonotape', etc. Alternatives are: (a) generic term in title, high in the entry, with specific term in collation, low in the entry; (b) specific term high in the entry; (c) generic term alone, in collation; or (d) specific term in collation. We suggest going back to first principles, and trying to appreciate why this information is given, namely to inform the catalogue user if, or how, he can use the document which he has traced in the catalogue. So, it would not be sufficient to give merely 'sound recording', because a phonodisc needs different apparatus for reproduction than does a tape, and a simple tape needs different apparatus from that required by a tape cassette. Therefore, we suggest that a specific designation may be named. Since this information is vital to a user, it should be high in the entry, *eg* in the uniform title as mentioned above. Also, as we have admitted, AACR is inconsistent in this respect. Note that this basic recommendation is qualified in more detail in the section on music recordings.

Finally, we have to decide which words of various synonyms to use. It may not be sufficient to prescribe simply local practice. As we explain in the last chapter of this work, we anticipate that some form of central cataloguing, whether or not machine-readable, may become accepted for special materials, just as we have come to accept centrally produced entries for normal books, whether as magnetic tapes, or as printed cards, or in list form. We suggest, in such a case, that local variations should give way to whatever terminology a central agency may use. AACR has given a lead in using the generic stem 'phono-' as in 'phonodisc' and 'phonotape'. However, if local practices can be conveniently implemented, *pace* such systems as MARC, they should be used. The understanding of the user is paramount, and if he cannot be made to understand semantically correct but incomprehensible terms, the catalogue becomes valueless unless explained at every turn by suitably trained library staff.

Concerning (d), separate in relation to integrated catalogues appears to be a vexed question. It is dealt with in the final chapter of this work which, having considered pros and cons, is written on the assumption of the integrated catalogue. However, at this introductory stage, it must be admitted that many librarians are actually using separate catalogues for the various forms. The reason usually given is that a user knows what form of document he wants. In the final chapter, we give our arguments against this attitude, but we offer a reconcilement of the conflicting views—that computerised storage makes it possible to have both complete integrated catalogue and separate catalogues for each form. We suspect that separate catalogues have grown up because: (a) various types of physical form have been added piecemeal to libraries' acquisition practices; (b) it is convenient—if there has to be an either/or choice for economic and labour reasons—for each departmental head to have his own catalogue for stock use and control; (c) each department has obtained its own staff, as the department has evolved, and that staff has justifiably come to be regarded as specialists in their particular field; and (d) there is lack of faith in the effective applicability of general codes, for author/title and description, and index languages, for the subject approach, to any and every form.

The subject approach, under (d), is not relevant in relation to AACR, as we have said. Concerning the other aspect named, we have admitted that AACR is not faultless in its content. Another fault—if fault it can be called—is that AACR, as an integrating code, came out too late: trailing rather than anticipating the introduction of various media. Irrespective of its intrinsic value, and arising from the lateness of AACR's publication, is the conservatism of some cataloguers. Having evolved systems of their own, and having become wholly acquainted with them, they are reluctant to change to a new externally produced code, irrespective of its value in the abstract. Rather parallel is the situation obtaining two or three generations ago, as public access to libraries' stock became acceptable, and there was forced upon librarians the need for detailed shelf classification. Some librarians had their own ideas, which they implemented rather than adopt an externally compiled scheme. During our professional lifetime, we have seen some British public libraries reluctantly giving way and reclassifying to, normally, DC. Admittedly, an important factor is the cost of changing to a different system, especially in a long-established library. But librarians, like other technicians, must expect to retool their production lines, as new systems emerge.

At the moment, librarians who have evolved their own systems can point to the dissatisfaction with AACR as expressed by 'media' librarians in the literature. They may say: Why adopt AACR when better codes for special materials are even now being written? Yet, to quote GELLAR (p 250) at least one tentative code does 'not criticize the AA rules as much as explain them in highly simplified terms, elaborate on them and suggest variations to suit the needs of cataloguers in media centers'. The code referred to is the (American) Association for Educational Communications and Technology's *Standards for cataloging nonprint materials,* 1971. We feel it would be unfortunate if individual libraries continued to evolve their own systems without reference to the one code which we feel has a chance of being accepted throughout the English-speaking world. This feeling applies especially in relation to computerised catalogues, for so much time and expense goes into planning, programming and debugging computerised systems that, once they have been evolved, there is a great risk that they will not be substantially changed in less than a generation. At least, we feel, such local systems should be MARC-compatible, hence automatically AACR-compatible, as, for example, has been done with the Bath mini-catalogue where some corporate authorship headings preferred locally differ from AACR British text rulings.

Much of our general discussion of special cataloguing problems has hinged on AACR, and it is no doubt evident that we advocate the use of this code as far as its admitted limitations allow. Our own view, from studying the literature as far as this has been available in writing this book, is that very few radical changes are being proposed, even during the present time of ferment. The indications are that most changes suggested will be small in number and that they can be coped with when the time comes. This policy is preferable to that of defiantly going one's own way, and running the risk of being permanently out on a limb when central cataloguing of special materials comes, as come it will. For when it does come, it will surely be based on AACR, even if in a somewhat revised form, and it will just as certainly be computer-based. Librarians who wish to pursue or establish local variations would be advised to do so after consulting the various official MARC publications, and to ensure that their variations are compatible with MARC format. We suggest that local librarians' efforts should be directed towards getting changes, where they are really needed, effected at the top. Having done their best in this direction, they should have the patience to accept those things which they cannot have changed. It is becoming patently evident that local librarians cannot build up a 'grass roots' system for their own libraries. They must accept some centralised decisions if their staff salaries are to be kept in hand. They cannot expect their authorities to continue to finance ad hoc activities when a service is available at a lower overall cost from a central source.

A vital aspect of special cataloguing not dealt with in detail so far is that of the subject approach. Our concern in this book is to deal with only verbal (cataloguing and indexing) parts of the storage and retrieval of special materials, and not classification, storage, and shelf arrangement. However, inevitably the various aspects of processing special materials impinge upon each other. One obvious example, judging from the literature, is that some librarians seem to be under the impression that if special materials are stored in separate collections, they must then be recorded in separate catalogues. Conversely, some librarians seem to be under the impression that if there is an integrated catalogue, the actual documents recorded must be integrated on the shelves. We suggest that this attitude shows a misunderstanding of the catalogue, whose purpose is to collocate surrogates of documents irrespective of where the documents themselves are stored.

There have been suggestions that subject entries should be interfiled, in whatever catalogue subject approach is used, while author-type entries are filed in separate sequences. This latter incredibly ignores the fact that, say, a user wanting a score of a musical work, and looking under a composer's name, will not be told that there is in stock a disc recording of the work in which he is interested. However, this topic is covered by later chapters, and at the moment we are concerned with the collocation of entries for subjects, although it is introduced here to point a parallel between author approach and subject approach.

There is possibly a feeling of need for individual divergence for the subject approach to the various physical forms which is stronger than the feeling for an integrated author-type approach. Each local departmental librarian may have put a lot of work into evolving a subject listing for a particular form, *eg* slides, which might be markedly different from that evolved by his colleague for, say, 'spoken word' records. We suggest that there may be ways of dealing uniformly with the subject approach to all forms, which can be acceptable to all the departments concerned. Subject integration proposals and systems have been put forward in particular for school libraries, or resource centres as modern media libraries are now called. Hence we suggest that a similar system, *eg* classification scheme, should be used for the subject approach to all forms of media in a library, if possible uniform between similar libraries, in turn common to all libraries, and finally coinciding with that of any central cataloguing agency which may evolve, or an existing agency which takes unto itself the recording of special materials.

Unfortunately, unlike author/title and descriptive cataloguing, there is no recent, generally acceptable single index language for the subject approach. LC uses three main systems: LC classification, DC classification in many documents, and LC verbal subject headings. BNB uses DC classification, UDC for documents for which UDC notation is available in the relevant documents, LC subject headings, and PRECIS entries. These subject approaches are being incorporated into MARC data, at the moment confined for the most part to English-language monographic works. As time goes by, other documents will be incorporated into the system, just as at the moment, one can buy LC cards for motion pictures, with tracings for the subject approaches. As more time goes by, one hopes that documents not at present covered by American and British legal deposit will become incorporated into the system. In fact, as we mention in the final chapter of this work, BNB is experimenting with MARC processing of audio-visual materials, which at present are not covered by British legal deposit. Because of the international nature of many audio-visual documents, 'non-English' such documents are more likely to be of use to English-speaking clienteles than, say, non-English language books. This vital aspect of some special materials is recapitulated in later chapters of this work. Therefore, because of the international nature of so many special materials, and because of the hope of international cooperation in storage and exchange of bibliographic data, there is a case for the use of a symbolic, non-verbal, index language for the subject approach to special materials, namely an internationally recognised notation of a general classification scheme.

The most universal, general, classification scheme on the market at the moment seems to be UDC. This system is widely accepted and understood in Britain and many European countries, including France, Germany and the USSR. However, it is not well known, so not yet accepted, in, say, the US and Australia. So, there would undoubtedly be difficulty in having it accepted as a universal subject approach in MARC. Nevertheless, we feel it is the most suitable system available at the moment, and we would like to see it incorporated into MARC format as a matter of course.

However, as we have said, our terms of remit do not cover classification, so we turn now to verbal indexing. Evidently, on current practice, we have a choice between LC subject headings and PRECIS. LC headings are incorporated into all MARC-based entries, while PRECIS is used only in entries coming from BNB. Nevertheless, we feel that PRECIS is, almost by definition, more precise and consistent than LC, and we should wish it to be accepted as a standard in the English-speaking world. On the other hand, LC headings are used in all current MARC entries, both British and American, and they are familiar to most of the English-speaking world outside Britain. We take exception to the patently inconsistent construction of headings in LC, and we should like to see a new list of subject headings and references constructed, possibly using LC's basic vocabulary but paying more attention to syntactic consistency. However, because of the 'vested interest' of libraries using LC headings, we cannot envisage such a work happening, or, if it did, being adopted. As a compromise, we would, then, suggest that both PRECIS and LC headings be made available for special materials.

Depending on the use made of UDC, it should be possible also to use chain procedure in the generation of a verbal subject approach based on UDC construction. An example is given in the chapter on maps, on p 199. We feel that UDC is sufficiently flexible and comprehensive to cater for all approaches, whether subject or form, and for integrated collections as well as special departments. From its notation, and using (adapted) chain procedure, it would be possible to work out verbal subject and form approaches to all special materials.

To sum up this chapter, and to generalise crudely. We would suggest the basic use of AACR for author/title headings, and, suitably extracted from, for description. All this with an option on adopting revisions to AACR or parts of it when they are issued. For verbal subject/form approach, ideally we would prefer PRECIS, but we would accept LC, especially if it could be reconstructed along consistent lines. We would recommend UDC as a classified approach, in which case adapted chain procedure could be used as a companion verbal subject/form approach.

Readings

Checklist of works cited in or relevant to this chapter. Reference may also be needed to the checklist following the last chapter, on p 302-303. Full bibliographic citations are given in the consolidated Bibliography, p 304-312. A list of abbreviations is given on p 7. The titles of periodical articles are given within quotation marks.

ALA 1941
ALA 1949
AACR 1967
ASHWORTH *Handbook of special librarianship . . .*
AECT *Standards for cataloging nonprint materials*

BM
BADTEN 'Commercial media cataloging . . .'
BOHANAN 'Cataloging A-V materials'
BRADFORD 'New media—new methods'
BROXIS *Organising the arts*
BRYANT, P *The Bath mini-catalogue*
BURKETT *Special materials in the library . . .*

CCR
CARSON 'Cataloging non-book materials'
COLLISON *The treatment of special materials in libraries*
'COMMERCIAL media cataloging . . .' *Library journal*
COWLEY *Bibliographical description and cataloging*
COX 'The cataloguing of nonbook materials . . .'
CUTTER

DAILY 'The selection, processing and storage of non-print materials . . .'

GAMBEE *Non-book materials as library resources*
GELLER 'A media troika and MARC . . .'
GERLETTI 'Digital apoplexy . . .'
GILBERT *Non-book materials: their bibliographic control . . .*

HALL *Potential use of* MARC *records in three libraries . . .*
HENSEL 'Treatment of non-book materials'
HICKS *The organization of nonbook materials in school libraries*

ICCP

JOHNSON *Practical cataloguing*

LCRDC

MCNALLY *A guide to the practice of non-book librarianship . . .*

MASON *A primer of non-book materials in libraries . . .*

MASSONNEAU ' Cataloging nonbook materials . . . '

NEEDHAM *Organizing knowledge in libraries*

NOLAN 'Audio-visual materials '

PIERCY *Commonsense cataloging . . .*

QUIGG ' How to make a union catalogue '

QUIGG *Theory of cataloguing . . .*

RIDDLE *Non-book materials: the organization of integrated collections*

RUFSVOLD *Audio-visual school library service . . .*

CHAPTER TWO

Music

WE HAVE decided to include music recordings under music because, after all, music is intended to be heard, whatever physical form a music document may take. Problems associated with music scores apply also to music sound recordings; this should be assumed, and applied, throughout the first part of this chapter.

Music has four main areas of interest to the cataloguer: (a) works about music and musicians, whether reference type or through-reading; (b) music scores, usually printed, but possibly in manuscript form or as facsimile reprints of manuscripts; (c) the subject/form approach to works about music and the music itself; and (d) music recordings, in various physical forms, but mainly as discs, tapes or cassette-tapes.

At first sight it seems that music is not inherently different from any other type of recorded information. It would appear that one has only to understand the composer as the author-equivalent, and one can go on from there in applying the basic principles of heading assignment and descriptive cataloguing. But before long, two factors start to emerge: (a) music notation is an international language, with repercussions similar to those emerging from the use of mainly graphic forms such as maps, photographs, pictures, slides, films, etc—*ie* the visual image potential is much broader than with verbal communication; and (b) composers' treatment of music highlights in a special way the various applications of the 'intellectual responsibility' principles of assigning headings to works. The international nature of music notation means that a performer, student, or critic may just as likely use a score printed for, say, German, Italian, or Russian consumption, as one produced for the use of the English speaker. Many scores include instructions in Italian, but many others give them in a variety of languages, including of course English. The latter probably applies particularly to scores produced in North America, although even in conservative Britain it is increasingly becoming accepted that, say, either 'piano' or 'soft' can be used without loss of face in the musical world. Depending on the country, and for which audience a score is specifically produced, a title may be in any of half a dozen languages. Also, composers, whatever their nationality, may themselves baptise a work in a variety of languages. We can get a Russian work, or a German work, with a French title, say *Casse noisette* or *Marche militaire*, and not regard it as unusual. On the other hand, it is unusual for a writer of verbal works to give his work a title in other than his vernacular. As with all materials, it may be important in academic bibliographic cataloguing to know what title a composer used initially, but at the same time it is just as important to be aware of the equivalent of that title in several languages, as mentioned above.

Possibly a greater difficulty arising from the international nature of music is that of composers' names themselves, especially in relation to those of countries not using the roman alphabet (looking at the problem from the English speaking librarian's viewpoint). As with titles, various publishers may use a wide variety of ways of representing composers' names, and any or all of these may be different from the form of name by which a composer is known popularly, or by which he is cited in basic reference sources, or even in published catalogues. Specific examples arising from this problem will be taken up later.

Yet another problem arising from the internationalism of music is that literary works used with music, *eg* songs, choruses, operas, may be in a variety of languages. In some cases the work in hand may be acceptable, for its music value, even if the language used is unfamiliar; in other cases, it may prove unacceptable. It is important, then, that a statement of language used should be made clearly, and high up in the entry; this, as will be seen, is one of the many ways in which the uniform title can be utilised.

It has become accepted, then, that the music cataloguer must know a variety of languages, at least as used in music. Even in a general research library, the cataloguer of books can probably get by with a more limited language knowledge. Also, and partly leading on from this, the music cataloguer must have some sort of knowledge of music, such as recognising key signatures and knowing the difference between, say, a theme and variations, an arrangement, and a transcription. If he has a knowledge of the basic repertoire as well, he can save himself a great deal of time and trouble spent on research in establishing, say, with which composer a particular work is commonly associated, or from which symphony, concerto or opera a movement or excerpt is taken. In sum then, we suggest that the music cataloguer needs to have a knowledge of languages, at least as used in music, and a knowledge of music itself.

Unprofessional as it may seem, we suggest that these two qualities may possibly be more important as initial qualifications in music librarianship and music cataloguing than professional qualifications in library science and even in the core subject of cataloguing. It may be easier for the suitably motivated professional musician to acquire cataloguing ability than for the professional cataloguer to acquire music knowledge. We realise we are not alone here: there is quite a body of opinion that the 'modern' so-called information scientist should be a subject expert first and an information retrieval expert second. However, this may be a conclusion based on one's own experience and observation, which may not coincide with that of others in librarianship. For example, we have known an ex-oboist who quickly picked up sufficient cataloguing techniques in a few tutorial sessions to be able to catalogue gramophone records, for retrieval as opposed to bibliographic purposes, in a public library context. On the other hand, we have also known chartered librarians who had passed a general cataloguing examination, but who seemed lost when confronted with gramophone records as part of their libraries' daily acquisitions. Of course, a practical solution is to enable potential music librarians to specialise in a music librarianship option, or elective, during their professional education, during which they would enhance and orient their musical potential towards library science. The difficulty here is that at the moment there are not many music librarianship posts as ends in themselves. The ambitious librarian may 'work through' being a music librarian in pursuit of, to him, higher things in the library world. We realise that a similar situation may well apply in other specialisations. However, we venture to suggest that if a librarian becomes really proficient in the cataloguing of music, including the acquiring of music and language knowledge (already dwelt upon), he may find the experience and discipline useful in dealing with other 'special' materials and other subject fields. Perhaps there is an analogy here with Plato's view (in the *Republic*) that music can be regarded as an integral part of the education of all people: certainly a high proportion of children seem to respond readily to a 'music and movement' element in their pre-school education.

Much music is issued in a ' fugitive material ' type of format, usually referred to as sheet music. Many items may consist of only four pages; but even if having more pages, they may be flimsy and not have proper title pages, *ie* they pose both physical and intellectual problems. It is as though the bulk of a book library's stock consisted of separate chapters from books, articles from periodicals, pamphlets, and physically slight ' report ' material. A physical solution is to bind together various similar works to make up something approaching a ' book '. This then might be catalogued as if it had been issued in a comprehensive form in the first place. This method has a great deal to be said for it, except that it is vital for retrieval purposes to include detailed contents in catalogue entries, and possibly analytical entries. A better solution still is to acquire ready-made collections in the first place, if at all possible complete works of composers arranged in such a way that the retrievalist can readily tell in which volume a specific work will be found. Failing this, this is where at least some elementary musical knowledge is relevant, since parts must be brought together to represent a coherent whole. For example, much of Chopin's piano music is difficult to play, and various arrangements have been made which are more approachable for the beginner than the originals were. In such a case, only arrangements of the same standard should be brought together; these will certainly be selections, and so a contents list will be needed in the main catalogue entry. At the same time a title page and contents list should be made for binding into the work itself. Whether analytical entries for individual works are to be made depends on time available; the knowledgeable cataloguer may select certain well known items only for such treatment, although it is difficult, even if one does know the repertoire well, to make subjective judgements. To some extent one can rely on uniform titles (dealt with later), and bring together works of a specific form, *eg* sonatas, nocturnes, preludes, and thereafter rely on careful use of the catalogue if a particular individual work is requested.

Another characteristic for binding together is that of instrument. This criterion can apply particularly where comparatively few works are issued for the less popular instruments for playing purposes, *eg* the horn. The cataloguer will have to construct an explanatory title, and a detailed contents list. In such a case, one can plead more firmly for analytical entries, by composer and title. Again, degree of difficulty of playing may have to be taken into account in selecting items for binding together.

In both types of binding together, *ie* by composer, or by instrument, all items do not have to be exactly the same size. Provided a knowledgeable and biddable binder is found, works of slightly different size can be brought together fairly conveniently.

One shibboleth which must be pinpointed, however obvious it may seem, is not to bind together parts, *ie* scores for different instruments intended to be played at the same time. One has come across instances of music for 4 hands 2 pianos, or for piano and violin, being bound together. Such is the musical ignorance of some allegedly cultured librarians! No amount of analytical cataloguing can overcome such follies.

A more satisfactory solution with 'fugitive material' sheet music, from the retrieval point of view, is to keep it separate in, say, vertical files, horizontal files, or pamphlet boxes. In fact, this treatment may be used while accumulating items for binding together. The problem arises as to whether: (a) to catalogue fully, under composer, with whatever form and medium approaches are used for other materials; or whether (b) to catalogue under just one approach, either composer, or form, or medium; or whether (c) not to catalogue at all, relying on the 'self-indexing' nature of fugitive material files, as often happens with other materials. The cataloguing decision depends to some extent on the physical method employed. If, say, the material is filed by composer, irrespective of form or medium, one or other of the latter might be used in the catalogue to supplement the physical arrangement. One would be inclined to use a classified approach for physical arrangement, following the classification scheme in use in the library, often by medium (instrument), and to supplement this by composer entries in the catalogue. If some material is intended for ultimate binding together, temporary manuscript entries on slips could be made in the catalogue, say in red, with coloured edges on the slips to facilitate easy recognition. When the time comes for binding together, the temporary slips can be withdrawn for use by non-professional staff in building up complete entries, including contents lists, both for the final catalogue entry and for binding into the work itself.

The problem of parts, for individual instruments or voices, is peculiar to music. If a work is represented in stock by a single combined score, *eg* piano-vocal arrangement for an opera, this should be shown in the uniform title. However, if a work, as represented in stock, consists of parts for performance, this fact is usually shown lower in the entry. Suffice it to say, at this point, that there is an obvious difference between a conductor's or a 'following' score, and a set of parts intended for use by performers; and the type of holding should be clearly represented in a catalogue entry. It is fairly common for the various subsidiary parts to be limp-bound and kept in a pocket at the back of the main score, or, if there is no main score, for all parts to be so treated. If sets of 'part' scores are kept in a separate sequence, especially if closed access, this fact should be recorded in the catalogue entry. It should be remembered that parts may be of use to someone other than a prospective performer, *eg* a student or research worker, and so all the usual approaches, such as medium and form as well as composer, should be represented in the catalogue. It is possible that the 'parts' scores may be the only, detailed at least, representation of a work in stock. Where identical copies of a work are needed for performance, *eg* vocal parts in an opera or similar work, the catalogue should state clearly how many copies there are in stock of, say, a piano-vocal score.

As has already been inferred, a score may be needed for various purposes: *eg* performing (both instrumental and singing) as a group; performing on one's own, as in say a piano arrangement of a work for orchestra; 'following' a performance; and conducting. Such information should be brought out in the description of a work in its catalogue entry. Whether such factors should be used as approaches is open to question. Some libraries physically shelve or file miniature scores in a separate sequence alphabetically by composer, thereby giving an approach which may cut across conventional classification, *eg* by instrument or by musical form. In such a case, the catalogue should clearly indicate in its call number the sequence in which such works will be found. We suspect that some librarians shelve miniature scores in a separate sequence purely for physical convenience, but that is another story.

Another factor to be contended with is the title page, or lack of it, with music scores. There are two problems here: (a) lack of information; and (b) where there is information, it may be contradictory. As we know, the title-page is traditionally the 'boss-page' or primary source in 'normal' cataloguing. Much sheet music is issued without a title page, which obviously upsets the preconceptions and training of some traditional cataloguers. Most books do have a title page; in fact, methods have been worked out of simply facsimile-copying the title-page, reducing the image in size and adding a heading to the result to form a catalogue. Music usually has a cover title, possibly giving more detail than its equivalent in other materials. In fact, cover titles of music may give too much detail, as when one cover includes titles of several related works by a composer and put out by one publisher. There may be a serf employed by the publisher or printer who underlines the title of the work actually within the covers, although this indication may not always be obvious to the uninitiated.

Music usually has a caption title (at the head of the first page of the score), which gives more information about a work than a caption title usually has in a normal printed work. In some cases this may in fact be the main source of information. Unfortunately, caption titles do not always emphasise typographically the principal contributor to a work, *eg* the writer of the words may be given on the left and the composer on the right, while in fact the composer is usually regarded as more important and more 'sought' than the poet or librettist. Or the word-writer's name may appear above that of the composer, thus confounding a basic rule of, if in doubt enter under the person first named, *ie* highest in the work. The cataloguer may have to select from the information given on the cover, the title page and the caption, including reconciling any inconsistencies, *eg* different ways, and even languages, and to add information from external sources to ensure that sufficient information is given to identify a work and to differentiate between similar-seeming works and editions of the same work.

As we shall enlarge upon later, music manifests a particular need for the use of uniform titles. These obviously try to ensure that all versions of a work are brought together at the same filing, or sub-filing, term. In addition they help the cataloguer in two ways: (a) they save the cataloguer the agony of deciding in what order the components of a title should be given; and (b) they ensure that the cataloguer does not overlook any essential component in a title.

Many musical compositions are messed about with by other composers—and pseudo and quasi-composers—to a greater extent than usually applies with 'normal' book-form materials. Or at least, if verbal writers do it they commit quiet plagiarism unknown to the cataloguer, while if they are writing on another thinker's writings they say so. The latter applies in music of course, and there is no doubt that, say, a verbal work on Beethoven by Grove has its author entry under Grove. The trouble arises in the numerous cases of 'shared' and 'mixed' authorship, unique to non-verbal materials, in which one artist's creation is developed, adapted and refined by another artist using a similar general medium, whether it be music, painting, or sculpture. Where, say, a symphony by Haydn has its notes re-presented for use in the form of 2 pianos 4 hands, we have a very near-parallel to translation of verbal works. In such a case, *ie* of re-arrangement for another medium, it is natural to give the main entry heading to the original composer. At the other end of the scale is the case of the composer who takes merely a theme from another composer, and builds a whole work upon it. Admittedly, one can say the former helped inspire the latter; however, it is both intellectually accurate and sought to catalogue such a work under the later composer. Unconsciously it may be that our decision, in the two cases instanced, is helped by the fact that the academically correct solution is very often the better known name, *eg* Vaughan Williams compared with Thomas Tallis. Liszt's *Fugue on B-A-C-H* does not really count, although we might well make an added entry under Bach in the way that we may make one under a 'Festschriftee'—it is a name permanently and inherently associated with the work. The same applies to Malcolm Williamson's *Epitaph for Edith Sitwell.* Between these two extreme cases—the simple arrangement and the theme and variations, is a great diversity of contributions between composers. One tough and perhaps typical example is an item by Tchaikovsky from music by Chopin known as *Un poco di Chopin* and used in one version of *Swan Lake* (surely one of the hardest stretches of water in the world to chart when one gets down to individuals' contributions: if it had not been for Petipa's contribution after Tchaikovsky's death the work would possibly be less known today than, say, the *Winter reveries* symphony). Some transcriptions, if they are to be catalogued accurately, can cause a great deal of research in external sources as well as a drawing upon internal evidence.

Another factor which applies particularly to music, even if the principle involved is not peculiar to music, is the number of approaches which may be used with it, each of which in certain circumstances may be regarded by some library users as paramount. Composer is an obvious aprpoach, as has already been assumed. Another possibility of 'intellectual responsibility' is the arranger, transcriber, and so on, again as already mentioned. A further possibility is the author of words, as in operas and poems set to music. This approach becomes very relevant when one poem or cycle of poems has been set to music by several composers: an example is A E Housman's *A Shropshire lad.* Another type of case is exemplified with folk songs, when the title, or first line, of a song may vie with the various composers who have arranged it, even if using the same basic theme. Which is more sought: 'Seventeen come Sunday', or 'Vaughan Williams'; again—'Foggy foggy dew', or 'Britten', or even 'I am a bachelor'? Subject/Form approaches are dealt with in detail later.)

In many cases, as in the standard or so-called 'classical' repertoire, music is fairly static. There is a body of works which is likely always to be wanted in the foreseeable future, irrespective of various editions of them which may appear from time to time, whether in score or in sound recorded form. It may be felt then that music could be a suitable topic for use in basic composer-title printed catalogues, for use primarily by the users of a library and secondarily by other librarians as a check list. Now, we acknowledge that editions of scores may come and go; and certainly recordings come and go so rapidly that we cannot keep pace with them. When a particularly noteworthy edition of a work is likely to remain in stock, perhaps one of the expensive and careful products of the Gregg Press, the edition in stock may be noted. It is suggested that, even in those popular libraries with a liberal acquisition policy, there is still likely to be a basic stock which could be recorded, for home, study and office use, in the form of a semi-permanent printed catalogue. In libraries with a recorded music collection, the holdings of records could be integrated with those of scores, using a symbol to indicate 'record'. The compilation of such a catalogue may, indeed, have a useful by-product in reminding the librarian of scores in stock with no records to match, and, if necessary, vice versa. If such a short-title catalogue could be computer-compiled and printed it would be possible to cater all the more conveniently for the more common of the author-type and form/subject approaches. The need for such a catalogue is most readily apparent in library systems with a far-flung membership, and whose members commonly borrow items by post, *eg* county and state libraries. From the computer store, suitably programmed, the library could compile 'sectional' lists: of miniature scores, operas, music for children, film music, and even 'mood' music, *eg* for weddings. There should come a time when a special search, and printout, could be made for special individual requests, as happens in various fields of science and technology at the moment: MEDLARS (MEDical Literature Analysis and Retrieval System) is an example. This type of flexibility in catalogue production will, one hopes, become commonplace when MARC becomes more common than at present, both in basic acceptance by librarians, and in coverage. Such 'tags' in music as form and medium should be easily machine-handleable, along with more common characteristics as intellectual level, and period or date ('musical epoch').

THE ENTRY

Part of this subsection crystallises some of the introductory observations; part has not been touched on before in this work; and part looks ahead to the Codes subsection, which may be used in conjunction with this one.

With music, there is not usually the (arid, one suggests) argument as to whether the author-equivalent or subject/form approach is more important, or more sought; and so we can go straight into problems of author-type entry. Whether the author-type approach is allegedly the main entry, as in the dictionary catalogue, or a so-called subsidiary approach, as in the classified catalogue, is immaterial here. We are concerned primarily with the unit entry, assuming that whenever an entry of any type is needed, the unit entry will be used with an appropriate heading inserted at the top, *eg* typed or printed on in the case of a card catalogue.

HEADING: FORM AND CONSTRUCTION

We assume here that the person primarily responsible for a work has been decided upon, and we then have to decide how the heading is made. Now and again, a corporate body may be an author, *eg* English Folk Song and Dance Society, but these occasions are too rare for comment here: a standard code—we suggest AACR—should be consulted in such cases.

Concerning, then, personal names: first as to fullness. Some codes, and therefore certain libraries, persist in spelling out surname, all forenames, and dates of birth and death. Is all of the following really necessary: Mozart, Johann Chrysostan Wolfgang Amadeus, 1756-1791? Bearing in mind the number of entries we are likely to have under Mozart, think of the labour involved in reproducing, checking and filing such a heading. This all began for two reasons, we suggest: (a) there was a need to distinguish between people with the same surname, and then even the same forenames; and (b) cataloguers' pedantry, or to put it more politely, cataloguers' search for full accuracy, the stated reason usually being (a). When (a) does arise there is some point in giving full details—although possibly some sort of appellative could serve to distinguish between people with at least the same surnames. Mozart's father may appear as a composer in a catalogue, and his son and sister may possibly appear in a catalogue as the subject of documents. Amateurish as it may seem, there is some point in adding *father*, *son*, *sister* to the headings of the minor Mozarts on the assumption that these terms will automatically be associated with *the* Mozart, who would be filed first in catalogues. (Perhaps it would be too much to suggest adding the Irishism *himself* to *the* Mozart? The other extreme has actually been practised, when only MOZART appeared as a heading in the gramophone record catalogue of the Lambeth Public Libraries (London) in the 1950's; one sympathises with the reaction against librarians' finicky exactitude. One has come across the plea that catalogues can be used as a source of information in themselves irrespective of the documents they record. We suggest that occasional needs of this nature are best answered from reference sources rather than causing the involvement of staff in hours of searching and writing, against this possible contingency. Surely it is easiest to give a composer the shortest possible heading; this can be extended if (ever) another composer with an identical name is later represented in the catalogue. When a new work is added to stock it is customary to check the catalogue or authority file, and any duplications would be brought to light then. If a comprehensive catalogue of all of a library's stock is maintained, *ie* including entries for all works in one sequence, obviously the need for distinguishing between author headings will become more apparent, and sooner, than if a separate music catalogue is maintained.

The spelling of some composers' names is sometimes a matter of opinion and personal judgement. This applies most strikingly with composers whose countries do not use the roman alphabet. Perhaps Tchaikovsky (to use what one regards as the 'normal' spelling) is one of the supreme examples. His name came into 'English' via German, and this accounts for the spelling 'Tschaikowsky'. According to literal transliteration the name should be Chaikovsky—but who on earth would look first for that in a catalogue? We do not know how Tchaikovsky would have his name spelt in English-speaking countries. But we do know that Strawinsky would have his name spelt thus, because the middle consonant should be a v-sound, while if the name were spelt with a v people might pronounce it as 'Strafinsky', as though it were a German name. In cases like this, in which the composer is known to have expressed a preference, we suggest that the composer's desires should be adhered to. Generally, however, we recommend that common usage should be followed wherever this is known. Only when a common usage cannot be established should one fall back onto official transliteration alphabets, *eg* 'The new Russian orthography' in ALA 1949, p 245-246. 'Common usage' can be investigated by consultation and comparison of basic reference works like Grove and general encyclopedias which are widely used by both librarians and library users, and from the cataloguer's own musical knowledge and 'habitual way of looking at things' (as Cutter would say). So, again, the sensible cataloguing of music comes back to the librarian's own knowledge and experience. As with other aspects of entry compilation, usage of codes is summarised in the subsection of Codes.

Similar difficulties can be encountered over forenames, but we do not regard decisions in dubious cases as being so critical as with surnames, as these are comparatively rarely needed for filing purposes. Whatever is done about transliteration from non-roman alphabets, we definitely do not support the *translation* of forenames which are common enough to have equivalents in several languages. Tchaikovsky remains Piotr, and J S Bach Johann. This would apply even in catalogues used mainly by children. The reason is simply that there seems no point in bothering. It is rarely necessary even to spell out forenames, as inferred above. Obvious exceptions are prolific musical clans, *eg* the Bachs and the Goossens, members of which are quoted as often by their full names as by their initials. In such cases: if in doubt, spell it out, and do not waste time on conducting a public opinion poll. We might mention here the possibility of actually changing headings if events prove the cataloguer to have, apparently, made a mistake! Some cataloguers seem to regard making amendments to any parts of entries as nigh unto heresy, as though the original decision were handed down on sacred tablets. In these comparatively few cases, recataloguing should be a normal and continuous process. Time spent on such recataloguing improves the efficiency of a catalogue, and gives satisfaction to all catalogue users as well as to the cataloguer, and is therefore well worth while. However, cataloguers may want to keep a record of such amendments. When a later grand recataloguing project is contemplated a scanning of a list of past ad hoc amendments, caused by day-to-day needs, may show that a general precedent is being crystallised, and this can be of use in any large-scale decisions. While on this topic of small-scale recataloguing, we suggest that limited but calculated experiments could be built into such day-to-day activities, the results of which, again, may help in deciding future large-scale policy decisions. Such experiments may, in fact, be more needed in subject/form cataloguing, which is probably subject to a greater need for radical overhaul from time to time.

HEADING: CHOICE

Some considerable space has been devoted to the construction of headings, since decisions, practices and possible amendments apply to the cataloguing of every work added to stock. Choice of heading decisions have to be made in only some instances. Although, such decisions may indeed be far-reaching in their effect on catalogue use and compilation, since what the user may regard as nonsensible decisions—however justifiable they may be according to various codes—can affect a user's faith in a catalogue as a whole.

We are confronted at once by two principles, which, in music cases, very often transpire to be contradictory. These are (a) intellectual responsibility; and (b) soughtness: the use of a 'tag' as approach term through habit but not based on any conscious working towards academic accuracy or even justice. As a basic recommendation, we would suggest that where these two principles clash, preference should be given to the sought tag. This recommendation is made because of the likelihood that most libraries are cataloguing primarily for retrieval rather than in the interests of academically accurate and full bibliographic description.

At this point, a reminder may be needed that a decision is not made solely academic, or irrelevant, by the provision of added entries to cover the approach rejected as main entry heading, as previously summarised on p 17, chapter 1. Even if a central catalogue agency is used for supply of multiple copies of cards, the local library still has to type in the various added entry headings and file the cards—with an ensuing increase in bulk of an expensive piece of library equipment. Also, it seems to have been established that some users at least are put off by a large catalogue with many—to them—superfluous entries and references.

Admittedly, it is not always easy to be sure what is the one and only sought tag: one difficult example is whether people will look for a well-known arrangement of a folk-song under the composer of the arrangement or the title of the song.

We shall now attempt to summarise individual conditions, and cases, of individual types of work. The 'shared' and 'mixed' authorship condition can be divided into two sub-conditions: (a) where the contributions of the two or more contenders are verbal and musical respectively; and (b) where all contributions are musical.

In the past, some codes have felt it important to bring into (a) what are now regarded as 'related and dependent' works, as exemplified by thematic catalogues. The sought approach term, as with literary concordances, may most often be the person whose works are indexed. However, this approach is covered by a perfectly valid subject entry, and it is still reasonable, even in strictly limited cataloguing, to expect an author-type entry as well. The type of entry to be excluded would be a form entry (in the subject sequence if separate) for 'Thematic catalogues'. In the rare event of, say, a musicologist studying the structure and detail of thematic catalogues as such, recourse must be had to various catalogue substitutes. In any case, there may be doubt over the sought term, *eg* Schubert or Deutsch, Mozart or Köchel. So, as with the supposed conflict in maps between area covered and author-type entry, we suggest that the problem virtually does not exist. As we explain in some detail in the chapter of this work on maps, one can claim with works in any physical form, whether book or other, that there may be doubt over whether the subject or the author approach is more important to the searcher in various cases of specific works. These specific cases do not have to make us deny the reasonably well-established need for both author and subject entries for virtually all documents in a library's stock. In music, the same principle applies to studies of a composer's works, *eg* a *study* by Grove of Beethoven's symphonies is no different in essence from Köchel's *catalogue* of Mozart's works.

Possibly a more valid example in our present context is where words and music are 'mixed' in a work itself. This situation exists in cases of previously existing poems being put to music, and in cases of librettists being commissioned to write words, or 'books' in the case of musicals, for a composer to integrate into a verbal-musical work. When the whole work is issued, *ie* music and words, in whatever form, *eg* either full scores or piano-vocal scores, there is little doubt that the composer wins. In fact, the most likely other contender may well be, not librettist or poet, but title, and we suggest that even in very limited cataloguing a title approach of some sort should be provided, especially in popular and children's libraries. Apart from title added entry, added entry for librettist or poet is obviously likely to be useful where not prohibited by limited cataloguing needs. In the latter case the librarian wishing to offer a reasonably complete service may need frequently to fall back upon catalogue substitutes. Possibly underrated and humble layman's reference works relevant here are *Everyman's dictionary of music* and the *Concise Oxford dictionary of music.* It may be worth a library's investing a few dollars in buying copies of such works for prominent display on catalogues, if the expense of title added entries rules out the latter. Even the alleged scholar may, quietly, wish to use a title approach occasionally. Admittedly a library does not necessarily have in stock all the items listed in such reference works. This is, of course, one of the disadvantages of catalogue substitutes, since their use necessitates cross-checking listed items with the catalogue. However, a service-oriented librarian will attempt to obtain any wanted items, whether or not they happen to be in the local library's stock. We are touching now on the possibility of a library's using as its main bibliographic tool, not its local catalogue, but a more general listing, *eg* a union catalogue of the stocks of related libraries, local holdings being marked with their local shelf locations. Such a possibility is realised in some limited areas, *eg* the marking up of government publications lists with local holdings. With MARC and various other computer-compiled and printed catalogues in the offing, such possibilities are not merely an 'ivory tower' lecturer's pipe dream. Naturally the MARC programs make provision for local libraries' use, and these fields can be employed for inserting local locations. However, there are two main requirements before catalogues produced in this way become viable: (a) acceptance of the principle, and practice, by local librarians; and (b) coverage of required subject areas by the central agency or agencies concerned.

We have already mentioned that the 'word' approach should include provision for author and title, the inference being entry for complete works, as exemplified by *A Shropshire lad*—the reader can no doubt readily supply examples from operas, *eg* Sonnleithner as author and *Fidelio* as title, supporting Beethoven as composer—and possibly even Edward J Dent as editor of a series of librettos. However, in addition, we may encounter a need for various types of analysis of works. A notable example is first lines of songs or poems, the likely emphasis being on folk songs and other songs of long standing, *eg* well known arias from operas and oratorios. Examples are not only *Foggy foggy dew* but also *I am a batchelor,* as well as 'Britten' as composer, and possibly 'Folk songs' as form approach; not only *Aida,* but 'Celeste Aida', as well as 'Verdi' as composer, and 'Ghislanzoni' as librettist. A concomitant need is that for English-language equivalents in certain cases, *eg* not only 'Visi d'arte' but also 'Love and music' from Puccini's *Tosca.*

Even in a unit entry-based catalogue, some of these approaches may be catered for by references; this provision can apply further where a number of editions (whether scores or recordings) are stocked. It must be left to the cataloguer to decide whether references or added entries are used in the small library; with a small number of different editions, the added entry principle may be preferred to references. A 'cut-off' point may be decided upon, *eg* when four or more editions are stocked, it may be decided to go from added entries to references. This number is consistent with AACR's 'cut-off' point for transferring from author entry to title entry for general works of multiple authorship. It must be appreciated that a reference in a catalogue necessitates double referral, with attendant irritation and frustration on the part of the user. Against our basic preaching, we may mention here the possibility of what we dub 'added references' as used in the BM catalogues. An 'added reference' consists of a reference structure, *ie* heading, with a 'referred-to' heading, but in addition, at little trouble, the shelf location of an item is given. For example, under a title or first line of a folk song, we refer to the main entry heading and title, but we also include the call number(s) or shelving number(s) of the work(s) in stock containing the item in question, *eg* 782-1/VER for 'Celeste Aida'.

Another 'word' approach may be that of a literary work from which a musical work is derived. As, presumably, in AACR, it may be that the relevance of the original work is rather nebulous; also is the ever-present possibility of there being several editions, or renditions, of both the 'foster-parent' and the 'child' of the liaison, so that the use of a reference may be preferred, in the interests of economical cataloguing. It may be thought that someone interested in *The chocolate soldier* by Oscar Straus is indifferent to George Bernard Shaw and the sugared-pill moral in his play *Arms and the man.* In this case, the connection may be suggestively catered for by a reference. However, the teacher of Shaw and his morals and politics may like to take advantage of the ultimate in sugared pills by using *The chocolate soldier* as an entrée to *Arms and the man.* This is where the catalogue can serve as an intellectual connector between apparently unlikely manifestations of the human intellect. Therefore, we express here a hope that different documents and forms may be integrated by the library's catalogue in the interest of ultimate learning in its broadest sense. This situation is parallel to that of novels and plays on which moving films are based. In sum, we positively recommend that some catalogue indication of the connection between different intellectual products and physical formats should be established, in the interest of the basic theme of such works, however tenuous it may be in some cases: the final judgement should be left to the library's clients. In conclusion on this point: we cannot assume that the connection between different works is always known to users of the library. Not only teachers, but school pupils and students, have to be considered. Regrettably, not even all teachers are necessarily aware of the possible broad cultural value of tying up the various representations of not only musical but also moral, social and political themes. Here, again, as so often, we come back to the knowledge and awareness of the music librarian. As elsewhere in this work, we plead for the retrieval value of catalogues, as—sometimes—differentiated from, or opposed to, their bibliographic value. The multi-media catalogue is dealt with in the last chapter of this book.

Another, equally important, aspect of multiple authorship is that in which all the various contributions are musical, even though the value of various contributions may vary. Specific cases include: arrangements; transcriptions; 'free' transcriptions; adaptations; 'inspired by' or equivalent; 'in the style of . . .'; pastiches; and 'variations on a theme of . . .'. A further, rather different, type of multiple authorship is a cadenza in a concerto or similar work, composed by a performer or someone else other than the original composer. These are given here approximately in their order of adherence to the original composer's apparent intent. Somewhere between simple arrangements and 'variations on a theme' comes the point where the original composer 'cuts out' and the later composer 'cuts in' as primarily responsible for the resultant work, and therefore worthy of main entry status. We suggest that arrangements, and works dubbed 'transcription' or similar by the later composer should likely receive entry under the original composer. From 'adaptations' onwards, there is likely to be a good case for main entry under later composer, under both academic accuracy and soughtness principles. When a later composer has absorbed an earlier work into a format and orchestration structure of his own, as is the case with Tchaikovsky's 'Un poco di Chopin', in *Swan Lake,* already mentioned, there seems little doubt that Tchaikovsky should get the main entry. We suggest a parallel case is that of the cadenza; whether or not the original composer is aware of it, the cadenza is 'absorbed' by the parent work, and we suggest then that the latter should take the main entry. The only exception would be when a virtuoso publishes a set of cadenzas from a variety of different composers, an unlikely event anyway. If the set of cadenzas relates to one composer and one form and, of course, one medium, we suggest that the original composer gets the main entry. The fact of the cadenzas being by another person can be brought out later in the entry. Again, with a work in the style of another composer, as with Percy Grainger's *Handel in the Strand*, there is little doubt that, on both intellectual and sought grounds, Grainger wins. In all these instances there is a case for added entries under the other composer: whether as author-type, or title, or inverted title is immaterial, we suggest. The same applies to Liszt's *Fugue on B-A-C-H* which may, in fact, be regarded as an 'in the style of . . .'. There is little doubt that variations on a theme of another composer should go under the composer of the variations. An interesting further variation on this theme is Brahms' *Variations on the theme of St Anthony's chorale*, often in the past inaccurately called *Variations on a theme of Haydn*. For purely sought reasons, an added entry may be made under Haydn, though musicologists nowadays seem to agree that the attribution of the original theme to Haydn is spurious. Those cataloguers who are worried about the academic correctness of their catalogues can work out whether they wish to have in their added entries 'spurious composer', 'attributed' or some similar qualifier. More to the point, there might well be a title entry under *St Anthony's chorale*. A slightly knottier problem is Purcell's *Trumpet voluntary* by Jeremiah Clarke. In the past this work has been attributed to, or accepted unquestioningly as a work by, Purcell. However, research over the past few years seems to have established that it is in fact by Jeremiah Clarke. It seems likely that the Clarke label will become more and more associated with the work, and we would therefore recommend a main entry under him with an added entry under Purcell. The title approach could be absorbed by a subject/form entry, although a title added entry could be made if desired.

A concluding summary, then in cases of multiple 'composership', is that the composer most generally associated with a work should be given the main entry. A qualifying explanation should be made in cases where there is genuine doubt as to his intellectual contribution in relation to another composer. This would best be given in the form of an explanatory author statement or a note lower down the entry.

To add a designation or function to the heading may cause unnecessary complications over filing and arrangement. An added entry should be made, if possible, for any other composer associated with the work. If the work has a distinctive title an added entry should be made under that, again if possible bearing in mind local circumstances as to both users' needs and cataloguing economies.

For the most part, it has been assumed that multiple copies of unit entries are available. However, not by any means is all music covered by the large central catalogue agencies. Further, it may be that a library cannot conveniently make its own multiple copies of unit entries. If, therefore, it is necessary for each entry to be individually produced, on a non-automatic typewriter, added entries may well be subjected to simplified cataloguing procedures, *ie* made shorter than the main entry. Any headings—author and uniform title (explained below) should be reproduced fully, as should the location, or call number, of the item, thereby vouchsafing both the way into the catalogue and the way out, so to speak. The only other data needed is (possibly) the title-page title and an explanation of the significance or status of the added entry in relation to the main heading of the work, usually covered by an author statement. From the information given the work can be located on the shelves, so we recommend it in preference to a simple *see* reference from the added heading and title to the main heading and title. If there are two or three different editions of the work in stock, there should be included, too, an edition statement and date. If there are four or more editions in stock, a simple reference could be reverted to, in the interest of economy, as already suggested.

A further, brief, postscript is inserted here in relation to 'pop' songs, and their entry in catalogues. Those libraries which do stock some pop usually do this in the physical form of gramophone records, and what is said here should be specifically applied to records where relevant. Pop has two basic differences from so-called 'classical' music (in its broadest sense of 'art' or 'serious' or 'repertoire' music): (a) it is often cited by title, as opposed to the composer, who may not be well-known; and (b) when cited by a person's name or persons' names, these are usually in the form of pop groups; even a household name like Mick Jagger probably comes less easily to the mind than the Rolling Stones. Incidentally, there may still be doubt about whether a pop group is 'officially' a corporate author entry, since the latter is usually reckoned to be more or less permanent, irrespective of the comings and goings of individual members. In the pop world even well-established names like the Beatles and the Bee Gees disband, perform on their own, and possibly reform, with no sympathy for cataloguers and other retrievalists in libraries. The Rolling Stones, for example, are still with us as such despite the death of Brian Jones. Despite this fluidity, names of groups may be associated permanently with certain songs, even though the groups may be brought together mainly or solely to give a personal sought tag to individual songs, *eg* the Flowerpot Men for ' San Francisco '.

We suggest, therefore, that such works receive a main entry under the name of the group which launched them, with added entries (or references) for titles. The latter would also collocate reminders of other versions of a song, if such are stocked. A significant reason for selecting group name, and not title, as main entry is that many sets of songs, whether as LP albums or as corresponding piano-guitar-vocal scores may be issued as collections, and the catalogue can thus conveniently collocate ' generic titles ', such as the Stones' *Big hits*, with contents lists of the songs in such albums. This can obviate the tedious compilation of many composer-title analytical entries or references. We must admit that a more likely practice is to cut entries down to an absolute minimum, and to rely on the memory and interest of music library staff: a noteworthy example of utilising the musical knowledge of staff as a human catalogue substitute.

To sum up our recommended treatment of pop music: Main entry under group, or individual name—composer and original singer, where relevant; with a very firm recommendation for added entries or references for titles. Also, make references both ways between a group and the individual members, or onetime members, of the group, as represented in the catalogue, *ie* in the library's stock.

UNIFORM TITLES

The title part of a catalogue entry serves two basic purposes: (a) to identify a specific document, in hand or of which the user has a note, with the entry in a catalogue; and (b) to bring together as one bibliographic unit entries for all the editions, arrangements and physical representations of, as well as excerpts from, a work in stock. A combination of both objects has been attempted in many catalogues in the past by accurately transcribing the title page title onto the entry (purpose (a)), and then by indicating a filing term by underlining or using upper case for the relevant word, or by bracketing parts of the title preceding the filing word. If the required arrangement word did not appear in the transcribed title, some libraries have practised inserting it within brackets; however, this practice could not be used if brackets were also employed to indicate ' ignore in filing ' when they enclosed parts of the actual transcribed title. It would be just possible to use different typographical devices, *eg* brackets for inserted and used words; parentheses for existing but ' unused ' parts of the title transcript. However, the clearest method is to use upper case for the filing word, irrespective of whether or not it features in the transcribed title. So brackets could be used for any inserted words as in normal cataloguing whether or not they were used as a filing medium. An example of this practice would be as follows:

> Die Bajazzi (PAGLIACCI: opera) . . .
> PAGLIACCI: an opera in one act . . .
> On with the motley (PAGLIACCI) . . .
> PAGLIACCI: Overture . . .
> Overture to PAGLIACCI . . .

Each of these would be followed by further information, as given on the title page or inserted by the cataloguer, relating to arrangement, form of score, etc.

The method outlined may look clumsy, but it does at least combine both objects of the title in an entry. However, it has two disadvantages: (a) cataloguer and user alike may find it irritating; this applies especially to the cataloguer, who has to work out carefully what typography is used, and who may have to extend his patience to supervising typing; (b) it does not cater readily for subfiling after entries have been collocated at, say, the short title. Both of these factors are demonstrated in MLA, which lists nine possible forms of title page titles for Beethoven's so-called *Moonlight sonata.*

We suggest, therefore, that the uniform title principle should be used—even if the title transcript itself is omitted. The latter applies particularly to recordings. On the occasions when words on the title page must be known, these can often be reconstructed from the very full information given in the uniform title.

The uniform title is recommended in AACR for use with any type and form of material, but it achieved acceptance principally, we suggest, from its use with music, both scores and recordings, as worked out in LCRDC and MLA, as the ' conventional ' title. Also, a noteworthy contribution was made through the cataloguing of so-called 'anonymous classics' (the *Bible*, *Arabian nights*, etc) where its use was particularly necessary because the title of such works is the main entry point into the catalogue.

We suggest that, even in small libraries, all the components of the uniform title form as laid down in AACR should be followed. We emphasise that the uniform title should include, where relevant, a 'popular title' or 'nickname', and a statement of the physical form, *eg* 'gramophone record', or 'phonodisc' or 'phonotape' to use the AACR form. Full details, with comments where necessary, are given in the AACR part of the subsection dealing with Codes. Whatever we think of other parts of entries as advocated by bibliographic-oriented codes such as AACR, we firmly recommend for serious consideration the parts dealing with uniform titles.

Some examples of title pages are given here as a short appendix, to demonstrate the need for uniform titles:

1 Eroica symphony
  Sinfonia eroica
  3rd symphony
  Symphony No 3 in E flat
2 1st piano concerto
  Piano concerto No 1
  Concerto for piano and orchestra in B flat minor
3 Waltz of the flowers
  Valse des fleurs
  Nutcracker's Waltz of the flowers
  Casse noisette: Valse des fleurs

Uniform titles are further dealt with in the section on individual codes.

TITLE TRANSCRIPTION

As inferred above, this part of the entry may overlap with, or even be made superfluous by, the uniform title. Nevertheless, however full a uniform title may be, it is often necessary to supplement it by further information, some of which may be given in the title transcript. If a transcript is not given, however, as already suggested for certain retrieval-oriented catalogues, extra information normally given at this point may be given lower in the entry. The principle we advocate is the fairly obvious one that the more important an item of information is, the higher it should appear in the entry, to catch the eye of a user in a hurry before he gives up reading the entry.

Strictly, the title transcript should give—as its name implies—a copy of the title information as given on the title page, or title page substitute if a cover title or—especially in music—a caption title is drawn upon. If a title page substitute is used, we doubt whether, in many catalogues, the source need be identified. When it comes to examining the document in hand itself, it is natural to turn to the cover and the caption, or even to information given at the foot of a page or at the end of a work (colophon-equivalent) if the bibliographic information seeker is particularly keen on identifying a document with a catalogue entry.

Even if the title page proper is omitted, having been subsumed by the uniform title, some author-statement type of information may be needed. The uniform title may state that the document is an arrangement, and even for what, but not by whom; and it may state the language(s) of any words, but not the name of the translator. A uniform title could be constructed to include names of collaborators, but it would then probably become too unwieldy for filing and arrangement purposes. So, after some thought, we suggest that it be allowed to remain as a statement of, in effect, what has happened, but not who is responsible for the happenings.

Whether or not the names of various collaborators are given, and the prominence they are given, *eg* part of the entry in which cited, will depend on the individual library. Yet again, this is where musical knowledge is important. If it seems important that the name of a musician responsible for an arrangement shall be given, obviously it should be given. However, if say, a piano work is 'fingered' by an insignificant person, however worthy, it may be considered unnecessary to name him.

A similar principle applies with added entries; we suggest that the general AACR principle of giving added entries where they are likely to prove useful should be followed. It must be left to the (knowledgeable) cataloguer to decide when to name a collaborator in a main entry; and, of those names, whom to represent in added entries. One thing only is certain: if a collaborator is worthy of an added entry, then he warrants mention in the main entry in some way or other.

As suggested in part by AACR, the following information may be considered for inclusion in the transcription of the title, etc if not already stated in a uniform title and of course if considered really necessary: edition; arrangement; arranger (or transcriber, etc); author of words; translation and translator; type, and editor of, score. We doubt whether the use of brackets need be religiously adhered to, as prescribed by most codes, unless the entry would otherwise become so distorted as to detract seriously from the bibliographic value of the entry.

If, as already suggested, reliance is placed on the uniform title and the title proper is not transcribed, it does not seem incongruous to start the transcription part of the entry with, say, a statement of arranger, edition, editor, etc; even if this practice may be unorthodox.

eg

[Boheme. Vocal score. English & Italian]
Translated by . . . [etc, etc]

However, if the title page title is meaningful on its own, and may in fact warrant an added title entry, both uniform title and it should be given:

[Works, piano. Selections; arr.]
Beethoven for ten little fingers

(In fact, if both of these do not clarify the intention of the work it may be considered necessary to add a note later on: 'For children', or 'For dwarfs' as the case may be.)

In general, in case of doubt over what to include in an entry's title page transcription, may we suggest: if in doubt, leave it out.

IMPRINT; PLATE AND PUBLISHERS' NUMBERS

Traditionally, this includes: (a) Place(s) of publication; (b) Name(s) of publisher(s); (c) Date of publication; and (d) Plate or Publisher(s) number in the absence of other publication information. In a catalogue in a retrieval-oriented library, say, the average popular or children's library, it is unlikely that there will be many documents of bibliographic interest. Any of this type may be in a special, often local, collection of some sort, and special extended rules may be needed for them.

For the average library, we doubt whether place is awfully significant. As we have established, music notation is largely an international language and whether a work is published in Leipzig or London does not necessarily affect the value of a score. Possibly place of publication may help to indicate language of words, if any. However, we assume that this has already been given explicitly in the uniform title. So, if in doubt, leave it out, especially since several places may appear on the title page anyway. In any case, any 'place' information of significance is likely to be country of origin rather than town, and this is not catered for directly in conventional rules.

On the other hand, some musicians, including amateurs, are sensitive about publishers. Some prefer, say, Eulenberg rather than Boosey & Hawke; some vice versa, for various reasons which we need not investigate in detail here. Suffice it to say that name of publisher may be important, even to the retrievalist enquirer, and so should be included.

Over date of publication we feel more doubt. Three dates are relevant: (a) that of original composition and/or publication; (b) that of the true edition of the copy in hand; and (c) that of the issue of the copy in hand. We suggest that (c) can be ignored. (a) may mean little to many users: few people wanting a score of a Beethoven symphony will care whether the symphony first came out in 1790 or 1805. A reprint of an original manuscript is a different matter; it may be of great importance to a user to know that the document he is requesting is a facsimile copy of a composer's actual script (autograph), and it is possible that almost any type of library will have some in stock. The form 1797 (1972 facism reprint) can be used, with a mention in the Notes, later in the entry, that the copy in stock is a facsimile reprint of an autograph copy: if considered necessary. Some composers are addicted to continuous revision—Vaughan Williams, always an individualist, was a notable contemporary culprit. In addition, older works may have been revised or re-interpreted by scholars from original published editions or autographs. Therefore it is important to give the date of true edition of any work if this can be readily ascertained, together with date of source. In this respect we feel that edition and editor statement and edition date should be juxtaposed, and so there is something to be said for bringing date forward in the entry to the author-type statement following title. Date can well be more important than publisher, and certainly more important than town of publication.

Bibliographic-oriented codes may well be justified in the importance which they attach to plate and/or publishers' numbers. However, since most libraries do not maintain catalogues for such purposes, we would suggest applying 'if in doubt, leave it out'. When a date is lacking, the use of these devices is usually advised. We suggest that, for most purposes, either an approximate date, or failing that, nothing is as much as is normally necessary. Even in a research library, the type of research requiring these numbers does not crop up often.

COLLATION

In general cataloguing this is used to summarise number of pages, or volumes in a multi-volume work, presence and types of illustrative matter, and spine height. As to size: this is very unlikely to be needed since the call or location number in the entry will indicate if a score is shelved in an unusual sequence. In any case, much music, *eg* piano works, most miniature scores, have fairly standard and recognisable sizes of their own, and there seems little point in endlessly repeating predictable sizes in centimetres. It is unusual for scores to have illustrations, so it seems worth recording those few cases which do, *eg* a portrait, or a sample autograph page. In libraries which are very retrieval oriented, even analytical entries may be warranted in some cases. Number of pages is as suspect as spine height: one doubts if this information is likely to be at all significant. If a work has so few pages that it is not worth individual binding and cannot stand on its own, the location or call number will have a prefix indicating the sequence in which it is filed, *eg* P for pamphlet box, VF for vertical file. Number of volumes can be very important when interpreted as number of parts for performance, as frequently happens with music. We suggest following AACR (see later) in this respect with two exceptions: (a) omission of number of pages for scores; and (b) simply stating '2 copies' where two scores are needed for performance and are in stock.

SERIES

Series statement should be included if it helps in the choice of a work from the range of those in stock. As with books, users may get to know the characteristics of certain series, and any information which is likely to be used frequently should of course be included.

NOTES

In general, we suggest that too much important information is relegated to the Notes, *ie* low in the entry. In many instances such information could be inserted higher in the entry, usually as part of the title or author statement without obtruding unduly. Typical examples from AACR are: Opera in two acts; For voice and piano; Arranged for guitar. Such information is often found as a sub-title to a work, or at least appears prominently on the title page or its substitute in some form or other. Information for performers may possibly be given in the uniform title. Certainly information for performers concerning medium of performance may be critical in a decision as to whether or not to call for a particular item. Such information is often more important than certain parts of the Imprint, and certainly the collation and so, in accordance with our basic principle of 'the more important the higher' it should be given in the title if at all possible. There must obviously be a cut-off point, and this could be left to the discretion of the cataloguer, *eg* we suggest that the AACR example 'Songs in languages other than English are accompanied by translations' could not readily be condensed without loss of intelligibility and it is too long to appear with the title. So, long items, and others in which not many users may be interested, should be given in their usual place, in the Notes. These include particularly works with which the one in hand are associated, especially the author and title of a work on which the work in hand is based, often a novel in the case of an opera, or parts of the Bible for oratorios and sacred cantatas. Added entries may be needed, also, in these cases. If an added entry is made, the reason for it must be made explicit somewhere in the main entry. Duration of performance is giving in the BBC catalogue, for obvious reasons; in fact several, or a range, may be indicated. whether or not this is practised in the average library's catalogue depends on two factors: (a) as usual, potential demand, *eg* from people building up a programme; and (b) catalogue substitutes available, *eg* printed catalogues such as the BBC's, and such works as S A Aronowsky's *Performing times of orchestral works*.

Contents lists are an item too often omitted on the plea of lack of time—even by some cataloguers who spend time on what we consider to be rather pedantic imprint and collation data. Any collection should be carefully considered as a candidate for a contents list, even if it is very long, as in, say, some collections of folksongs. In fact in such cases, contents lists may obviate the need for analytical entries, with a little drill in patient catalogue use. It may be decided that it is worth the extra labour of combing contents lists of entries brought together by specific subject cataloguing or classification than to anticipate occasional requests for songs, say by making numerous analytical added entries, 'added references', or simple references under composers and titles. Contents lists are necessary for complete works of a composer in several volumes. According to custom, the number of volumes in multi-volume works is usually given in the collation. However, it may be worthwhile considering putting this with contents lists, in the notes. They need not necessarily list each work if the volume title gives a clear indication of the type of work included, say, all the piano sonatas by a composer. However, if a volume is not comprehensive in its field, but includes only selections, then a detailed contents list should be given. Titles here can be edited to omit information already given in the title or uniform title.

In a catalogue intended for use by children, or the uninitiated, it may be useful to expand on level of difficulty of some items, and even to include a very brief account of plots and background to dramatic or programme works such as operas and certain orchestral works, and connection with other works, where relevant, usually novels or plays. Accompanying material, *eg* gramophone records, should be named.

LANGUAGE

As far as possible the home language should be used in all music cataloguing, especially in popular libraries. In a uniform title, the vernacular, if not English, say, would be used as a filing medium only if there were no accepted English title, or if it were impossible to decide fairly that the English form is more likely to be sought. An example of the first type might be *Cavalleria rusticana*—the English title *Rustic chivalry* is virtually a joke. An example of the second type might be *Die Meistersinger/The mastersingers*; however, we would opt for the English version in this case.

Language decisions may be needed in other than uniform titles. A likely example is in contents lists: we suggest giving the form in the document, with the English translation in parentheses, as in AACR. Another common example is in names of instruments: following our basic rule, we suggest English if reasonably possible. An example of unreasonable use of English would be 'English horn' for 'cor anglais'. We also suggest such an accepted abbreviation as 'cello' rather than 'violoncello'.

TRACINGS

Records of all added entries should be included in the main entry. These will automatically appear on added entries if the unit entry principle is practised, *eg* entries produced by facsimile copying or by an automatic typewriter. If entries are typed individually, there is little point in repeating the tracings on added entries. One—controversial—exception would be if tracings are intended to give information to the catalogue user, *eg* when subject/form entry tracings are used instead of subject/form notes. A less controversial economy is not to spell out titles and individual analytical entries; these can be covered in the tracings by 'Title' and 'Contents' respectively. Further, it may be necessary to differentiate in tracings between uniform title and transcribed title, if both are used in the entry. Since these tracings are intended for staff use only, cyphers can be used, *eg* 'UT' for uniform title and 'T', 'Ti', or 'Title' for transcribed titles.

ADDED ENTRIES

An added entry, in our view, is a copy of a (full) unit entry filed under a heading additional to that of the 'main' (usually composer) entry. In a classified catalogue, academically, the main entry is filed under the class number at which the document is shelved; however, we still envisage the composer entry as being virtually a replica of it. Whether music entries are interfiled in a general catalogue, or in a separate special catalogue, makes no substantial difference.

However, all music is not well covered by central agency services, so libraries may well practise simplified cataloguing. In such a case, if sufficient information is given in an additional entry to enable a work to be identified and located, without reference to the main entry, such an entry can still in fact be an entry and not a reference. But if any additional approach to a work is catered for by referring the user to the main entry, before location is possible, this constitutes a reference. A midway point is when a work is actually identified but very very briefly, but in effect only a reference is made to the location of the document, as often used in BM practice. As already mentioned, we dub such an approach as an 'added reference'.

We suggest that in general many approaches are needed in the case of music. So, even if added entries are very brief, even to the point of being 'added references', this is preferable to economising to the point of simply failing to cater for a variety of approaches. We suggest further that for most libraries at least it is preferable to have many short entries than very few detailed entries giving a great quantity of bibliographic data such as minute imprints, plate or publishers' numbers and collation.

Alternative approaches are likely to be useful under: significant title of main work; 'nickname' or popular title; title(s) of excerpt(s) if uniform titles are used; titles in various languages; authors and titles of 'related' and 'source' works; arrangers, editors, and transcribers; collaborating composers or names of composers whose works, or themes, are drawn upon; authors of libretti, 'books' of musicals, and of poems set to music. Analytical entries may be useful, in the case of collections, under composers, titles and occasionally first lines of songs, depending on whether or not catalogue-substitutes are available for ready use. Despite what is said above, composer-title and certain title references could be used in certain instances. Such a case would apply where an excerpt is entered in indirect form, via the 'parent' title, *eg*

WALTZ of the flowers
see
TCHAIKOVSKY, P. I.
Nutcracker. Waltz of the flowers

VALSE des fleurs
see
TCHAIKOVSKY, P. I.
Nutcracker. Waltz of the flowers

and possibly

TCHAIKOVSKY, P. I.
Valse des fleurs
see his
Nutcracker. Waltz of the flowers

and even

TCHAIKOVSKY, P. I.
Waltz of the flowers
see his
Nutcracker. Waltz of the flowers

(But see also AACR for uniform title construction of this work: R 240A, p 238, examples.)

SUBJECT AND FORM APPROACH

Previous recommendations and comments have been confined for the most part to the author/title approach. However, the 'matter' of music is important just as much as the need for known and cited individual works, however imperfectly cited (hence our recommendations for composers, collaborators, titles and quasi-titles as approaches). From this point of view, music has two chief approaches: (a) forms, or types, of music itself, and (b) the subject of music, in the way that authors may write about any subject. A further type of form is music in the physical form of sound recordings: this aspect is dealt with in the next subsection.

In a subject catalogue (in the broad sense) it is essential to differentiate between: (a) subject, in the sense of works about music; and (b) form, in the sense of entries for works themselves under headings for 'types' of works. Classification schemes have two basic ways of differentiating between scores and music as a subject of investigation. The Dewey Decimal Classification in the past fell back on using a prefix like M or S with a number for an instrument or form; later it introduced a stage-by-stage differentiation, in that there is a notation, for, say, one instrument and a subdivision of that notation for scores for that instrument. Thus in principle, scores and works about scores would be interfiled; in fact librarians almost always maintain separate sequences, if only for physical convenience. Other schemes may arrange whole sequences of separate notation for scores as differentiated from works on music; examples are the Library of Congress Classification, and the British catalogue of music classification by E J Coates. This method is usually preferred for shelf arrangement, for obvious physical reasons.

However, for catalogue purposes, it is preferable to represent actual items immediately adjacent to works about those items, *ie* not only to have works about Beethoven listed immediately after entries for works by Beethoven as a whole, but to have entries for works about Beethoven's symphonies given immediately after those for scores of Beethoven's symphonies, and a book about Tchaikovsky's *Swan Lake* listed immediately after scores of that ballet.

Therefore, in a classified catalogue the DC arrangement is preferable —despite the contumely which is heaped upon it by some critics. Using the separate sequence principle, 'works by' and 'works about' form separate blocks, and their inter-relationship has to depend on the subject index to collocate these distributed relatives by proxy. Therefore double referral is needed to get the user from, say, Beethoven's *Choral symphony* as a score to that work as a subject of a monograph or article, the subject index being the intermediary. But, to take another example, using DC 18th ed, the subject index will give, *eg*

VIOLIN 787.1

and from this number in the classified file of the classified catalogue one is led (we hope) by guiding to 787.15 for violin scores.

At this stage, however, we should differentiate, further, between not two, but three types of document involving instruments:

(a) scores for music for an instrument, or instruments;

(b) works about music for an instrument or instruments; and

(c) works about the instrument as a physical object, *eg* its history or manufacture. The subject index to a classified catalogue may then use

a) HORN : INSTRUMENT
b) HORN : MUSIC
c) HORN : MUSIC : CRITICISM

However, if chain procedure is used—and strictly—a different citation order may emerge depending on the structure of the classification scheme. The type of structure exemplified above could be used also for the dictionary catalogue, but using, if preferred, the conventional dash—and not colon—to separate isolates in the heading. However, librarians preferring direct phrase construction may finish up with, say, HORN MUSIC; HORN MUSIC—CRITICISM; and HORN—INSTRUMENT.

The Music Division of New York Public Library uses differently coloured tops to its cards which partly takes care of the above problem, and also another—the differentiation between scores and musical works consisting of words only: music itself—green; words only—yellow; works about—white. Since colours of course do not have any filing significance, a filing order then has to be established: first sequence—white; second sequence—green and yellow interfiled. It should be mentioned that some works entail multiple entry; *eg* a work 'about' but including also music will have one white entry and one green entry.

It should be remembered that headings, usually for scores, can become extremely complex, and in fact so clumsy as to make filing difficult. This applies especially in 'conventional' dictionary catalogue headings which attempt to be co-extensive with the nature of the work yet retain at least some direct phrase construction. An example from the New York list is

FLUTE IN TRIOS (FLUTE, OBOE, CLARINET)—ARR

A little structuring would obviate giving insignificant connecting words filing significance, *eg*

FLUTE—TRIOS [etc]

A further complication is that when a heading includes the names of several instruments, a decision has to be made on the citation order to be used. There are two likelihoods: (a) alphabetical; and (b) score order. Whatever decision is made obviously affects the type of collocation emerging when a number of entries have to be filed. Assuming that most people using such entries are reasonably knowledgeable musically, we would recommend (b), since quite firm conventions have been established arising from the type of instrument (strings, woodwind, brass, etc) and the range of each instrument within its type.

So far we have used instruments to exemplify various problems. But there are likely to be several components of various categories in a fully coextensive heading.

Some forms are fairly stereotyped in nomenclature and the compositions in such forms do not always have individual titles to confuse approaches; examples are symphonies, concertos, sonatas. Other examples of forms traditionally always have their own titles, *eg* operas, oratorios, and songs, already mentioned. These may be less likely to be asked for by form, but the possibility exists. Possibly just as important is medium—instrument and/or voice. Other possibilities, though perhaps less likely, are approaches by period, national school, and 'types' (subject relevance) of music. An enquirer may be interested in Romantic, or Classical, or Baroque music. Another may be interested in English, or German, or Viennese. Yet another may want martial music, or even 'deathbed' music. The latter type of request is rather nebulous, and embraces a subjective choice as in the need for incidental music for, say, play productions ('mood' music). However, the first two are reasonably cut-and-dried and one might expect a catalogue to cater for them in some way in a formal manner. The 'types' of music, or 'characteristic' music or 'mood' music, may best be catered for by the compilation of special lists by the (knowledgeable!) music librarian, based on a library's stock, whether in score or sound record form. We suggest at this point that music has at least four approaches which should be considered: Form; Medium; Period; Schools (usually national); and of course individual composer where not covered by the author approach.

REDFERN (p 19) lists the following, which we consider comprehensive, except for the omission of Voice:

'Facets in music

1 Facets in literature and music

  1 Composers

  2 Instruments

  3 Size of ensemble

  4 Forms

    a Major (*eg* concertos)

    b Minor (*eg* binary)

2 Facets in literature and possibly in music

5 Musical character
6 Space (*ie* country etc)
7 Time (*ie* baroque etc)

3 Facets in literature and unlikely in music

8 Elements (*ie* harmony etc)
9 Techniques (*ie* orchestration etc)
10 Theory (*ie* appreciation etc)
11 Forms of presentation (*ie* catalogues)
12 Phase relationships (*ie* music interrelated with other subjects)'

A librarian may make or use such a list if designing a new classification scheme, or refining or explaining an existing classification scheme. Classification does not concern us immediately here, but we must acknowledge that such categorising is very useful in the consistent construction of headings for: (a) a dictionary catalogue; (b) an information file; or (c) a file of music in 'fugitive material' form. It is evident that not all of the components given are likely to be needed for one heading, but if any degree of coextensivity is to be aimed at, it is also evident that not only Redfern's facets apply, but that there may be even further complications, as has already been demonstrated in the case of instruments. 'Instruments' seems simple when listed as such, but there may be a wide variety of combinations of instruments, not only as such but linked with certain forms, *eg* concertos and chamber music ensembles, and with voices; an example is Britten's *Serenade for tenor, horn and strings*. Composers may, in fact, use such a variety of combinations that it is impossible to cater for them all without virtually representing both the title of a work and the instruments listed in the score.

A basic decision has to be made at the start: shall each heading be purely pre-coordinate or shall some form of post-coordinate structure be assumed? If one adopts pre-coordination, each heading will include: (a) all the components present in the work; and (b) a settled order in which these components shall be combined, or cited. Even so, a decision has to be made (a) whether to use one entry for each work, with supporting references; or (b) whether to use multiple entry employing some form of permutation of the components of a heading.

A simple example is, say:

(a) HORN—CONCERTOS

and CONCERTOS

see also

HORN—CONCERTOS

or (b) 1 HORN—CONCERTOS

2 CONCERTOS—HORN

It can be seen that (b) could result in a very bulky catalogue. In fact, when three or more components are needed for a heading, the situation could get out of hand. The reader may like to work out the combinations, and number of entries, possible for a work with the heading TENOR—HORN—STRINGS. It seems evident that multiple coextensive entry in all cases is not practically realisable in most catalogues, and that some form of a simple coextensive entry backed up by references is the only feasible solution, that is, if coextensive headings are insisted upon.

An alternative, practised by many 'conventional' dictionary cataloguers whether they realise it or not, is in effect multiple post-coordinate entry. That is, a work is entered two, or even more, times under headings which are not fully coextensive with the coverage of the work. Our simple example from above would give:

1 HORN, *or* HORN MUSIC

and 2 CONCERTOS

This method is used by SEARS.

A halfway mark between single and multiple-concept entry is practised by many 'conventional' dictionary catalogue libraries. The New York list, already mentioned, would use two overlapping headings for a particular work, *eg*

1 FLUTE IN TRIOS (FLUTE, OBOE, CLARINET)—ARR.

and 2 SUITES (CHAMBER ORCHESTRA)—ARR. FOR TRIOS

ie medium and form entry respectively.

Many librarians use LC for general works. Current editions incorporate music headings, previously published separately, and so LC is a good example of a—possibly *the*—general list of headings. Generally the New York Public Library uses multiple entry, as already shown. On the other hand LC generally uses single entry with supporting references, *eg*

HORN MUSIC

see also CONCERTOS (HORN)

and HORN AND PIANO MUSIC, ARRANGED

see also CONCERTOS (HORN)—SOLO WITH PIANO

VARIATIONS (HORN WITH ORCHESTRA) SOLO WITH PIANO

Nevertheless, it would seem that Britten's *Serenade for tenor, horn and strings* cannot be accommodated at one LC heading, despite the great volume of combinations of media enumerated in the system. For full, or as nearly as possible full, representation, we might possibly use:

1 HORN WITH STRING ORCHESTRA

and 2 SONGS WITH ORCHESTRA

although we do not feel very happy about this.

We have already mentioned the cumbersomeness of some headings incorporating a variety of instruments. LC has its share, *eg*

STRING TRIOS (VIOLIN, VIOLA, VIOLA DA GAMBA)
STRING TRIOS (VIOLIN, VIOLA D'AMORE, VIOLA DA GAMBA)
STRING TRIOS (VIOLIN, VIOLA D'AMORE, VIOLONCELLO)
STRING TRIOS (VIOLIN, VIOLONCELLO, DOUBLE BASS)
STRING TRIOS (2 VIOLINS, VIOLA)
[etc, etc]

Incidentally, LC uses plurals here, but one is liable to encounter the singular elsewhere, *eg* PIANO QUARTET.

When a library has a very extensive stock, and when any degree of specificity is hoped for, it is indeed very difficult to avoid cumbersome headings. However, LC could be more consistent in its various citation orders. It seems to oscillate between medium and form in an arbitrary way, as demonstrated by using HORN and STRING as entry words sometimes and CONCERTOS and VARIATIONS at others.

Another slightly disturbing fact about LC from the music librarian's point of view is that music headings get interfiled in the direct phrase alphabetical sequence with non-musical headings. One finds, for example:

HORN (MUSICAL INSTRUMENT)
. . .
HORN AND PIANO MUSIC, ARRANGED
HORN CARVING
HORN FLIES
HORN MUSIC
[etc, etc]

In a general catalogue, one should surely expect to separate music from non-music headings, even when homonyms are concerned.

Music librarians who wish to be radical, consistent and hard-working may consider using chain procedure as a way of constructing headings and references. Chain procedure is, by definition, derived from a classification scheme. A scheme based on analytico-synthetic (faceted) principles, which therefore responds well to chain procedure, is the *British catalogue of music classification* devised by E J Coates. Despite this scheme's use for some fifteen years in BCM, the classification does not seem to have been widely adopted. One reason may be that not many potentially extensive libraries have been established since BCM started. One example is the Music Division of the State Library of Western Australia, which uses BCM for scores, but DC for works on music. Whether or not a library adopts or changes to BCM, it could still use BCM as a basis for the construction of its alphabetical-subject approach, in particular for dictionary catalogue headings and references. We propose to take and analyse for our purposes an example given in the preface to the BCM scheme: Military marches for trumpet, which would be classified at WSGM/KG. The notation for Trumpet and Marches has to be combined in reverse alphabetical order, *ie* W comes before G. The oblique stroke /, introducing in this case ' character ' of music, comes after the main notation.

Specific entry in the chain index to the classified catalogue gives:

MILITARY: MARCHES: TRUMPET WSGM/KG

The rest of the chain produces:

MARCHES: TRUMPET	WSGM	
TRUMPET	WS	
BRASS WIND INSTRUMENTS	W	(notation in BCM scheme is not expressive)
WIND INSTRUMENTS	V	
INSTRUMENTAL MUSIC	L	
MUSIC: SCORES	C/Z	(not needed in catalogue for music only)

These produce the following chain of headings and references:—

MUSIC *see also* INSTRUMENTAL MUSIC
INSTRUMENTAL MUSIC *see also* WIND INSTRUMENTS
WIND INSTRUMENTS *see also* BRASS WIND INSTRUMENTS
BRASS WIND INSTRUMENTS *see also* TRUMPET
TRUMPET *see also* MARCHES: TRUMPET
MARCHES: TRUMPET *see also* MILITARY: MARCHES: TRUMPET

When other musical forms for trumpet are added to stock, further references would be needed, *eg* for trumpet concertos:

Heading:— CONCERTOS: TRUMPET
Reference:— TRUMPET *see also* CONCERTOS: TRUMPET
This preferably going onto the same card as TRUMPET, etc above: *ie*
TRUMPET *see also* CONCERTOS: TRUMPET
MARCHES: TRUMPET

An easier but less satisfactory method would be the general or 'blanket' *see also* reference:—

TRUMPET *see also* names of musical forms with subdivision TRUMPET, *eg* CONCERTOS: TRUMPET

In addition, since the cornet has something in common with the trumpet it may be considered useful to connect the two with *see also* references both ways, provided there is cornet music in stock:

TRUMPET *see also* CORNET
CORNET *see also* TRUMPET

It is suggested that such collateral ('sideways') references should not be made automatically, but only when the librarian considers that the two have sufficient in common, *eg* being possibly interchangeable, or often played by the same player. This is an example of the music cataloguer needing some sort of musical knowledge or education.

Despite the need for care, as mentioned above, BCM responds well to the technique because it does not skip stages of division. Compare a random example from the Library of Congress Classification:

LC:— Instrumental music—Organ
BCM:— Individual instruments—Keyboard instruments—Organ

However, we must remember the possible basic disadvantage of the system as a whole: combination order for compound headings is decided by the scheme. So, if the citation order (1) Form, (2) Medium is not wanted, then the method would not be used for a dictionary catalogue, even though it may well be acceptable for a chain index in a classified catalogue. (It may be of interest to note here that the Music Division of the State Library of Western Australia, mentioned above, has a classified catalogue but constructs its subject index from LC subject headings.)

One may prefer to go back to first principles and design a citation order according to what one considers—from knowledge of users' requirements and of music—is most likely to be useful, or 'sought'. The basic decision to be made is medium—instrument or voice—in relation to form. We suggest (1) Medium; (2) Form, *eg* HORN—CONCERTOS, not vice versa. If 'orchestra' is not assumed as in the 'concertos' example, this could be cited as a second medium, *eg* CELLO (and) ORCHESTRA, such connectives as 'and' and 'with' not having filing significance, *eg* CELLO (and) ORCHESTRA—VARIATIONS. A collective noun denoting a group of instruments would count as 'medium', as STRINGS. Where the number of instruments also inferred a form, *eg* normally, sonata form, this would itself be counted as 'form' *eg* STRINGS—QUARTETS. A *see also* reference would, of course, be needed, *eg* SONATA FORM *see also* STRINGS—QUARTETS, and similar numbers of instruments; when the type of instruments is inferred in a term like 'quartet' there seems little point in enumerating the individual instruments. A similar situation exists for other numbers of instruments, *eg* trios. However, whenever the number of instruments includes a variety of instruments, the 'instrument' compound becomes superfluous or so diffuse as to be irrelevant. Schubert's *Octet* would be best represented by the simple entry OCTETS, in the same way that a symphony is obviously best represented by SYMPHONIES and not by the artificial term ORCHESTRA—SYMPHONIES. If such an approach word has to be catered for this can be done by *see also* references, *eg* ORCHESTRAL MUSIC *see also* SYMPHONIES.

A further complication is a combination of both a voice and an instrument as leading components, as in Britten's *Serenade for tenor, horn and strings*, already cited. In such a case, we can—we suggest—accept the composer's word, as expressed in the title, as to which is the most significant component. We can involve a second round, and give both media—voice and instrument—followed by subsidiary elements, in this case yet another medium.

eg TENOR—HORN—STRINGS *or* TENOR (and) HORN (and) STRINGS with appropriate *see also* references. It might be mentioned that a combination of 'tenor' and 'horn' is not a common combination (not to be confused with the instrument 'tenor horn') and so—relying on the librarian's musical knowledge—an added entry for the Britten work may be made under HORN. 'Serenade' is a 'minor' form—applying REDFERN's apparent principles. It can probably be ignored, even in a catalogue pretending towards a coextensive structure of headings. In this case, as it happens, a user using the approach term SERENADE would be catered for by a title added entry.

Redfern does not appear to cater for certain 'types' of music like operas, oratorios and cantatas unless these are included under 'Forms—major'. Again, terms like these assume voices, including chorus, and primary entry term can be the form itself. it has to be remembered that we are catering here for the pure subject/form approach as such, and what we say here does not necessarily affect the construction of uniform titles under composers. Having accepted entry under form term, we must then decide as to 'types' of form, *eg* operas are 'grand' or 'light', or even, now, 'rock'; cantatas are 'sacred' or 'secular'. It is worth considering following the citation order suggested by COATES (though in a different, technical, context, in his *Subject catalogues* and in *British technology index*), and use the citation order of (1) Thing, (2) Type. So we get OPERAS, GRAND or merely OPERAS, OPERAS, LIGHT, and OPERAS, ROCK; and CANTATAS, SACRED and CANTATAS, SECULAR. This is not alphabetico-classing, as some over-simplifying writers may suggest, but merely indirect, as opposed to direct, entry. (However, personally, we prefer direct entry whenever possible—admittedly a subjective judgement.) So, Mendelssohn's *Elija* comes under ORATORIOS, and Vaughan Williams' *Toward the unknown region* comes under CANTATAS, SECULAR: Puccini's *La boheme* is under OPERAS, and Johann Strauss' *Die Fledermaus* is under OPERA, LIGHT. There may be a rather nice distinction between OPERAS, LIGHT and MUSICALS, the latter term usually being applied to comparatively recent works with a less symphonic structure. Further, we should respect composers' nomenclature and use, *eg* MUSIC DRAMAS for Wagner's main works. *See also* references can be used to connect, both ways, similar types of works which have different form entries, *eg* OPERAS *see also* MUSIC DRAMAS, and MUSIC DRAMAS *see also* OPERAS.

Despite our suggestion for reasonable attempts at coextensivity of headings, we suggest that REDFERN's facets of 'space' and 'time' need not be included in headings for musical works. However, they should be included in headings for literature about music. It may seem inconsistent, but we feel that under, say, OPERA, direct subdivision by composer for actual works is preferable to indirect subdivision by period or place, even though, say, a document on 18th century German operas goes under such a heading as OPERAS—GERMAN—18th CENTURY, while the entry for a study of a particular Mozart opera immediately follows entries for the work itself under, in effect, OPERAS—MOZART.

To sum up, works on music might approximately use the following citation order—not that all components are likely to occur simultaneously: (1) Instrument/voice; (2) Form; (3) Musical character; (4) Size of ensemble; (5) Space; (6) Time; (7) Form of presentation. It is not very likely that such factors as harmony, orchestration, appreciation, and music in relation to other subjects are likely to occur in combination with all the others, but if and when they occur they should precede, or replace, (7) Form of presentation. Composer would be the final factor for arrangement, especially since, in a dictionary catalogue, there would be added entries for composers as subjects immediately following composers as authors, as mentioned already.

Some of this may seem a little indefinite, but we suggest it is preferable—assuming one could start again from scratch—to such apparently blatant inconsistencies as in LC's:

PIANO MUSIC
PIANO QUINTETS
SONATAS (PIANO)
QUINTETS (PIANO, OBOE, VIOLIN, VIOLONCELLO)
CONCERTOS (PIANO)
PIANO, FLUTE, VIOLIN WITH STRING ORCHESTRA
Piano—Tuning *see* TUNING

to name but a few random examples. There may be some musicologically subtle reason for these constructions, but if—after some thought—we still cannot reconcile them, what of the more casual user?

Music recordings

We count a sound recording as a music recording, not only if it consists solely of music, but also if it includes enough music to warrant added or analytical entries for the music element. The latter category would include such records as those by Michael Flanders and Donald Swann, Peter Ustinov, and Peter Sellers—which would normally be regarded as Comedy or Humour in a ' reader-interest ' classification applied to records. Also included would be ' talking about music ' types of record, of which music is the subject and which include musical examples. As elsewhere in this work, comments are oriented towards the retrieval or finding-list catalogue, since this is of most interest to most librarians. The bibliographic catalogue is well served by current codes, we suggest to the point that the more-used retrieval type of cataloguer is almost made to feel apologetic about not giving the minute detail expected for permanent and exhaustive bibliographic data. However, we feel that the latter is needed, in fact, by very few libraries and users. Record collections are fairly common in the United States and in some British libraries. They are also (too slowly we feel) becoming accepted in Australia. It would be unfortunate if their progress were inhibited by fear of this very common non-book medium as part of library materials. Records are indeed complex to catalogue, but limited cataloguing can be practised to help in making a record collection economical and viable. No librarian should feel that he cannot stock records because of having to catalogue them.

All that has been said about music scores applies to recorded music. Examples are the need for added entries, or ' added references ', or references, for popular titles for certain ' form ' works like symphonies, for titles of such works as operas and oratorios, and for excerpts if the main approach is to be via name of composer and title of ' parent ' work. As with scores, there is doubt if added entries (or even references) are needed for many librettists. But they may more often be needed for poets whose works are set to music and for the author and titles of literary works on which an opera or musical is based. This is part of the wide' retrieval ' basis required in many popular libraries, both adults' and children's. Few popular users are likely to know, and therefore use as an approach term, a librettist of an opera; more are likely to be interested in an approach to an opera or musical via a writer such as Shakespeare, Dickens or Dumas. Such sources are dwelt upon here, as being more palatable via gramophone record form than score form; more amateurs are likely to listen to a record than they are to follow a score meaningfully.

It is an obvious economy to integrate a record and a score catalogue, including, too, entries for works about music. Title and similar approaches can then score the double, or even treble, purpose of approach to the three physical forms of: (a) records; (b) scores; and (c) 'works about'. The catalogue can really earn its keep in a music department since it is usually the only medium—other than interested and aware staff—for integrating the use of all physical forms of stock. An entry for a record can be filed immediately behind that for a miniature score of the work. To make the connection even more pointed a note can be put onto each entry that a score or a record, as the case may be, is also available in stock. Rubber stamps, neatly applied, can save typing time, if, say, cards are received from a central agency or if one form comes into stock at a different time from the other.

A complication occurs when a library uses a record's main catalogue entry as an 'indicator' to show readily whether a record is 'in' or 'out'. This may happen in closed access libraries, *ie* when the catalogue is the only means of approach to records. It may be that such an apparatus is likely to be a reason for a public library's not initiating a collection of records in the first place on the plea of 'too much admin'. So, if such a procedure can be obviated, and if records can be treated as like books as possible, this may help to get either a new collection started, or an existing collection liberated. A ready substitute for book browsing exists now because of the increasingly common use of attractive and informative sleeves for at least 45 EP (extended play) and 33 LP records. Ordinary 45's do not have such sleeves; but again many libraries do not stock them—for better or for worse. In the many cases where such sleeves do exist, some libraries use the sleeves, as though they were documents, for display and shelving in classified order. Whether or not the record itself is in the sleeve, such a practice amounts virtually to open access, and there is, therefore, some doubt as to whether an 'indicator' catalogue is needed also. What we are pleading for here is ordinary treatment of what are in fact ordinary documents in a library's stock. This, then, can lead to what usually happens with most library's stocks: a classified shelf arrangement of some sort, use of which is aided by (a) helpful guiding; and (b) of course, a catalogue. It is possible to operate, physically, a parallel shelf display of scores and of records in some cases. One very obvious disadvantage of this is that some tracks on some records, especially long players, make strange bedfellows (disc fellows, track fellows?) compared with scores. So, from the cataloguer's point of view, they cause complications. It is common now for one disc to have works by various composers and in various forms or of various types (and possibly with not even the same performers, although that would not matter for shelving purposes). A substantial difference, then, between records and books is that records are very likely to have several and diverse works on one disc far more commonly than one finds disparate literary works being bound together. This seems to be dictated by the playing time of the 12″ LP, which is now virtually the standard form of physical presentation of much music, while a bound book can viably range from about 100 pages to over 1,000 pages. Miscellaneous collections of recorded music could be put at the nearest general orchestral works subdivided by composer. However, even when one disc is devoted to one composer, one often has to have recourse to the catalogue and its analytical entries or its contents lists—this applies to records called 'Orchestral favourites of . . .' or '" So and so ", and other works by . . .' A fairly typical example is a Vaughan Williams record which includes 'Fantasia on Greensleeves', 'Overture to The Wasps' and the cantata 'Toward the unknown region'. This record, in a 'retrieval' oriented catalogue, involves title entries for the works mentioned, also approaches via the keyword 'Greensleeves', the ancient Greek playwright Aristophanes, and Walt Whitman who wrote the words used in 'Toward the unknown region', not to mention subject/form entries.

We suggest that, if unit entries are not readily available, it is more useful to give entries for the many approaches to such a work, however short they may be, rather than, say, a single entry giving such minute bibliographic detail as matrix number, or even manufacturer, of the record concerned. We suggest that the uniform title principle is the most useful for the main (composer) entry of such a work,

eg VAUGHAN WILLIAMS, Ralph
[Selections]

with a detailed contents list. If necessary, the briefest of references can be given to this heading

eg TOWARD the unknown region
see
VAUGHAN WILLIAMS, Ralph
[Selections]

If there are several records at this heading, the one required can quickly be ascertained by glancing through the contents lists of each entry. But see again the comments on the possible use of 'added references' on p 45.

Codes usually remind us firmly that an extra, very necessary approach for records of music is the performer element. This could possibly include orchestra, conductor, vocal and instrumental soloists, name of chorus and even chorus master. Possibly codes overrate the performer element in many cases? One very noteworthy exception is when a performer becomes a unifying, hence sought, element: what we call the 'Night with Joan Sutherland' syndrome. Lubetzky, in his *Code of cataloging rules,* thought this element significant enough to include it in his first rule. AACR skirts around this approach, and in the end usually finishes up with title entry. We suggest that entry under name of performer can satisfy both principles of intellectual responsibility and soughtness in catalogue main entries decisions. It may be that one's suggestion appears to the catalogue code historian to hark back to the British Museum rules, which advocate entry of apparently anonymous, and diffuse authorship, works under a name within the title. However, we suggest that, if indeed it matters, the Joan Sutherland syndrome is different from the 'Little Harry's troubles' syndrome, exemplified in BM Rule 18. As already suggested, many short references to the chosen main entry heading, in this case from composers and titles, may be preferable to only one or a few full entries. Approaches to records for subsidiary performers can often be found via such catalogue substitutes as manufacturers' sales catalogues.

The sought principle applies, too, to sound tracks from films, *eg Lawrence of Arabia* is likely to be more in average enquirers' minds than Maurice Jarre, the composer of the music featured on the recording. The same applies to musicals, such as *Sound of music.* If title entry is used in such cases, one further has the satisfaction of being consistent with the entry of films themselves, if they are stocked.

Also, one is driven back to soughtness in the case of pop albums, if they are stocked. Whether or not an organisation like The Rolling Stones is, or is not, technically a corporate author becomes of academic consideration if people ask for records by this group. Admittedly a personality like Mick Jagger can vie with the parent group, as already mentioned. The same applies with the Beatles, whose components are becoming more accepted as sought personal authors since the break-up of the group. In such cases explanatory *see also* references in all directions is the best solution. Whether or not analytical title entries are given for groups' albums depends on time available and basic knowledge of both staff and users. A knowledgeable public library user wanting, say, 'Honky-tonk women' or 'My sweet Lord' will probably be aware enough of the pop scene not to need analyticals to guide him to the required group or individual entry. In addition, we may hope that the music librarian may serve as an adequate catalogue substitute.

THE ENTRY

Gramophone records are liable to be even less helpful than scores as to fullness and sometimes even accuracy of information. Information may be obtained from the manufacturer's label, sleeve, or container for tapes, or if necessary external sources, preferably a reputable bibliography or a printed catalogue of a library practising very full cataloguing. Commonly information from both the record and its sleeve has to be combined to give enough detail.

HEADING

This is covered by the Heading part of Music scores, and by comments above, and little more need be said here. Headings for scores and recordings by the same composer, etc must be consistent, whether or not the entries are interfiled, as there is bound to be, or at least should be, a lot of turning from one to the other in a well-exploited library. As with scores, we would not normally recommend use of designations in headings, *eg ed*, or even *cond*, as there is no limit to the numbers of cyphers with which a cataloguer could become involved—with, we suggest, an increasing perplexity on the part of the user, especially if headings for a person were then sub-arranged in some order of importance of contribution inferred by the designation. The part played by a person in a recording emerges in the body of the entry if other than composer.

UNIFORM TITLE

The form of title given on a label is very often different from that given on a sleeve, the latter often highlighting a 'nickname' for a 'form' work or a performer. Also, data from the two sources may have to be reconciled. Occasionally, neither may give information on a work actually included on a disc as a fill-up. One has heard of cases of records having to be played throughout by an expert in order that their contents can be accurately pinpointed. However, we are not suggesting that all records should be played before cataloguing, however pleasant this might be for the cataloguer. Since a record cannot be scanned or flipped through like a printed work, a chance has to be taken in most cases. If a completely wrong disc, say, has become attached to a certain label and therefore supplied in a wrong sleeve, this information will no doubt be forcefully brought to the library staff's notice by a user of the library. However, as we say, such irregularities are comparatively rare, and when they do occur the catalogue will simply have to be amended or the record exchanged through the supplier.

For most records, the main problem is to represent the full and accurate title, and in such a way that the entry is integrated with other entries for the same work and other works by the same composer in a meaningful and helpful way. Because of the great diversity of title representation, or misrepresentation, we suggest most firmly that the uniform title principle be used, as advocated by AACR, Ch 4 Uniform titles and Ch 14 Phonorecords. This is outlined and discussed later under Codes.

At this point, we would make two interconnected suggestions: (a) that the use of brackets be dispensed with for records; and (b) that a title transcript, from the item itself, need not be given. To take (b) first. Strictly, the label title should be transcribed; the label is the nearest approach to a title-page substitute, the information on a sleeve of a disc being the cover-title substitute. However, records are more likely to be identified by a sleeve title, assuming open access. Yet, as we have said, sleeve titles may be so ill-constructed, for cataloguing purposes, as to render their word-by-word identification value void, bearing in mind the need to reconstruct catalogue filing titles in the interests of systematic catalogue use. There seems little point in giving both label title and sleeve title in catalogue transcripts, because of the labour, bother, etc involved for a dubious reward in usefulness. It seems likely that many users will quickly get used to the formula used for uniform titles, and they are likely to accept readily the fact that catalogue uniform titles will not correspond minutely with sleeve or label information. Those who rely on the title approach can be served by added entries or references to the uniform title via composer. So, if the uniform title becomes *the* title part of an entry, there seems little point in bracketing it, especially since it will lead naturally on to an author-type statement giving necessary information not included in it. Following on from this reasoning, we further suggest that source of title need not be stated lower in the entry.

If the catalogue consists of interfiled entries for music scores and records, it will be necessary to identify the latter, and we agree with AACR that statement of physical form should immediately follow uniform title. If the library stocks various physical forms of recordings, *eg* discs, tapes, including tape cassettes, these characteristics too will need to be identified. However, if there is a separate catalogue of recordings, and if all the recordings are discs, there is no point in including such a statement on every entry. In fact, if most of the collection is discs, with just a few tapes, only the tapes need an identifying statement.

We acknowledge the system implicit in AACR's use of 'phono . . .' for all physical forms, but many librarians may wish to stick to old-fashioned terms even if they are not semantically sound, *eg* merely 'record' and 'tape' (or 'cassette') may be regarded as sufficient. We probably all know the joke about the correspondent to a newspaper who said 'I have a round, flat, black disc with a hole in the middle; is this a record?'. 'Record' still usually connotes disc when used in a 'phonorecording' context, and the terms mentioned above are likely to be both readily acceptable and unambiguous to most library users. In any case, there should be a general instruction on top of the catalogue explaining this element of entries among others.

To facilitate filing, hence tracing, of titles, usually under a composer's name, we suggest that a fresh line is started for such of the author-type statement as is necessary for each record.

TITLE TRANSCRIPT

If, despite our advice, a title transcript is still used, this will follow the label since it is the most likely to remain with the record: a sleeve could become lost or worn out. For tape recordings, there is little choice except to use the reel label, even though the reel could become detached from the tape. There is something to be said for a spoken title page substitute at the start of a recording giving composer, full title and performers and even date of recording and manufacturer; however, this does not seem likely to happen, at least with commercial tapes. If it were done, it could be drawn upon by the cataloguer in the way that film 'titles' are used.

IMPRINT

In most cases, there is virtually no point in giving place (town) of publication, as commercial manufacturers are known to belong to a particular country. See also AACR Rule 252C for further details if required. It is not much trouble to include the manufacturer's number, and since this is unique—a standard book number-equivalent—it should usually be included to help identify a record. This may occasionally be particularly useful if a detailed title-transcript is not given. There seems little point in giving matrix number in most libraries, although it may well be needed in the few bibliographic catalogues which are compiled, *eg* by 'record archives' organisations. Date of recording is more likely to be of value than date of issue, especially since many records nowadays are dubs from a previous issue, possibly a 78 recording dubbed onto a 33. To make matters more complicated, the originals may be a series of separate 78's or 45's themselves having possibly widely different dates. It is particularly important that early records later re-released should be identified. This applies especially when the original was an acoustic recording. If the latter is ascertained for sure, it should be stated in a note. The fact that a record is a re-release may be obtained from the sleeve, even if indirectly. Such information can also sometimes be gained from reviews. We suggest that this date, even if approximate, should be given at this point, *ie* high in the entry, using the AACR form for books, *eg* 1944 (1973 reprint), even if further, lengthy, details must be consigned to the Notes later in the entry. If it is known that the release date is not the original one, and the original date cannot even be approximated, it is best to confirm that current release date is in fact a re-release, *eg* just giving (1973 reprint). Possibly the parentheses might be omitted, *eg* 1949, 1973 reprint; and 1973 reprint.

There is a case for using 're-release' rather than the book-style 'reprint'.

COLLATION

This obviously differs from a score or book equivalent because of the unique physical form of records. As in other parts of the entry, more than full details are given in AACR: Rule 252D.

A basic factor, for the cataloguer in a hurry, is that there is no need to give information which applies to all records in stock, *eg* diameter, speed, microgroove if all records are, say, 12″ LP's. If a few items are different, then merely the exceptions can be noted, *eg* 10″. Although stereophonic records are increasingly common, for the moment it is advised that 'stereophonic' be given where applicable, since such a warning may obviate spoiling a disc through its being played on inadequate equipment. Nowadays, it should be noted if a record is 'quadrophonic'. There is some doubt about whether number of sides or discs is needed in all cases. If the information is needed for programme planning purposes, more positive and direct help could be given by a statement of playing time in minutes in the Notes. A reason for giving number of sides or discs arises when a very extensive work is involved, *eg The history of music in sound*; a user may wish to select certain discs from the Contents list lower in the entry. In such instances, applying what we mentioned when dealing with scores, there is a case for giving number of records in Contents list. Part of the physical description of a record is a statement of printed and similar accompanying materials. Officially this should go as part of Notes, but we see no reason why it should not be given here if it is very relevant to the use of the record and can be stated concisely. This accords with our general rule that the more important information is, the higher it should come in the entry. Included here might be useful information given on the sleeve of a record, *eg* mention of words of a poem set to music or of a song. However, since sleeves almost always give background information on a work or its performers, this factor as such may not necessarily be worth especial notice.

SERIES

This does not require much special comment. In addition to AACR recommendations, it can be used for (a) a statement of the series or similar set to which an individual disc belongs, *eg* if items from, say, a *History of music in sound* are catalogued individually—although we would not normally recommend this practice; and (b) a statement of a record club if this is not clarified in the Imprint.

NOTES

As with scores, we suggest that vital information about a work should be taken up the entry where, we hope, it will more readily be seen and in fact where it is in a natural position as part of or immediately below the uniform title.

Probably the main use for Notes is to give details of the performers and the performance. Some information will be needed for all recordings, *eg* orchestra and conductor for symphonic works, plus soloists for concertos, and possibly performers in significant obligatos. Works including words will need statements of vocal soloists, of choruses, and language of words if not given in uniform title. The ' occasion ' of a recording may be useful if significant, say a live recording of a London Prom.

An explanatory note is needed for any special aspect of a recording. One example might be that the record is a ' minus one ' recording, the solo part in, say, a chamber work being omitted, so that the playing listener can try his luck. Another is that, say, one side of a disc consists of rehearsals of a work, and the other side is the final performance. Yet another is a recording which, say, on one side demonstrates the evolving thoughts of a composer, as interpreted from his notebooks, while the other side gives the final version. Allied with the last mentioned topic to some extent is the fact, as already stated, that a few composers are inveterate revisers even after publication and performance of a work; in such a case a note should attempt to clarify the operative date of various movements. Occasionally research workers unearth a different, or even an extra, movement or other part of a work; there should be a note explaining if such a recent discovery is incorporated into a performance, giving if necessary the date of discovery, name of discoverer and source. Occasionally there is doubt, possibly arising from research after a work has become established under a certain name, as to the true composer of a work. As with scores, a note is needed, to help identification, pointing out rival claimants to authorship. A recent example, already mentioned, is the apparently inaccurate association of Haydn with Brahms' *Variations on the theme St Anthony's chorale*. A current example is the emergent opinion that the so-called *Toy symphony* was composed not by Haydn but by Leopold Mozart. We suggest that, whoever is decided upon for main heading, there is no need to add *supposed author* or equivalent in the heading, but that a note mentioning the doubt, and the rival claimant, is sufficient, with of course an added entry or composer-title reference. All scores and recordings of such a work should be entered consistently —it is better to be a hundred percent wrong and consistent than only fifty percent wrong and half-consistent.

A Contents list is very necessary for collections, selections, anthologies, etc of all sorts, whether or not analytical entries are used. Exact details of excerpts should be given, including English titles of vocal works where relevant. Uniform title technique could be used for listing items fully yet concisely. Relevant here is a ' with ' note when a record is backed up with a distinctly different work, as the information may be taken into account by a user in deciding which recording of a work to request.

Finally, where relevant, information should be given about accompanying letterpress or score material, if not taken up to Collation, mentioned above. As mentioned under Collation, there is no need usually to mention information about a work or performer given on a sleeve: this can usually be taken for granted. However, exceptions can be considered, as always in cataloguing. One example might be if the words of choral or vocal music are given fully or fairly fully on a sleeve. Very occasionally it may even be felt necessary to make an analytical entry in such a case. At this point it would be relevant to note that the library has a score of the work or works in stock. We have already mentioned the possibility of using a rubber stamp; however, if the luxury of individual notes can be included it would be helpful to name the type, and shelf location, of scores, to obviate the need to be referred to another entry.

TRACINGS

These are required on a main entry, as in any other cataloguing procedure. Since there may be many added entries in some cases, it may be worthwhile considering, say, underlining in red names and titles in the entry which generate added entries. Some libraries give tracings on the back of cards, where this physical form of catalogue is used.

Codes

BM: 'Catalogue of music' section, p 59-60

Consistent with the structure of its *Catalogue of printed books,* the British Museum has main entries under composers. These are shorter than entries according to more recent codes, but we suggest detailed enough for most purposes at least, possibly even in a large research and national library. It should be remembered that all the BM's stock is at present very strictly for reference only. Therefore works can be called for if any minute points need to be checked. The main entries are supported by a variety of so-called 'cross-references', which we call 'added references' since usually they consist of a hybrid between a short added entry—usually sufficient to identify a work—and a reference to the main entry. Cross references are made quite freely for: arrangers; editors; song titles; and titles of choral works.

BM follows its traditional use of form headings to some extent. Anonymous works where relevant are entered under so-called 'class-headings', *eg* PSALMS; HYMNS; CHRISTMAS CAROLS. Form headings also are used for PROGRAMMES, including 'word-books', and PERIODICAL PUBLICATIONS, the latter being established BM general practice, although recently there have been some moves towards giving periodicals more direct entry. Anonymous instrumental works go under title; where there is no title, one is not supplied for main entry purposes, and such works, again, go under relevant 'class-headings'. Anonymous vocal works have their main entry under first line, with a cross-reference from title—the reason for this inconsistency is not apparent. It may be remembered that in BM practice a work is usually 'anonymous' if the author's name is not given in the work, irrespective of whether it is in fact known. This accounts for the apparent Irishism that a cross-reference is given from the 'name of the composer, if known' to main entry for anonymous works.

Form headings are normally used only for anonymous works, and what we would nowadays call diffuse authorship works. Normally relevant works are entered under names of editors or collectors, but with a cross-reference from the 'class-heading'.

As with other voluminous authors, a systematic arrangement is used for sub-arrangement under composers, etc with a large output. Normally, a clear indication of the system used for each author is given before the actual entries under his name.

It is customary to make fun of the BM's cataloguing in some quarters. And, indeed, there is little doubt that with the hindsight of some 140 years, BM cataloguers today would do things differently. However, we suggest that once one gets used to BM's idiosyncrasies, and once one reorients oneself from the very different methods used according to newer codes, searching in BM catalogues can be reasonably straightforward. However, one lack—admittedly judged retrospectively—is that of uniform titles or some other regularly applied way of bringing immediately adjacent to each other entries for editions of works issued under varying titles, with which music abounds.

In the main work, music is dealt with summarily: Section 11, p 29. Composer is main entry, assuming a card catalogue, but otherwise 'Enter music works doubly, under the author of the words and under the composer of the music'. Under Cutter's method of approaching what we now call limited cataloguing, 'short' and 'medium' catalogues would normally not give added entries for librettists, though we are still recommended to give 'references' for 'important authors, as Shakespeare, Tennyson, Omar Khayyam', especially for songs. However, the Bible does not require an entry. We agree completely with these terse rules, and we do not make apology for Cutter's relying in general on the cataloguer to decide who is 'important'. We realise that judgements are sometimes subjective, but an occasional misjudgement, viewed retrospectively, is surely better than numerous never-used entries for rarely cited librettists and minor poets.

The main treatment of music in CUTTER is the lengthy Section 367, by O G Sonneck, p 138-140.

Parallel with Phillips' supplement on Maps and atlases in the same code, this section starts by asserting 'Music cataloguing and book cataloguing are essentially the same'.

As one might expect, composer receives main entry, there being the usual added entries for authors of words. The intellectual responsibility principle is adhered to for librettos (presumably separately published); and Sonneck rejects without argument the case for what one calls here 'cataloguing by attraction' in entering them under composer of the relevant opera; however, added entries are prescribed for composers. If Cutter himself had made this particular rule one can imagine the see-saw arguments in which he might have indulged. No reference is made to a possibly parallel decision, that of liturgies, which in the main code, Section 59, go under the name of the relevant church along with such works as prayer books, creeds and catechisms. Presumably any such religious words set to music would have main entry under composer, with added entry under the name of the relevant church.

A brief summary of title page problems for sheet music is given, with ultimate preference emerging in favour of cover title or caption title, although the fact has to be noted in the entry. As we have already mentioned, since it is such common practice to use these sources for cataloguing purposes, we doubt if notes to that effect are really needed. There is no mention of any attempt to collocate variously titled versions of the same work, either by typographical devices or by uniform titles. Since CUTTER was compiled with a conventionally printed catalogue in mind, it would have been easy to recommend, say, bold type for a collocating filing word. It should be noted that for title entry, in the body of the work, multiple entry is recommended, with entry under first title, references from later forms lying second in preference (Section 144). Also, a form of uniform title is recommended for titles using various spellings, the obvious intention being collocation and ready location (Section 140). The form recommended is:

History.] The hystorie of the saints

('History' being in bold). These precedents might well have been followed up and applied to music, and it seems likely that this might have happened if Cutter himself had integrated the music supplement in his code with the main body of the work.

Under Imprint, considerable space is devoted to dates, although they are admitted as being 'generally either omitted by bibliographers, or given with the wide margin of centuries . . .' A lot of detail is then given to methods and media used in dating undated editions. The use of Hofmeister's *Handbuch* . . . , musical periodicals, publishers' (plate) numbers and publishers' catalogues, and the substitution of (US) copyright date and date of first performance (suitably indicated typographically) are mentioned as possibilities. This advice can still be useful to cataloguers compiling a bibliographic-oriented catalogue. However, as we have already suggested, this is not likely to apply in many libraries.

Collation is not mentioned as such, and in fact to some extent Cutter himself seems to confuse this with Imprint (compare in the body of the main work Sections 257 and 276 ff), despite his definition on p 18. The usual content of the collation is subsumed under the part on Notes. The latter, as recommended by Sonneck, would include information which nowadays might appear in a uniform title, title transcript, imprint, and collation, as well as in the notes themselves. We are told to distinguish sheet music with an 's', but reasons are not given. We doubt the value of this, since the only significance of a score being sheet music is that it may be filed out of the normal sequence, and this should be made clear in the call number. Some space is devoted to terminology relating to, for example, what are now often called ' vocal scores ', but which more accurately should be called ' piano-vocal scores ', although Sonneck uses the more cumbersome ' vocal scores with pianoforte accompaniment '— surely not needed nowadays. Also he seems not to like ' score and parts ', which to oneself seems to have an acceptable meaning nowadays. At one point, instead of giving firm advice over terminology, which a code should do, he despairs with ' it seems hopeless to suggest a fixed terminology . . .' !

The section concludes with four examples. These seem to manifest a fussiness in some instances, *eg* one heading is given as Gaynor, *Mrs.* Jessie L[ove (Smith)].

Admittedly, this is not peculiar to music cataloguing, but it makes one sympathise with users who themselves despair at the pedantry of some cataloguers. On the other hand, another example seems to demonstrate a useful application to detail, in supplying a Contents list. However, never to be satisfied, since the contents list consists of six of Goethe's poems put to music, we would like to have seen mention of the original German titles.

In conclusion, we suggest that, although much of the content of this code has been absorbed by later codes, it may still be of some value to music cataloguers requiring detailed bibliographic description of some, often older, works.

AA 1908

There are two mentions of music in this code, under an LC supplementary rule, p 53, and in three rules about music entry, p 5.

The first merely states that the word ' music ' is not to be used in Collation, and that if a book contains music this fact is brought out in a note when not stated in title. One would have thought that ' music ' should qualify for mention in Collation, one of whose purposes is to indicate the nature of illustrative and other non-verbal information in a work, *eg* maps. However, there is a great deal of finicky detail in the rules given here, and we suggest that for the most part this exposition can largely be ignored. We feel in retrospect that ' love's labours lost ' is the kindest way of referring to such instructions, at least in relation to most cataloguers.

The chief relevance to music of this code's contents are Rules 8 Music; 9 Librettos, and 10 Thematic catalogues.

Rule 8 gives what is now regarded as standard instructions. Main entry goes under composer, with added entries under editors, arrangers, and authors of words. Variations go under later composer, with added entry under the original composer. In common with other early codes, the use of uniform titles has not yet been lighted upon. AA 1908 does not specifically cater for limited cataloguing, it being usually stated without qualification that added entries are required for all collaborators. As we know, such a rigid instruction has been traditionally more honoured in the breach than in the observance.

Rule 9 states that librettos go under librettist, *ie* it shows a respect for intellectual responsibility. Even if the librettist is not known, we may still not succumb to composer main entry, title entry being prescribed. Added entry is made under composer. As with other codes, we feel that this rule could make clear that it deals with librettos published separately; this may seem obvious, but some students do not always appreciate the significance of it.

Rule 10 states that thematic catalogues have their main entry under original composer, added entries being prescribed for editor or compiler. This decision is inconsistent in principle, we suggest, with Rule 7, since it succumbs to 'cataloguing by attraction', in effect in this case subject entry. It is noteworthy that there is no ALA alternative rule here, as applies at Rule 16 Concordances at which the American option is for entry under compiler, only added entry (in effect subject entry) being prescribed for author concordanced. These two rules provide an excellent example of how 'case' codes can result in inconsistency of principle, as opposed to 'conditions' codes, which would treat both thematic catalogues and concordances as 'related works' and presumably give consistent treatment, according to intellectual responsibility.

Other rules throughout the code can be invoked for application to music. We do not propose to go into details here, but some relevant rules are as follows: 2 Joint author entry; 13 Commentaries; 14 Continuations, which could be used as a precedent for cadenzas, entry being under the author of the continuation, not the original; 151 Indexes, which could be used for thematic catalogues, entry being under the parent work; 17 Epitomes, favouring the original author; 18 Excerpts; 19 Revisions, preference being for the original author; 22 Manuscripts, allowing for construction of a sort of uniform title, naming title followed by (*Manuscript*); all the rules relating to construction and choice of names as authors, whether personal or corporate, *eg* music conservatoires could follow the precedent of Rule

94 Observatories, with place as entry word; 112 *ff* Anonymous works, which, unlike BM, favours entry under author when known; 120 Epics, etc, which might be invoked when a traditional epic is used as a source for a musical work, as in Wagner's music dramas—English form is preferred unless 'vernacular is decidedly better known', an example of the latter being *Nibelungenlied*; 121 Periodicals and similar, following rules for various 'cases'; 139 Additions to titles; 143 Same work published in different languages; all other rules relating to description—Rule 167 Contents includes a music example; 169 Added entries, including titles; 170 Punctuation; 174 Figures—*eg* enumeration of symphonies, concertos and similar forms.

ALA 1949

This code is confined to headings decisions, unlike, say, AA 1908, which attempted to rule for both heading and description. ALA 1941 (a preliminary edition) included description, but the description element was taken over by LCRDC 1949; ALA 1941 is not dealt with here specifically, since we deal with LCRDC itself later.

The rule concerning music is no 12, in many substantial sections and subsections. A footnote mentions the frequent necessity of establishing 'a conventional or standard title' to be given between in effect the heading and title transcription. The reason for such a title, and its content, are not given; strangely, LCRDC is not referred to, although this is the source needed to make up for the deficiency at this important part of a music entry.

The basic part of the rule deals with in effect the composer as an author-substitute, and need not be dealt with at length here. Examples cited are: instrumental work; single song; collection of songs by one composer; opera. Added entries are given for authors of words where appropriate, but in one case involving a cycle of five songs added or analytical entries for authors of words are not prescribed.

Folk songs go under arranger, with added entry under title. Title entry is prescribed for anonymous songs, and, interestingly, we are told in a footnote to construct a 'uniform heading' according to the rule for anonymous classics. This rule, no 33, is one of the most detailed in the code; it takes eleven pages, and leads on to Rule 34 Bible and Rule 35 dealing with other sacred literatures—these being virtually also anonymous classics, and taking some seven further pages. To be cruelly brief, the sum of these rules is that an 'anonymous classic' goes under its vernacular title unless it is 'known equally well in many languages' (p 63), in which case the English form is used. An extra point is that the language of the text is added to the uniform title. An interesting harking back to BM is the ruling that certain titles including place names are entered under the latter (p 66). Similarly works (in our application, songs) whose titles include a proper name, real or fictitious, may have a uniform title consisting of the name (p 66-67). Again the similarity with BM anonymous works is striking.

Librettos go under name of composer of the music, an interesting example of cataloguing by attraction or sought tag approach (p 29-30). An alternative rule, in small footnoted type, allows entry under librettist, with title entry for anonymous librettos, *ie* not composer even then, thus displaying a consistency within this alternative rule not always evidenced by the code as a whole.

Another ruling worthy of thought is that liturgical music goes under the name of the church (p 31-32). Yet psalters go under the composer (p 32); this time we have intellectual responsibility as the principle.

Contrariwise, cadenzas go under the composer of the whole work: cataloguing by attraction again (p 32).

The decision over arrangements, etc is left to the cataloguer, depending on his conclusion over 'the extent of new composition involved' (p 32-33).

The treatment of thematic catalogues demonstrates one of the inconsistencies which we had in mind above. For while librettos go under composer according to the obviously preferred rule as already mentioned, soughtness gives way now and thematic catalogues go under compiler, and we are told, significantly, to make a *subject* entry for the composer. Also significantly, provision is made for publisher as author heading when compiler is not known.

It will be seen that ALA 1949 displays an apparently arbitrary mixture of intellectual responsibility and soughtness. However, taken all in all, it presents a reasonably comprehensive coverage of music and related works, and with on the whole commonsense decisions. In fact its detail helped to pinpoint contradictions for Seymour Lubetzky to draw upon in his incisive *Cataloging rules and principles*. Another aspect in its detail also served a purpose in bringing to a head the use of needless detail in author headings. Consider the following:

Koechel, Ludwig Alois Freidrich, *Ritter* von, 1800-1877. How much of this is really necessary? However, some moderation at least is displayed in:

Mozart, Wolfgang Amadeus, 1756-1791.

This omits the two unused forenames Johann Chryostom—surely known only to the detective-minded cataloguer—dragged in by LCRDC (p 86). This code is discussed next.

LCRDC 1949

This code served as the 'running mate' of ALA 1949 for some twenty years until the appearance of AACR; in fact some of its content was taken almost unchanged into AACR, especially that relating to many special materials. This applies to a considerable extent to its rules on music. LCRDC introduces itself by defining 'descriptive cataloguing' as in effect including author-type headings; yet substantially it excludes headings from its coverage. It strikes a half-way mark with music by including 'conventional titles', which, as 'uniform titles', are dealt with as part of the heading in AACR. These two terms are dealt with further, and clarified, in our section on AACR. Although this code came out, virtually as a consolidation of LC practice over more than forty years, its first edition at least did not include gramophone records. Nevertheless, this can be used for many gramophone record problems, obvious exceptions being lack of information on performers, and variations for inherently different data such as in Collation. (Records as such were dealt with in Section 9A in later editions.)

Since LCRDC deals with a variety of materials, the rules for music can be supplemented by reference to general information, for application as required, found in some sections of the code other than Section 9 Music. Examples are relevant parts of the Appendices: I Glossary (drawn upon below); II Capitalisation; possibly III Abbreviations; and IV Numerals.

It is emphasised early in the code that descriptive cataloguing serves two main objectives, which we sum up as: (a) to identify a document and distinguish it from other documents; and (b) to facilitate integration of the record of a document with those of other documents.

We suggest that objective (b) is dealt with very clearly and helpfully in this code, having been overlooked or assumed in some previous codes. However, a lack—despite the definition of 'filing title' on p 109—is that specific filing rules are not included. The definition may be taken to infer that strict alphabetical arrangement may be departed from, since reference is made to systematic arrangement. This question will be taken up again later, when we deal with MLA and its filing rules.

The need for 'conventional' titles is established at the outset because of the need to collocate entries for various editions and arrangements of a composition, and because of the need 'to bring together in a systematic arrangement general and miscellaneous collections of a composer's works'. Unfortunately, what is not specifically stated is the need to ensure collocation of entries for one composer's various works in a particular form, *eg* symphonies, sonatas, although in fact, this is implicit in the rules for conventional titles. Immediately, the code goes on to exemplify the ways in which one work, in a particular form, may be represented on a title page. The example used is Beethoven's so-called *Moonlight sonata,* drawn upon in turn by MLA and AACR. We feel that there ensues—judged retrospectively—some slight confusion between: (a) works which can satisfactorily be identified by an imaginative title, *eg* operas; *and* (b) 'form' works which may, or may not, have an imaginative title, *eg* Beethoven's third symphony appears at one place because it has an imaginative title, and the fifth symphony at another because it does not. We suggest that this possible confusion may exist because sufficient distinction is not established between (a) and (b). As we shall see, this distinction is clarified in AACR, dealt with later.

Many of the recommendations of LCRDC, and indeed actual examples used by it, are reproduced in AACR. Since the latter is the more likely to be used nowadays, and to obviate pointless reproduction of data, we propose to deal with these factors in the part of this work on AACR. One lack, we feel, which is evident in LCRDC, and which is made good in AACR, is the inference in LCRDC that a 'popular' title given to a 'form' work is not used in the construction of the conventional title, as shown in the example on p 76:

Sonata, piano, No. 14, op. 27, no. 2 C# minor. for the *Moonlight sonata*; *cf* AACR, p 233:

Sonata, piano, No. 14, C sharp minor, op. 27, no. 2 (Moonlight). We might note also the difference in citation order of components of this title between the codes.

We propose, therefore, while acknowledging the contribution made by LCRDC to music cataloguing, not to study its recommendations in detail. We will content ourselves by concluding with a note of the succinct statement of types of information needed for music, as given in LCRDC (p 75):

- a. Medium
- b. Whether the work consists of score and/or parts
- c. Statement of arrangement, noting original form
- d. Arranger
- e. Notation, if special
- f. Duration of performance

Even in quite simplified cataloguing, we would suggest that these six items should be kept in mind.

MLA

The latest version of this code was published in 1958. It consists of five main sections: I Entry; II Description; III Phonorecords; IV Simplified rules; V Filing rules. There is also a Glossary, and of course an Index. The code caters for popular libraries, as demonstrated by Section IV, and in general could be regarded as a complete code for cataloguing all forms and types of music. Unlike LCRDC, it has not been wholly eclipsed by AACR, since it caters specifically for simplified cataloguing and the actual arrangement of entries in a catalogue. The card catalogue is assumed, as demonstrated by the format of its examples, which could be reproduced onto the standard 5″ × 3″ card as to type measure. Its basic rules can be applied to any physical form of catalogue. However it does not directly cater for computer manipulation, as it relies on human interpretation of terms for arrangement purposes, *eg* interfiling singulars and plurals as though spelt the same.

The rules in the work are systematically numbered along the lines of a classification scheme with expressive (hierarchic) notation. This helps systematic use of the code, in working from general to particular, although criticisms have been made of the resulting cumbersomeness of rule numbering, as inevitably happens when expressive notation is used.

Section I is the same as ALA 1949 Rule 12. Since this is a music only code, librettos—strictly verbal works—are incorporated here, as indeed in ALA 1949, but unlike in AACR with its intellectual-analytical principles. For the most part, then, following ALA 1949, the sought solution is favoured. In addition to standard examples such as librettos and cadenzas, mentioned in the comments on ALA 1949, we might further mention also the treatment of medleys. If taken from several composers, these go under the compiler/arranger. But a medley of works by one composer goes under the original composer. The cataloguer is allowed or intended to use his own judgement, in the many types of work comprising the wide spectrum of arrangements, etc (R IA11), a decision resting on how much original composition is involved. To make such a decision would in some cases entail a great deal of work in comparing an arrangement with the original. However, in this respect the principle of intellectual responsibility obviously takes precedence. We suggest that typographical prominence on the title page might have been taken more into account. A similar principle might also have been applied to works of joint authorship (R ID). This observation is made here because Lubetzky took this type of factor into account in *Cataloging rules and principles* which appeared five years before this code was published. Obviously it could not have been taken into account in ALA 1949 itself, since that code was the object of Lubetzky's scrutiny. As on the broader front of AACR North American text's treatment of corporate authors, Lubetzky seems to have been a prophet going unrecognised in his own land.

In its heading construction MLA perpetuates what we cannot help regarding as the 'academic accuracy' pedantry of LCRDC, *eg* for Mozart, on p 28.

'Conventional' titles are still given under description, and nine variations possible for the *Moonlight sonata* are listed as in LCRDC. The resultant citation order is a copy of LCRDC's, again as demonstrated in the composer-title reference, except that the key has become flattened and is now C minor, not C sharp minor.

Although this part of MLA is virtually a copy of LCRDC, it is laid out more spaciously and clearly than the latter, with brackets in line and not lowered, as in LC's idiosyncratic practice.

Of course, the construction for collected works, whether complete, or of various media, or of various forms, follows LCRDC. However, variations in LC's actual practice in the past are mentioned, though in the Filing section of the code (p 67). Section III Phonorecords is derived from LCRDC Ch 9A.

Section IV Simplified rules is a rare entry into limited cataloguing by a published code with the authority of a reputable professional association. This section has not been supplanted by AACR, although at the time of writing (1972) an abridged edition of AACR British text was being prepared. From observation, we suggest that almost all libraries not relying on a central cataloguing agency practice limited cataloguing to some extent.

It may be necessary to reiterate here that limited cataloguing can include three main elements: (a) constructing shorter entries than prescribed in a standard code; (b) having fewer added entries than prescribed in a standard code; and (c) varying the amount of cataloguing given each document within a library depending on the need estimated for each document or type of document. In MLA, generally only (a) and (b) apply. There are no suggestions, *eg* on quick methods dealing with the many items of sheet music coming into a library, as compared with more substantial works physically.

A cause for regret is that the first casualty in simplifying some entries is the ' conventional ' title, although the examples without one leave a line space between heading and title page title. It is stated that conventional titles are not needed when there is no clash with other works in the catalogue. However, this does not cater for an expanding stock. On the other hand, one cannot predict how much work might be involved in using conventional titles throughout compared with the instances when entries have to expand if a clash occurs. As we have said earlier, a way of obviating this problem is to use only uniform (' conventional ' here) titles, and without brackets, the assumption being that a document can be identified when such a need arises by drawing upon and interpreting information from the uniform title.

One useful thing emerging from MLA simplification is that the difference is crystallised between what are called ' non-distinctive ' and ' distinctive ' titles, the former embracing ' form ' works and the latter works known by in effect what we call ' imaginative ' titles, but including too non-English titles for ' form ' works which cannot satisfactorily be translated into English.

Distinctive titles take the best known forms, with a preference for English, as opposed to a possible preference for that used in the first edition of the composition. Presumably Johann Strauss' *Gypsy baron,* given as *Der Zigeunerbaron* in the full code (p 17) would be given under its English title according to the Simplified code. The examples given are Mozart's *Marriage of Figaro*, with which we agree, and Debussy's *Afternoon of a faun*, with which we cannot bring ourselves to agree. There is a sub-rule allowing a Russian title to be given in its vernacular characters—about which we have even more doubt. Having to reproduce Russian characters on, say, several catalogue cards, and having to file them into a roman sequence, do not seem conducive to a library's being able ' to catalogue its music as quickly and yet as efficiently as possible ' (p 51).

No specific rules are given for the form of composers' names, but the examples given incidentally do not seem to correspond with what one might expect in the type of library for which the Simplified code is intended. Examples are Kabalevskii, Dmitri Borisovich, 1904- , Prokof'ev, Sergei Sergeevich, 1891- , Mendelssohn-Bartholdy, Felix, 1809-1847, and Chaikovskii, Petr Il'ich, 1840-1893. Surely one can expect more conventionally accepted spellings for Russian and Soviet composers, and the omission of ' Bartholdy '; and we wonder as usual how vital are dates of birth and death. Apart from anything else, like hoping for minimum searching (p 51), we visualise the poor cataloguer, hooked on academic accuracy and completeness, scanning obituary columns in newspapers each day, almost hoping for the demise of a musician represented in his catalogue so that he can rush in to work to complete a hitherto incomplete heading. (The really badly hooked cataloguer might even resort to crime to help complete his beloved headings . . .)

More unnecessary detail in headings, this time for corporate authors, can be seen in Catholic church. *Liturgy and ritual.* In the type of library which, apparently, can dispense with certain conventional titles, we doubt whether there is a need for subdivisions under many corporate bodies' names. As to the choice of authorising church, and not composer: there may be something to be said for this on grounds of soughtness since authorised music seems not usually to be by well-known composers, unlike masses, etc which presumably are not authorised, and which seem often to be by better known composers.

The bibliographic unit (unit of collocation) varies rather, because of an irregular application of what in the main code is a positive application of the conventional title principle. So, in the Simplified code we find *Fifteen songs and airs* under the umbrella supra-form conventional title of Collections, vocal, yet the *Gay Rosalinda* adaptation of Johan Strauss' *Die Fledermaus* (not, mercifully, entered as *The bat*) given individual entry. It will doubtless have been gathered that we recommend the use of the conventional title; yet we cannot accept such a vague collocating term as ' Collections ' for a particular type of music like songs, especially since the full code, presumably research-oriented, recommends the more direct ' Songs ' (p 26). In a ' popular ' catalogue there is much more to be said for the rule for entering certain excerpts directly under the composer, *eg* J S Bach's *Jesu, joy of man's desiring*, especially since a 'scope-card cross reference' caters for approach via the parent work (p 61). This certainly seems acceptable for this particular work, although there may be doubt about the value of other examples given for excerpts from Berlin's *Easter parade*. We cannot help suggesting that if there is any doubt, entry should be via a uniform title for the parent work.

As to description: as previously mentioned, we doubt if place of publication and date of printing of copy in hand serve a very useful purpose in general; and we wonder who, in the type of library presumably intended to use the code, is likely to have recourse to plate numbers. The code's suggestion that 'Collation may be omitted without destroying the value of the entry' is welcome, as is the further suggestion that data relating to score and parts might be combined with medium of performance note. However, as already stated, there is something to be said for carrying such information as the latter to a higher place in the entry, and if concise enough into the uniform title. Again, language of words could surely be named briefly in the uniform title, and not relegated to Notes. We agree that Contents should be given, although the qualification 'for the more important publications only' should be interpreted liberally. Analytical entries are, we suggest, rightly catered for. However, if economy is the keynote, the part of the entry referring to the main entry could be reduced to just author heading, title and call number, and omitting imprint. It might even be possible to manage by citing main author heading and specific call number. In fact, at one time, we compiled an index to songs in anthologies giving merely song title and call number. In the few instances when there were in stock two collections by the same editor or collector and at the same class number, a glance through the contents list at the main entry soon sorted out the collection required.

Section V 'Filing rules' for conventional titles represents an aspect of codes which is found too rarely. CUTTER, for example, is one of these rare codes to include filing rules. It seems sensible that a code devoting so much of its space to the construction of headings should logically go on with instructions for the arrangement of them. Although this code does not deal with works about music and musicians, it includes also filing rules for the arrangement of entries for 'by' and 'about' (R VG). However, its main purpose is the arrangement of conventional titles, which we regard as the code's chief raison d'être.

Following to a slight extent the principle most emergent from the

1st edition of the ALA filing rules, it assumes some degree of 'classified' or systematic arrangement. Its first rule is that 'Works' comes before all other titles. Collections of all of a composer's compositions, including all forms and media, are embraced by 'Works'. Conventional titles then give, say, media, so all of a composer's organ works receive the conventional title 'Works, organ'. So we get, say:

Works
Works, organ
Works, piano
Works, violin
[etc.]

The citation order for 'form' works using a particular medium, say, organ concertos, receive the citation order Form, Medium in conventional titles. Therefore, we would have, say:

Concertos, organ
Concertos, piano
Concertos, violin

It is seen that various 'form' collections, *eg* Concertos, Fugues, Sonatas, Symphonies, are put in their alphabetical place throughout the whole sequence, being interfiled between distinctive titles of such works as individual operas and oratorios—that is, if any one composer has produced such a variety of compositions.

It should be noted, then, that this code does not manifest a completely systematic arrangement, *ie* working by modulation from the most complete collections to specific works. The only non-alphabetical arrangement is for (complete) 'Works'; the rest of the sequence relies, for systematic arrangement, on the construction—citation order—of conventional titles. In constructing conventional titles for Works, perhaps it would have helped to precede 'Works' by, say, '*AAA*' to ensure that filers and users were not confused by finding a title beginning with W at the front of the sequence, within a composer's name. Otherwise, we would suggest that an explanatory note (card) be inserted at the front of the sequence explaining the filing construction. If a computer-compiled catalogue is to be made, the program would have to explain to the computer that the letters W-O-R-K-S precedes A—and hope that no individual composition happened to start with these letters. It might be mentioned in passing that BM uses a more thoroughly systematic arrangement under voluminous composers; something approaching this construction emerges in the 1st edition of the ALA filing rules.

A further feature of these filing rules, of which the user must be aware to use a catalogue effectively, is the filing significance of punctuation. The significance order (or 'vertical' filing order in UDC terms) is:

1 Closing brackets (*ie* 'square' bracket)
2 Semicolon
3 Period (full stop)
4 Parentheses (*ie* curves, or 'curved' brackets)
5 Comma
6 No punctuation: longer titles

Example:

[Die Fledermaus. Du und Du]
[Die Fledermaus. Overture]
[Die Fledermaus. Waltzes; arr.] *Phonodisc*
[Die Fledermaus (Gay Rosalinda) Libretto. English]
[Die Fledermaus (Golden Butterfly) Piano-vocal score. English]

The system is logical, and represents careful consideration of the need to arrange entries for a bibliographic unit in a helpful way. A human may build up an intuitive understanding of the system. But, again, a computer-compiled catalogue would need careful programming, even to the point of substituting, for computer purposes, symbols which represent an ordinal significance to a computer. This might entail reading a closing bracket as 1, or A; a semicolon as 2, or B; a period as 3, or C; etc. Similar techniques have proved necessary in computerising classified catalogues using UDC, which also uses various arbitrary symbols with a set filing order, such as (. . .), (O.), and =.

Further, a common computer problem emerging from the example given above is to get the computer to ignore initial articles, singular and plural, English or non-English. We cannot, say, make 'die' a so-called stop-word as there may be titles starting with 'die' as an English word. The only substantial solution is to suppress all articles at the input stage, and this entails professionally scanning each title, and editing where necessary.

Unfortunately, for ease of understanding, the period is not followed by automatic alphabetical arrangement. 'Special' terms such as Libretto, Piano-vocal score, and Selections, come before excerpts. So 'Boris Godunov. Selections' precedes 'Boris Godunov. Polonaise.'

Since punctuation with filing significance has been embarked upon, it would seem that excerpts, say, could be preceded by a colon, leaving the period for 'special' terms applying to entries for the complete work. Then the colon, not used yet, could become item 4 in the filing order given above, and the existing 4, 5 and 6 could become 5, 6 and 7. Apart from helping the human user, this type of positive signal could be used more readily in computerisation.

A final difficulty for both humans and machines is that plurals and singulars are interfiled as though in the singular. This situation is hard to overcome if one is to fulfil the intended sense of the resultant catalogue as envisaged in the code. Perhaps the compilers should have resigned themselves to some apparent lack of collocation and allowed singulars to come before plurals as in ordinary alphabetical filing. But we suggest that a more helpful solution would be to prescribe one form, say plurals, in all uniform titles, even though the resultant title would look rather incongruous in some cases.

A conclusion on the code in general is that it is still a necessary tool for music cataloguers, having not been by any means wholly supplanted by AACR. As we have said, AACR includes neither limited cataloguing rules nor filing rules; and, despite our critical comments on both of these components of MLA, we suggest that both of these represent a worthwhile starting point from which to evolve rules suitable for the present retrieval—and machine-oriented-age.

AACR (British text)

Chapter 13 Music and Chapter 14 Phonorecords are directly relevant here, but the structure and whole philosophy of the code is that of integrated principles of conditions of authorship, of titles, and in parts even of form, so it may be necessary for the music librarian to draw upon the whole code. Terms such as 'shared authorship', 'mixed authorship' and 'related works' should be understood in order to apply the conditions connoted by these terms to music works. It would, therefore, be pointless to attempt to enumerate all the rules in this fat work which could apply to music. Even some of the 'cases' given could apply to music, *eg* R 29 Liturgical works under certain religious publications. Apart from this, there are such rules as R 19 Related works, under which the case of librettos receives special treatment. Also, under R 19 the case of thematic catalogues is inferred, even though it does not receive specific mention.

However, bearing in mind the international nature of music, it is worth mentioning that particular reference may be needed by music cataloguers to the rules affecting forms of name. We commend especially R 43 Fullness, which, in summary, recommends that headings should consist of nothing fuller than the most complete form usually found in publications. This obviously obviates mention of unused forenames and dates of birth and death, these only being needed to differentiate between people whose names are otherwise identical (see our previous comments on Mozart as represented in older codes). Also worthy of attention, we suggest, is the alternative rule for R 44B Names not in the roman alphabet. This allows entry of relevant names in 'the form most frequently found in English-language translations and reference sources' (p 65). We suggest that this can dispose of the troublesome Russian and Soviet examples which we cited when commenting on MLA. Another rule which may be particularly relevant is that dealing with prefixed surnames, R 46E (p 71-74).

The generalised nature of AACR may seem disadvantageous for the cataloguer working solely with music. However, the code caters for the integration of entries for all types and forms of document into a single comprehensive catalogue. And we suggest that this can be a positive advantage. Even if separate catalogues are maintained for 'special' collections, the common theoretical basis of the code means that users can go from one catalogue to another and expect a consistent approach to apply to all. Further, when all central cataloguing agencies reach the point of being able to supply entries for all types of material, whether in list, card or computer tape form, worked out according to AACR, this means that libraries can participate in such schemes with the minimum of local effort, editing and adaptation. We might mention at this point that MARC potentially caters for physical form as an approach term. Therefore, eventually it should be possible for music librarians to be able readily to access a tape for entries relating to, say, music scores or music gramophone records. A difference between AACR and previous codes is that transcriptions of actual title pages are given, which help one to imagine what the original document looks like. However, size of typography is not shown, and this can be important in some instances. Also, solutions are given merely descriptively, *eg* 'Main entry under Bach'. Some cataloguers look regretfully back to previous codes which give the actual form of the heading decided upon. With AACR, if the cataloguer has not become accustomed to forms of heading decided on and exemplified in earlier rules, it is necessary to refer back to the relevant rules, thereby using up time and patience.

The rules for music, as might be expected, start with a reference back to Chapter 1 of the code, *ie* the rules for entry of authors. Chapter 13 then goes on to apply the basic principles of AACR to music. The first rule, R 230 (p 228), deals with 'mixed authorship' applied to music, *ie* works involving music and words or stage-action as in ballet. Examples given under the general rule include a poem set to music, an opera, a musical and a ballet. The main entry goes to the composer in each case. It is noteworthy that in cases of a literary work from which an opera or musical is derived only an author-title to composer-title reference is prescribed, not the added entry which we have come to associate with AACR and its assumption of the unit entry principle. We have to remember at this point that a libretto of an opera is dealt with in Chapter 1, as an example of a related work. The rule is under librettist, but an alternative rule allows composer (R 19B).

Ballad operas (exemplified by *The Beggar's opera*) go under the, later, dramatist (*ie* John Gay), presumably by analogy with works compiled under editorial direction. Certainly Gay is the sought name, and the individual most responsible for the resulting work in its form as published.

The question of collections from works by diverse hands receives different treatment, *ie* as for collections, as opposed to an integrated final work as in a ballad opera. R 230C Poet's works by various composers, causes a reference back to R 5, typical of AACR's structure and basic philosophy. Another example of AACR's integrated structure is the reference back to R 3 for pasticcio-type works when a later composer, or later composers, especially wrote music for a form of composite or joint authorship work. The answer here comes back to either the most prominently named of three composers, or title when the composers' names are not given. Actually, we feel that the two examples given here (R 230B2) seem almost to have formed the rule, rather than being a result of the rule.

Direct intellectual responsibility seems to be departed from in the case-rule for officially prescribed liturgies. The code departs even further from its apparently basic principles, by prescribing what seems to us to be form entry, *eg* Catholic Church. *Liturgy and ritual.* Incidentally, it seems unfortunate that the two examples given here (R 230F) both apply to the Catholic Church. Could not the Church of England, or the Church of Wales, or the Church of England in Australia possibly supply an example?

R 230D Incidental music, under composer, gives another example of an explanatory reference from source author-title to composer-title.

R 231 introduces the thorny problem of one composer's music which is re-presented by a later composer. The spectrum ranges through arrangements, transcriptions, versions, settings, etc. AACR does not make a marked distinction between 'arrangement' and 'transcription' as does Dove, following McColvin; incidentally, we are inclined to agree with the latter. AACR pays particular attention to terms on the title page; *eg* expressions like 'freely transcribed', 'based on', etc are used in coming to a decision over earlier versus later author. Also, direct information, *eg* apparently internal evidence, must also be used, *eg* 'if it is known that extensive new material has been introduced . . . '. Generally, the basic rules are followed in that if the work is anonymous, entry is under title, except that folk music goes under the arranger, with which we agree. Such cases are apparently works of mixed authorship, although we would think that some at least qualify for 'related music', which is suggested only tentatively under R 231.

R 232 continues the problem under the heading 'Related music' with the advice that it applies to 'a work that represents a distinct alteration of another work (*eg* a free transcription) . . .' Ensuing explanation shows that there is something in common with R 230B dealing with Pasticcios under 'mixed character' works. Possibly the basic principles of the code's conditions in general do not always fit comfortably into musical cases. We are thinking in particular of instances in which a work 'paraphrases parts of various works . . . ' of another composer. Those in 'the general style of another composer' seem straightforward, however; a common example might presumably be (the previously mentioned) Percy Grainger's *Handel in the Strand*, which would go under Grainger. The case of 'theme and variations on . . . ' is the most straightforward. The rule seems to rely to a considerable extent on title pages, although a reminder of this is not given under this rule; dependence on title pages in some cases is, however, implicit in the parent rule, R 19. Thematic catalogues ('thematic-indexes' in the code's index in another context) are related/dependent works, although they are not named among the many cases cited in R 19 or at this point. We feel this is a positive lack in this code, since R 19 in fact reverses the decision, for composer, given in AA 1908, and some librarians may not have been wooed away from this code via ALA 1949. Perhaps we should emphasise that we acknowledge that the composer may be more sought but so may be the subject of other documents, especially if it is, say, a well known person being written upon by a lesser known person. But to make a decision on this score causes unnecessary confusion between subject and author entry.

R 232 adheres to the intellectual responsibility principle by entering a cadenza under its composer, rather than that of the work with which it would be used. In the context of AACR, we sympathise with this decision, resisting the pull of the often more sought name of the original composer. The code could, however, have allowed an alternative rule for cataloguers using a sought principle, as it did in R 19B for librettos; we feel that a similar principle is at stake and the lack of an alternative rule manifests an inconsistency in the code overall.

The cases of cadenzas, librettos and thematic catalogues in general highlight a deficiency of the code as a whole, viz that it does not cater sufficiently for case-educated cataloguers. We feel that more explanation and cross referencing could have been included, although —bearing in mind the basic philosophy of this code—we do not disagree with the conclusions reached, for they help to consolidate the code as basically an author code, and not a subject-substitute code.

Rightly, considerable space is devoted to uniform titles: R 233 to R 243 (p 232-240). Chapter 4 of the code introduces and substantiates the idea of the uniform title. This chapter comes in Part I of the code dealing with rules for entry and heading, *ie* not description. This policy is perpetuated in the rules for music. It is not merely of academic interest, as some catalogue departments may possibly allocate headings decisions to professionals and description to non-professionals, and the code demonstrates, in such instances, that formulation of uniform titles is a professional job. As well as being a task for professional librarians, we suggest further that it is one for the musically knowledgeable.

For the first time, a differentiation is clearly made between uniform titles in general, and those for 'form' works. The uniform titles of the latter now take over the term 'conventional' title, used in previous relevant codes to cover all that AACR now includes under the generic term 'uniform title'. We shall return to AACR's conventional title later.

The purpose of the uniform title is stated simply to be a means of bringing together (entries for) 'all editions and arrangements of a work that would not otherwise be brought together' (p 232). At this point, a choice emerges between the academically accurate and the sought, since it may be either the original title or that by which it 'is cited in standard musical literature'. Unlike IAML, we are not given examples of sources which may be of use in the latter alternative. We would recommend—at the risk of gross generalisation—three standard works, all of which attempt in varying degrees to reconcile soughtness with academic accuracy: *Grove's dictionary of music and musicians*, current editor, of 5th ed, Eric Blom; Oscar Thompson's *International cyclopedia of music and musicians*; and *Musik in Geschichte und Gegenwart*, edited by Blume (MGG). Libraries which are not very comprehensive in music may use the very worthy *Oxford companion to music*, by Percy Scholes, while Blom's *Everyman's dictionary of music* may be useful in clarifying titles and their alternative forms, although it makes no attempt at completeness over a composer's various 'form' compositions. Whether a code should make recommendations or suggestions of this nature is open to debate. But we suggest that since AACR frequently refers the cataloguer to basic reference sources and similar, mention of what it regards as exemplary titles would not be out of place and would not add unduly to its 327 pages.

We have a supreme example of a need for authority in R 234, which states that the original language should be used for uniform titles unless a translated title 'is better known'. Composer-title references are recommended in the code for rejected forms of title; of course title references as such may be required also, not only for rejected forms, but also for used titles in simplified cataloguing.

R 235 *ff* deal with conventional titles, especially as to citation order of components of a conventional title and as to how components are represented. The basic structure is demonstrated by Beethoven's *Moonlight sonata*—the victim of past codes' demonstrations. The citation order emerging is

> Form, medium, series number, key, opus number, popular title if any

eg Sonata, piano, no. 14, C sharp minor, op. 27, no. 2 (Moonlight). Generally, English terms are preferred, whether for forms or for instruments.

Medium is not stated when implied by form, but it is given when in effect it is unusual, as in 'Symphony, organ'. Citation order of media follows score order.

A problem common to some composers, which we feel is not resolved by the rules for conventional titles, is the conflict between 'popular' titles and form names and series numbers. An example is Ralph Vaughan Williams, who notoriously did not cater for systematic cataloguers. His *Sea symphony* happens to be his first, yet it is rarely referred to as Symphony no 1. Similar problems occur with his *London symphony*, and *Sinfonia antartica* for which he deliberately seemed to use unconventional spelling. R 239C and D cater for various collections, so we might expect, under Vaughan Williams, 'Symphonies, no. 1-6'. We would favour the stereotyped form of entry for named symphonies when published individually, *eg* 'Symphony, no. 1, Sea Symphony' or similar for the *Sea symphony*. The rules seem to infer that what is apparently a 'form' work but which is peculiar in content should receive its own uniform title. We assume this would apply to Stravinsky's *Symphony of psalms*; but it could apply to Beethoven's *Choral symphony*, which would be entered as 'Symphony, no. 9 . . .'. A 'symphonic poem' would presumably be entered directly under its distinctive title, *eg* 'Tamara', not 'Symphonic poem, Tamara'.

Collections are catered for by 'Works' for complete editions; for medium the method used is 'Piano music'; for forms, the method used is 'Concertos', or 'Concertos, piano'; while 'Selections' is used for various media or forms, and 'Organ music. Selections' for selections confined to a medium. To some extent, then, AACR conventional titles differ from MLA's (*eg* 'Works, piano'), and reverts to the more direct form originally used by LC (MLA, p 67). We feel that the more direct form of AACR is preferable for an avowedly alphabetical author-title catalogue. Under the MLA ruling the front of the file under a composer would bceome bulked by conventional titles like 'Works, piano'. Admittedly forms receive priority, and so media become distributed relatives, as in 'Concertos, piano', but at least a key word is given an entry word, and not a very generalised term like 'Works'.

R 240 deals with excerpts. These go under the title adopted for the parent work. There is no alternative rule for libraries wishing to enter excerpts directly, as is given in MLA's Simplified code. However, as we have stated, we wonder if direct entry in all cases is necessarily a good idea in any library. Presumably, excerpts are sub-arranged alphabetically by title under the parent title. So an overture to an opera does not necessarily come first among the excerpts from that opera, *eg* 'Aida. Celeste Aida' would file before

'Aida. Overture ' or 'Aida. Prelude '. This even applies to movements from a symphony, which are identified solely by their tempo designation. Here, we are torn between an instinct for systematic arrangement and acquiescence to what amounts to an alphabetico-indirect, and even an alphabetico-classed arrangement—if suitable examples are chosen. Perhaps we could possibly—even though inconveniently in practical terms—suggest that a systematic, *ie* chronological, arrangement be considered in a classified catalogue when several excerpts finish up at the same class number. However, we do not suggest subfiling apparently verbal divisions chronologically according to an order implicitly understood by library staff but not explicitly expressed in the uniform title, whether ' distinctive ' or ' conventional '. Librarians intending to use computer-manipulation of entries for music entries compiled according to AACR will obviously have to do a lot of thinking. Concerning movements of symphonies: the number of the movement could precede its name. Concerning operas: some system at least could be manifested by including the number of the relevant act.

We cannot help pinpointing the fact that the examples given under R 240 include ' The nutcracker. Valse des fleurs ', and wondering if this mixture of languages crept in by design or accident. In such cases, we would suggest that libraries with largely English-speaking users prefer the English form throughout.

It may be worth noting that two excerpts published together receive in effect individual entry, and that three or more normally receive an entry under parent title followed by ' Selections '. To revert to another part of the code altogether (R 3), we are advised that a work with more than three authors may be entered under title as main entry. We cannot help wondering if this, as a general principle, could not be applied to musical excerpts, unless we are taking the consistency principle too far?

Several important rules for uniform titles are not mentioned here, because we do not need to make specific comments on them. However, of course, they need to be taken into account if a decision is being made about adopting uniform titles.

As one might expect, the section on Description starts with the usual comparison between description of books and music, with a statement that scores demand certain modifications and additions compared with rules for books. All parts of the description receive conventional names, and are given in conventional order. However, in the summary of the relevant terms, ' series ' is not mentioned although it is dealt with in its appropriate place according to the code in the rules themselves. Choice of source of information—title page, cover or caption—depends on whichever is fullest. We are not specifically told to name source if other than title page. We suggest 'if in doubt leave it out'. We have already made recommendations and comments on the detail and order of parts of the description of music in general, and the reader may wish to refer back to these and apply them to AACR's rules.

In accordance with convention, the title page title is transcribed in full, sub-titles including, where relevant, form, executants and genre, and possibly opus or serial number, or original key of work, 'although these last may be included in the title proper'—presumably depending on the order in which they are cited. After the composer statement, comes collaborator statements, followed in turn by type of score, in brackets if supplied by cataloguer. We suggest, as before, that it is pointless to repeat any information already given in the uniform title. Such repetition is liable to irritate users as well as possibly causing extra work in the catalogue department. However, a contrary point of view is that it may be easier and quicker merely to copy the title page than to have to spend time making decisions on what to leave in and what to omit.

The code rightly devotes some space to the problem of language of transcription, bearing in mind the international nature of music as reflected in its publication. One factor to be taken into account in selecting the language is the fullness of information given in rival forms. In general, preference is given to English. We are not told to give the English form of title proper if a non-English form is chosen, yet strangely we are told to do this in the case of subtitles.

Imprint is rightly emphasised 'in libraries where music is collected for research' (p 241). Early works are suggested also for full treatment, 1850 being put forward as terminating date, although the BM seems to have taken 1800 as a dividing line. In other cases, as we have suggested, name of publisher and operative date may suffice, though the code, not setting out to cater explicitly for simplified cataloguing, does not get round to this. Imprint is an example entailing reference back to the general rule, R 139. Considerable detail is given on plate and publishers' numbers. We have already suggested that such information is likely to be of use only in research-oriented libraries. It should be remembered that these are likely to be very few, and tertiary educational institutions are not necessarily included automatically by any means. An obvious case of need would be for a musicologist preparing a work for publication, and he would surely want at least to scan all the actual scores available. We cannot help wondering, then, if there is ever a need for inclusion of such detail, unless catalogues are to be used as a basis for published bibliographic catalogues or computerised records, *ie* for use away from the library compiling them.

Under Collation, we are reminded that scores, as opposed to score and/or parts, are normally pinpointed in the title transcript. This factor may be critical in deciding if a work is to be called for, and we agree therefore that such information should be as high in the entry as possible. In fact, score and parts could be brought out higher in the entry in many cases. Other aspects concerning this part of the entry have already been commented upon.

Concerning Notes, AACR repeats many of the instructions which we have already commented upon. As we mentioned at the time, some at least of the notes (as recommended by AACR, following other codes) could be represented concisely in uniform titles and need not be given again here. Also, other information may have been given already in the title transcript, if used, and, again, there is doubt about the need to reiterate it at greater length. At this point it is worth recalling that, in naming instruments, English forms are preferred, although an accepted term like 'cor anglais' is preferred to 'English horn': the English name brings home the incongruity of such a term, for the instrument is neither English nor a horn. The same rule, R 236C2, also clarifies some ambiguities, like recommending terms for the uses made of the piano, *eg* 'piano duet' is justly ignored in favour of '2 pianos', for two pianos four hands, and 'piano 4 hands', for one instrument four hands.

We have already commented quite fully on duration of performance and contents lists. Both are catered for in the code, as might be expected.

MUSIC RECORDINGS

Only aspects relating to music are mentioned here, and then solely where necessary to supplement our previous comments on music in general.

The code covers all physical forms of recording, and uses semantically consistent terminology, starting with 'phono-', *eg* phonodisc, phonotape. The term appears high in the entry, immediately following, and on the same line as, uniform title, if used, or transcribed title. This seems very necessary, for obvious reasons relating to whether or not a user wishes a document to be retrieved.

Main entry follows the rules for scores. No account is, then, taken of a performer as a unifying factor in a recording. This ignoring of Lubetzky's *Code of cataloging rules* R I is regretted. Lubetzky attempted to bring a new dimension into music record cataloguing, parallel with the acceptance of entering films under title: this, again, being the unique unifying factor in many cases. There seems little argument for entering 'Elizabeth Schwarzkopf sings' under 'Elizabeth', or *The world of Joan Sutherland* under 'World' except to satisfy other cataloguers, who have rejected BM's catchword entry.

Also, we wonder about what we call the 'Smith-Jones-Black syndrome' for treatment of 'popular music'. The code suggests an admittedly arbitrary choice, as composer, of the third-cited name. This rule is unsatisfactory on both criteria of: (a) soughtness; and (b) bibliographic accuracy or stemming from intellectual responsibility. The composer entry rule, which usually works for scores, is, then, arbitrarily forced onto a different medium. As we have already said, pop records are often 'made' by a particular pop group; and, luckily for cataloguers, the group often includes the composer and lyricist anyway. We suggest then that this AACR rule has not catered for the unique contribution of the audible contribution to a musical work. In sum, then, for pop group records we suggest that, while exceptions must always be catered for, the basic rule should prefer a form of corporate entry under group, but with a case for title entry. We concede that this suggestion may savour of a retreat into 'case' law, but this is no less faithful to conditions principles than the entry of some textual works having four or more authors under title (R 382), or the entry of serials, as a named case, under title (R 6A). There is a positive case for title entry for sound tracks from films, which obviously aids collocation in an integrated catalogue.

The code reminds us of the variety—or paucity—of sources from which to drawn information for the title transcription (*R* 252B). This unsatisfactory situation has already led us to suggest abandoning any differentiation between uniform and transcribed title, and so not bothering to name the sources. This suggestion would not necessarily apply to cataloguing in record archives, whose catalogues are likely to be drawn upon in the future by 'phonographers' in minute bibliographic research.

Imprint instructions (R 252C) acknowledge that place of publication becomes superfluous when a record is put out by a commercial company such as Decca. We agree that manufacturers' record numbers should be retained, in the way that we would recommend including standard book numbers on catalogue entries for books, as a rapid and unique way of identifying a document. Research-oriented libraries may wish to include matrix numbers, as inferred in a footnote (p 248); possibly even, these could have received more emphasis for the benefit of such libraries.

We have already dealt with Collation in principle. However, we think a reminder may be useful here that much detail peculiar to various physical forms could be ignored when most of a library's stock is confined to one form, there being a brief mention of other forms where relevant, possibly taken up to uniform title level, and there only. Collation caters basically for two types of information: (a) physical description to aid identification; and (b) that which tells the prospective user of playing characteristics, *eg* speed for a tape. We suggest that in general only (b) needs to be catered for. Other information adds up virtually to playing time. This can be inferred by the physical form, *eg* if the library stocks mainly 12″ LP's playing at $33\frac{1}{3}$ the approximate playing time is commonly known; but if exact information is required this can be given explicitly in minutes, possibly in the Notes. We might remember at this point that catalogues are not produced by cataloguers for their satisfaction in a completed work of art, like a wood carving is produced. They are merely tools in themselves serving as a medium to facilitate use of stock, and any information in them which is not used—however pleasing it may be to the manufacturer—is in fact worthless.

We emphasise the value of giving information on accompanying printed and similar material, as this can help in choosing a certain record, and it can enhance the value of a record (R 252D7).

We have already commented on Notes at some length. We reiterate here that some information given usually at this point is virtually covered by a full uniform title, and may not warrant repetition even in an extended form. Examples are musical form, and language of words if not English (or other home language). Information needed, in the notes, should include names and functions of performers, including of course orchestra and conductor where relevant. Original date of recording may certainly be useful if considerable advances have been made in recording techniques since then. Unusual factors should be named individually, *eg* at one extreme 'accoustic' and at the other 'quadrophonic'. Information like this could normally be rendered tersely enough to be included in Collation, where it belongs. 'Occasion' of a recording can be given, but only if it adds to the recording itself. One example we think of currently is a performance of Malcolm Williamson's 'opera' *The stone wall* at the London Proms in 1971, with its essential audience participation. We suggest that R 252E Notes be examined carefully to find out, in the context of each individual library: (a) what can be safely omitted; (b) what can be rendered more concisely than shown in the code, and transferred 'up' to its more appropriate place in the entry; and (c) what has to be given at some length and therefore must be retained in the notes —examples are contents of collections and selections, and 'with' notes.

R 253 deals with non-processed (*ie* 'one-off') records. In the field of music, this rule may apply particularly if a library, or a local organisation, makes ad hoc recordings, usually on tape, of local folk songs, ballads, etc, and possibly of local organised performances of standard works. Such examples warrant greater detail than with commercial recordings, since the local library becomes the record archive or ultimate bibliographic record of such recordings. Local history catalogues, especially if published and distributed, may well become sources for research workers, either in local information or in particular physical forms. Local librarians therefore have a special moral obligation to the profession in such circumstances, and we recommend not only that such recordings should be initiated (which is beyond the scope of this book), but that, once made, they should be fully catalogued.

Throughout the code, we are told to make added entries under performers as relevant. We suggest that in many cases the performer approach, as differentiated from performers in the description, need not be as significant as is inferred. In many libraries, it can be left to catalogue substitutes for the comparatively rare occasions on which it occurs, especially in relation to orchestras and conductors.

Our main criticisms of AACR are not of its detail, although this may seem to be the case, but of its basic intention. It seems to be aimed at what we call the bibliographic-oriented library and catalogue. In fact, most libraries, hence their catalogues, are what we call retrieval-oriented. This situation applies in most of the activities of popular libraries, including public children's libraries, school libraries, many special libraries, and, we take leave to suggest, most of the activities of academic libraries. It seems unfortunate that a new code, anticipated with hope by many practising librarians, shall have transpired to cater mainly for academic research-oriented catalogues, as shown by some of its rules for main entry and added entry and many of its rules for description. It may seem unfair to criticise a code for not being what it is not intended to be. However, our intention is to show that there is a need for a retrieval-oriented code, to cater for what we dare to call ordinary libraries, as differentiated from certain national libraries, national archives of all physical forms of material, and national bibliographies. We hope that the abridged edition of AACR, presently being compiled (1972), will remedy the lack. However, in the overall interest of central cataloguing, especially when mechanised as in MARC, we hope that a retrieval-oriented code need not conflict too much in its approaches, these being the most important code decisions. It is to be hoped that a central catalogue system could cater for all approaches. Unwanted approaches, as well as unwanted description, can be suppressed in local programming. The important thing, we suggest, is *not* to ignore approaches required by retrieval-oriented libraries but not necessarily by bibliographic-oriented libraries. This aspect applies quite a lot to scores, but considerably more to music records, especially those of popular appeal.

IAML, 1957—(in progress)

To date (1972) only the first three volumes of this projected five-volumed work from the International Association of Music Libraries have appeared: v I allegedly dealing with the author catalogue in relation to music but including various other factors; v II a limited code covering most aspects of music cataloguing; and v III dealing with 'full cataloguing' of music but in fact confined mainly to author-type decisions and description. V IV will deal with the cataloguing of music manuscripts, and v V will cover sound recordings. Overall, this work should, apparently, be the last word of our time in the cataloguing of all music, old, new and in various physical forms. We cannot attempt to pass final judgement on it as a whole until it is completed, and the contents of the five volumes assimilated and reconciled. Here, then, we deal with each volume on its own. This decision is justified because the first three volumes do not seem to us to have a unifying philosophy or principle. If the code is completed in our lifetime, we hope to deal with the work as a whole in a later edition of this book if this is called for.

IAML v I Author catalogue

Volume I, although supposedly concerned with author cataloguing, seems to us to deal principally with the background situation and general problems associated with music cataloguing. It is a rather heterogeneous collection of comments and principles which is difficult to summarise, and to generalise upon. It usefully includes twelve examples of facsimiles of title pages and entries from various sources.

The volume opens with the 'Cataloguing problems of a music library'. It attempts to embrace relevant works such as literature on music, librettos, programme notes, manuscripts, recordings, relevant illustrations and facsimile reproductions, as well as music in general and in relation to librarianship. A Hyatt King, President of IAML, introduces the difficulties confronting the music cataloguer, especially bearing in mind the fact that some collections of music were catalogued before any attempt at all was made towards a codification which might be acceptable not only in one library, but in various libraries—and we might add in different countries (p 6).

Later, emphasis is placed upon the variety of the impacts of music. Scores are taken for granted; and we are also reminded of the overlapping of music with other divisions, music in other, general, works, and literature relating to music. The vital aspect of subject cataloguing gives rise to at least two curious comments: viz that subject cataloguing of music requires no different treatment from other materials; and that the LC Music subject headings list (as it was at the time) constitutes a subject index to the LC classification class M Music.

Librettos are commented upon next. An interesting summary demonstrates their fairly equal treatment by various nationalities. In favour of entry under librettist are named Italy, Munich, Austria, Spain, and the Anglo-American rules. Composer entry is chosen by Basel, Belgium, Cambridge, Denmark, France, Norway, Prussian Instructions, and the Vatican rules. American rules oscillated from composer to librettist and back to composer. To sever this two-way pull the code suggests entry under title, but with the strange justification that emphasis, by users presumably, is 'placed on subject matter'. Some justification is attempted by citing O G Theodore Sonneck's *Catalogue of opera librettos printed before 1800*, published in 1914.

This seems slightly dubious reasoning, since both librettists and composers are liable to be better known for works issued since 1800, and in any case of course, wholesale title entry destroys the collocation of authors, as has been not only assumed in the past, but re-examined and accepted by authorities like Lubetzky and ICCP itself. There is mention of a, presumably main, title catalogue of librettos, with another catalogue of composers, librettists and all other collaborators, with additionally a subject catalogue to cater for the historical approach. Apart from querying main entry under title, we wonder now whether all libraries need an approach for all persons associated with librettos; and not just composers and librettists. We feel that here is a need for a centrally compiled and published index or bibliography to be used in conjunction with libraries' own catalogues: in other words a catalogue substitute. In due course there might be a central computer store which could be kept up to date and corrected as research brings new information to light, and to which enquiries could be sent on behalf of research workers requiring an exhaustive search on a particular type of approach. In the meantime, however, we cannot help wondering whether it is worth initiating such a project in each library, be it machine-stored or in hard copy form.

This volume deals briefly with programme notes, pinpointing the need for, in effect, analytical entries for composers and performers. This is a very noteworthy hope to fulfil a very real need, since more detail on certain individual works may be found in these documents than in any other source. Whether local librarians could actually undertake such a task is another matter, and no doubt many of them may maintain that they do not need a reminder of such a hope. Theoretically, since programme notes are printed publications, a copy of each should be deposited in national libraries, wherever they are produced in each country. If copyright deposit were enforced, then one might hope that indexes could be made by national libraries. Obviously, here is another need for machine storage, with rapid searches on demand or printouts available to local libraries.

Music publications in general are dealt with next. We must take exception to the assumption that it is 'quite natural that music publications are separated from other printed materials, and that they are collected in separate catalogues'. Even if they are shelved separately, as in libraries organised on a subject departmental basis, this does not preclude their representation in a general catalogue. The separate catalogue principle is recommended, or at least assumed, for other types of material, *eg* manuscripts and pictures of music interest, presumably because the materials themselves are stored in separate sequences. If this is the background to such reasoning, surely it is false. Currently there is considerable, and justifiable, talk of the concept of the so-called multi-media catalogue, and we feel that this concept should be taken into account. Music is surely a supreme example of the multi-media concept, *eg* a score and a gramophone record of, and accompanying information on, a particular work. And so, this idea should be at least considered in a work of international significance. Perhaps it will be taken up in the volume on sound recordings not yet published at the time of writing (1972).

This volume—vindicating its title—deals at some length with the content of a full catalogue entry for a music work. We do not propose to reiterate here the lists of items which may be needed in an entry since they are covered by AACR, and especially since the latter further recommends an order for the components of description, which the IAML volume does not attempt. However, some comment is called for on the types of Notes recommended. Included are such items as dedication and method of printing, but such information as duration of performance and type of notation are not mentioned. We must, then, suggest that at least the Notes section should not be regarded as either authoritative or comprehensive.

The volume then goes on to a citation of the practices of various libraries and authorities. Though interesting, perhaps these have since been overtaken by events in the form of ICCP and codes emanating since, and because of, it.

Later, we are advised that in the absence of a title page, we should draw upon the cover and caption titles. This is standard practice, and does not call for special comment, except that perhaps the complications of cover titles might have been emphasised more, since these often name several works issued in the same series by a publisher.

At this point there are tabulated details of which parts of entries are included, although no conclusions are drawn. Like the information given earlier, *eg* on which classification schemes are used by various libraries, the information may be of interest as a demonstration of precedents.

The next interesting point is the comment that film music should be entered under title—which itself could set an interesting precedent if acted upon. Other codes do not directly and specifically deal with this increasingly common situation. The suggestion deserves serious consideration, at least from the sought point of view. However, it could lead to problems when a film's music happens to be by a composer who made the music into a work of note in his own output. An example is Vaughan Williams' music for the film *Scott of the Antarctic* which later was ' recycled ' into the *Sinfonia antartica.*

The basic problem of cadenzas produces the solution of entry under the (original) composer of the concerto. This solution may be sought in many cases; nevertheless, it contradicts the ICCP-AACR principle of intellectual responsibility, and therefore could confuse the modern cataloguer. A ' cross-reference ' (not an added, unit, entry) is recommended for the cadenza composer.

Cross reference advice is then summarised. Examples given include arrangers, original composer when main entry is under arranger, composers of cadenzas, editors, authors of texts, titles, first line of texts, illustrators, and translators. We do not object to the need to cater for these approaches. However, we would have thought that the reference/added entry problem might have been clarified more satisfactorily. AACR almost invariably uses references to cater for differences in author or title *headings*, not usually for actual *works*. Various approaches to the latter are covered by added entries, not references; further, with an assumption of the unit entry. Perhaps, if the unit entry principle is to become more wholly accepted, we must become more accustomed again to very short entries, *eg* something like those used in the basic British Museum catalogues of the nineteenth century. The time may come when each country has one machine store of full bibliographic information on music works, while local libraries use a stripped-down and extracted version of this store as their own catalogues. When this happens, we can start to forget about the difference between a main and an added entry and even a reference, except for shelving purposes, in each library, of its own documents.

Finally, this volume attempts to deal with what it calls ' Catalogue organisation ': in effect the arrangement of entries under a composer's name. The actual construction of filing titles is, we feel understandably, introduced here, although some critics may maintain that such a vital topic should have been dealt with already. There is no need to reiterate here this volume's consideration of LC's conventional titles, since the essence of these is reproduced in AACR, and we deal with this aspect under our consideration of AACR, and in our general discussion of the parts of the catalogue entry.

However, incredibly—to us—the possibility of arrangement under a composer's name by opus number is considered—but mercifully, and sensibly we feel, rejected. There are tabulated various American practices in sub-arrangement which may be at least of academic interest to students. However, at the risk of seeming authoritarian, we suggest that such sub-arrangement has been reasonably resolved, for English-speaking libraries at least, by AACR, even though regrettably that code does not include rules for actual filing.

The problem of sub-arrangement applies particularly with prolific, or so-called 'voluminous', composers. This volume gives a full statement of the organisation of such a composer's entries in the Bibliothèque Nationale, which may be of use to librarians who wish to use a non-alphabetical and highly systematic order. If such an order is followed, we would suggest that very adequate guiding is needed. This applies especially in a card catalogue: the sequence may be more obvious in a bookform catalogue. Meanwhile, if the latest edition of the ALA filing rules is of any significance, it looks as though a more purely alphabetical arrangement is to be preferred.

Volume I of this code is difficult to sum up. In some ways it is annoying and frustrating, but in others it attempts to review and summarise various national practices—an endeavour which is surely needed in an attempt to establish an internationally acceptable methodology for cataloguing music. On the whole, as foundation for the following and future volumes it serves a useful purpose. However, we cannot help feeling that it is not wholly vital to, at least, the next two volumes to have appeared, since they themselves include quite a lot of discussion. And this appears to have been the basic objective of this volume.

IAML v II Limited Code

This volume appears to be intended to be used alone. It deals with author, title, including uniform title, descriptive, and alphabetical subject cataloguing of music, and with the classification for both shelf and catalogue arrangement of music and works about music. The idea of a short work dealing with the complete organisation of music sounds very desirable. However, we feel we should state at the outset that we do not feel that the volume manifests itself as the vade mecum of the music librarian in a hurry. This general comment is not based necessarily on the brevity of the volume—54 pages mainly in parallel texts in French, German and English. Incidentally, however, this structure can be of help to the librarian with slight command of languages since the equivalents in the three languages may easily be checked. We feel that a satisfactory short code for music could be compiled. Our imagined code would have its basic rules aimed at average libraries of up to medium size with a catalogue devised mainly for retrieval purposes. It would include also supplementary rules, and where necessary alternative rules, for larger libraries and those, whatever their size, whose catalogues were intended to serve a bibliographic function.

As it is, this volume seems to alternate, in its purpose, between the two types of catalogue, but with an emergent emphasis on the bibliographic catalogue. This needs stating at the outset, because, as said above, it does not seem to be aimed at the librarian in a hurry, despite its title and brevity.

LCRDC, then MLA, can safely be assumed to have established the need for some form of uniform title, conventional title, or filing title. Whatever it is called does not affect its basic purpose: the collocation of entries for editions of a work and possibly entries for certain types of work by a composer. The uniform title, to use the current comprehensive term, necessarily comes in an entry immediately between the composer heading and the title transcribed from the title page or its substitute. Yet in IAML v II the section on 'Conventional titles' comes as Appendix B, at the end of the code, with no reference to it at the start of the rules for title (p 20). Also, to add to the relegation of this vital part of music cataloguing, examples in the rest of the code act as though uniform titles do not exist, *eg* we find

LITAIZE (Gaston)—24 Préludes liturgiques [etc.] (p 23)
and RASOANAIVO (Charles)—Pièces pour piano [etc.] (p 21).

These reveal an obvious need for uniform titles of some sort.

Therefore, in this respect, we have to quarrel with the structure of the code and the presentation of its examples.

The code is structured as follows:

I Problems of conservation of works
II Preparation of cards
  A Catalogue of authors and anonymous works
    I Heading
    II Title
    III Imprint
    IV Collation

In the Preface (p [7]), we are told that the code is '. . . expressly designed for a music library or for a music section of a library, newly established'. The preface goes on to say that the code, in effect, is useful for cataloguing a music library for the first time or at least only superficially, or for cataloguing a music collection now separated from the rest of the library. It emphasises that the rules must be adapted for local usage. It does not mention any particular type or size of library.

The section on Conservation seems to assume that music score libraries are not usually classified, and that in any case classification is less and less used. From our knowledge and observation, we do not agree with this. It seems common practice, in libraries of English-speaking countries, to have a classified catalogue of scores and works about music, at least outside North America. The code, on the contrary, tends to assume arrangement on the shelves 'simply by format' (p 11). Yet on p 15 there is a statement that music cataloguing has no particular problems as to call number. We know that a call number is necessary to ensure that documents can be retrieved and it becomes vital to pay attention to call numbers when documents are arranged by format. The inference—from the code's rules for Collation—would seem to be that the code expects the user to ferret out and understand a symbol like 'fol.' embedded in the body of the entry in order to find out where the score is actually shelved or filed.

The code assumes cards as the physical manifestation of the music catalogue—and this in the 1960's, some fifteen years after the introduction of the computer, and despite the fact that noteworthy music libraries may well issue their catalogues in printed book form.

The code does not seem to assume the unit entry, judging by some at least of its rules and examples, which give references in relation to specific editions of works, or at least some compositions as a whole. We may have:

main entry: REBEL (Francois).—Ballet de la paix [etc.]
second entry: FRANCOEUR (Francois).—Ballet de la paix [etc.]

for a work written in collaboration (p 16). Yet elsewhere we find:

main entry: BEETHOVEN (Ludwig van).—Grand Septuor [etc.]
cross reference: LISTZ (Franz)
arr.
BEETHOVEN (Ludwig van).—Grand Septuor [etc.]

for an arrangement (p 18). Later in the code it seems to be assumed that there will be multiple production of cards (p 29); but this cannot be reconciled with the first pair of examples given above. As it happens, in the second pair of examples it might be difficult to squeeze two lines of, say, typing, onto the unit entry to cater for: (a) the collaborator; and (b) his designation of function. Presumably, the designation is included prominently because secondary cards are filed in a separate sequence after a composer as such (p 40). We feel it necessary to point out that such a separate sequence can be confusing to the user, who may not know or care who is 'main' or 'secondary' according to the cataloguer, in his initial approach to a catalogue, however necessary it may be, ultimately, to know who receives priority when it comes to locating a document on the shelves. A particular example of this occurs in the code where it deals with a piano arrangement by Beyer of themes by Flotow (p 19); the casual user might well look under either composer in the first place.

Concerning form of author (composer) heading, the code departs from accepted practice—or reverts to printed list-form practice perhaps despite its assumption of a card-form catalogue. On the good side, however, it does not give superfluous information such as forenames and dates where not needed to identify a person. In fact, it does not have rules for differentiating between persons who might be confused with each other. We are not complaining about this, since the code seems to be intended for a music-only code, and because in any case some codes devote undue attention to this fairly unlikely possibility. We suggest that enclosing forenames in parentheses and the use of a fullstop and hyphen between name and title are not necessary: this practice is demonstrated in examples given above in other connections. We suggest that it contrasts fussily with the example of current general codes, and in any case it would not be necessary in a card-oriented catalogue.

The code seems to take the title page as a partial arbiter to help resolve intellectual responsibility conflicts, *eg* 'if the title includes " adaptation ", " arrangement ", " reduction ", " transcription ", the author chosen is the author of the original work . . . ' (p 18). While if the title includes ' " fantasy on . . . ", " pot-pourri on . . .", " variations on . . .", etc heading chosen is the name of the arranger . . .' (p 18). Overall, this seems a possible rapid way of resolving such conflicts, although we still retain a degree of admiration for codes which attempt a more academically accurate resolution of the problem by using internal evidence from the score itself.

The problem of what we usually call diffuse authorship—though not mentioned as such in the code—receives interesting and sometimes casually controversial treatment. A work is dubbed ' anonymous ' not only when no author is given, but when a large number (not defined further) of authors contribute. In such cases entry is under title, though here there is no mention of any form of uniform title, *eg* for folk music and folk songs. An anonymous document is entered under author when the latter can be identified, as followed by other current codes. In certain, early, cases—sixteenth century and occasionally seventeenth and early eighteenth century—entry is recommended under name of publisher, although designation of publisher is not given in the headings.

eg PHALESE (Pierre), ed.—Paradiso musicale [etc.]

More usually, perhaps, corporate entry is recommended for non-commercial organisations. At this point, the code gives different examples in the three languages used in the code, the English translation citing

GUILDHALL SCHOOL OF MUSIC AND DRAMA. LONDON

although the code seems to advocate this treatment reluctantly for music as opposed to other works.

Cadenzas go under the ' true composer '. The code states that a cross-reference is made ' *to* the author of the concerto ' (our italics), although of course the example shows the cross-reference *from* the concerto composer, as given in the rule (p 19).

Librettos go preferably under the author, with (it says) cross-reference *to* the composer of the music, persumably, again, meaning *from* the composer (p 19). However, a useful point is made in favour of the decision to enter librettos under the author of the words, because of the use of some eighteenth-century librettos by several composers.

Concerning the title part of the entry, two factors are mentioned: (a) the form of the document, *eg* orchestra score, piano-vocal score; and (b) the need for an exact statement of the edition of a work. However, as might be expected, these two components are to be cited in the reverse order from that as cited above from the code: *ie* (a) title transcript; and (b) the so-called 'form', to be given in brackets. As in other codes, the three main sources of title transcript are mentioned: cover title, 'main' title, and caption. The 'main' title is preferred if none is the most complete. In fact, even when there is a normal title page, this may be less complete than, say, the caption. For certain works in 'several fascicles', we may in effect bring part of the collation up into the title transcript—rather dubiously, we suggest. If a uniform title is used, there might ensue here a confusion between numbered items in a form (called 'serial' in this code) and the fortuitous issue of parts in separate bibliographic format. As we have previously inferred, there is a great deal to be said, in fact, for binding such parts together, and therefore cataloguing them as a unit, the components being indicated as a Contents note.

The bibliographic bias of the code is shown in its statement that the title 'proper' should be represented in full in all languages in which it is given. This contrasts with AACR (R 133C) which allows selection in various degrees depending on the languages concerned; inevitably we prefer the latter—the document in question can still be identified satisfactorily, we suggest. Again, we feel, confusing title with collation, we are told that incunabula parts should be enumerated here; a reference is made to Section 31 (p 28-29).

Items given in brackets if necessary include (a) 'type' of work, *eg* sonata, and key; (b) medium, *eg* 1 voice and 2 pianos; (c) 'form' *eg* orchestra score; and (d) opus number. This citation order may conflict with uniform titles as recommended in other codes.

One example given demonstrates a significant difference from title, collation and notes as used by other codes.

> BARILLER (Robert).—Rhapsodie bretonne pour saxophone, alto et orchestra [Arranged for saxophone and piano. Score and parts.]

However, there is something to be said for bringing such data up into the title part of the entry, as we have previously touched upon.

There seems little doubt that this information is likely to be sought more often by users than, say, imprint is.

At this point, the code deals with 'series title', although it itself states that this information follows 'collation or in a note' (p 23).

Imprint information is similar to that in other codes, although printer is mentioned without further qualification as a next alternative to publisher; there is no mention here of publishers' or plate numbers, which surely are a natural component, if used, of the imprint. The bibliographic nature of the code is indulged in the detail mentioned for ascertaining dates of publication. The detail given for ascertaining dates of documents published from the sixteenth century forwards is likely to be of much use to only a limited number of libraries. At this point, mention is made of standard bibliographies, both general and those of individual composers' works (p 25). If reference is needed to standard published sources, it is indeed very useful if a code can find room for the more highly recommended works to be named. The code cites actual examples, *eg* Eitner's *Quellen-Lexikon,* and sources which themselves cite examples, *eg Die Musik in Geschichte und Gegenwart* (MGG), article 'Bibliographie'. Presumably any later editions of the code will mention the new basic source work sponsored by IAML itself, which obliquely replaces Eitner, *ie Repertoire international des sources musicales* (RISM). The code acknowledges that such works will probably not be readily accessible to the small library. However, it is very unlikely that the small library would need them for cataloguing purposes anyway.

The code seems to concentrate exclusively on date of publication of a document, and does not pay any attention to its operative date—surely of considerable importance in music since plates may be passed on and used again and again. The main check on this comes only indirectly via plate numbers, but even these are included in the collation, implying that their contribution to physical description is more important than their 'imprint' value.

This section does not give actual examples, but elsewhere in the code examples show place and publisher's name inexplicably in italics.

Collation, according to this code, includes four types of information: the usual ones of size, pagination and illustrations, but in addition plate numbers, as already mentioned.

The bibliographic nature of the code is again brought home with mention of wire lines and chain lines as a means of determining size—and this in a so-called limited code! However, it is admitted that, from

1820, (spine) height only of most documents is sufficient. A workman-like aspect of the code is introduced here, with the expression of height as 16° (up to 20 cm), 8° (20 to 25 cm), 4° (25 to 30 cm), and fol. (over 30 cm). However, since the code seems to assume shelving by size, these symbols would be more obvious and useful in the call number than in the collation, since they seem to be critical in shelf location of documents.

Two examples of collation given are:

fol., 410 p., decorated title, plate, portrait

and 5 part obl. 4°, 1 preliminary leaf, 46 p. each, decorated initials

which definitely smacks more of bibliographic description than retrieval-oriented information.

The plate number follows within brackets. Strangely, for this code, no mention is made of publishers' numbers.

'Contents' as a heading (misprinted as 'Contens' in the code) is followed by 'There are two types of *notes*' (our italics) (p 27), although there does not seem to be provision at this point for non-contents types of notes. Despite the great detail, of dubious value in most libraries, assumed elsewhere in the code, we seem to be excused giving such essential information as what individual works a collection may contain. At a stretch we may just about list the names, only, of composers concerned. Yet we are told to make cross-references from their names: imagine the frustration of a user who follows such a reference through, only to find solely the composer's name repeated at the alleged main entry. We are advised that if in doubt the extra information may be confined to fifteenth and sixteenth century works.

A second type of 'note' under Contents is that relating to parts. To the hypercritical, it is surprising that no mention is made of earlier parts of the entry at this point. In the section under Title, for example, we are told to include in brackets details of scores and parts.

Section VI deals with 'Secondary cards'. A contradiction in this section has been demonstrated already; apart from an obvious endorsement of the need for various approaches, little further comment is necessary. We might mention, though, the recommendation to use *arr.*, *harm.* and *adapt.*, but no others, hence perhaps the incongruous *see* which is used illogically for other secondary entries.

Part B of the code deals with Secondary catalogues. These can comprise: (a) authors of words; (b) subjects; and (c) titles and incipits. It is emphasised that such entries stand on their own, since they include call numbers (p 31), that is, they are not references. We are given a free choice of interfiling all entries, with main entries, or maintaining separate sequences. In the pure dictionary catalogue, mention is made of the possibility of variously coloured cards. We doubt the need for these, as long as call number is clearly given, and as long as special arrangements at one entry term do not have to be pinpointed—though the possibility of the latter is not mentioned.

The ' words ' catalogue needs no further comment.

The subject (*ie* form) catalogue receives rather short shrift, when compared with the, we suggest, inordinate detail accorded to some parts of description. There is a brief mention of what transpires to be a classified catalogue, with in this case entry under medium, but with no reminder of a later part of the code dealing in great detail with a particular classified construction. We are then more or less recommended to use an alphabetical structure. This uses multiple single-concept entry, *eg* Beethoven's piano and violin sonatas receive four simple-heading subject entries: (a) Piano; (b) Violin; (c) Sonata; and (d) Chamber music. 2 instruments. This corresponds approximately to the broad headings used by SEARS, and contrasts with the attempts at single multiple-concept headings used by LC and to a slightly lesser extent by New York Public Library, dealt with already in the section of this book on the subject/form approach.

The code suggests an economy, by excluding entries for forms. This would result in ' upwards ' see references

eg Symphony *see* Orchestra
and Concerto *see under* the name of the solo instrument.

Obviously, on arriving at say ' Violin ' we would need to turn over numerous cards not relating to violin concertos to find in passing the required entries, interfiled presumably by name of composer. In fact, we encounter the usual disadvantage of the over-broad subject entry, made notorious by SEARS, but contrasting with the cumbersomeness of the single multi-concept headings in LC.

The code gives a list of eighteen ' terms of types ', including, *eg* Air; Folksong; Song; Manual; and Treatise (p 33). This seems a very arbitrary list, for it is too long to be merely exemplary, yet it does not attempt to be exhaustive as is explicitly stated. Even such a short list can cause cross-classification, as is shown by the above-named samples. Needless to say, we do not suggest that this code should be followed for the alphabetical subject/form component of a music catalogue. The advice on such entries brings to a head the feeling that this code as a whole is rather amateurish and ill-balanced. This is strong language, but it has been considered carefully, and we can only be incredulous that such an organisation as IAML should sponsor such a code as, one might have hoped, the international code to end all codes.

The title catalogue, we are told, 'permits the finding and identifying of a piece known only by its title' (p 14). Presumably this statement means 'known by certain enquirers', since we are then told in effect that all works possessing a title need a title entry; although of course many such works will be known also by their composers' names.

Despite the assumption elsewhere that unit entries will be made by a 'multigraph' process, the sample entries for this catalogue receive a completely different format consisting of (heading) title; 'type'; and composer (p 34-35).

Part III deals with Arrangement of the author catalogue. It starts with a clear statement on the need for a 'conventional title' citing the following examples of titles for the same work.

Concerto
Konzert für Violine
Violin-Konzert
Solo du concerto de violon

This topic is left at this point, but with a mention of the appendix to follow on how to establish consistent titles.

If, then, we are told, a library does not adopt conventional titles, it will still need to bring together (entries for) 'different editions of the same works' (p 39). Paradoxically, the code then goes on to outline a system for bringing together, not editions of a work, but works of a similar type, *ie*

Theatrical works
Vocal works
Instrumental works
Pedagogical works
Cross references

with in most cases further systematic subdivision under these group headings.

Those interested may wish to examine these methods of sub-division in detail, and they will not be outlined here. However, we cannot help taking exception to the recommendation to arrange, say, symphonies by opus number. Why not simply 'serial' number for the form in most cases? Also, there seems to be so much latitude allowed under 'Instrumental works' as to make the code meaningless in the sense of being a set of rules to provide guidance, *eg* Stravinsky may be sub-divided by instrument, Bach by forms.

There are three appendices to the code: A Manuscripts; B Rules for establishing conventional titles, and C Plan for the systematic classification of a subject catalogue (by Hofmeister). In an attempt partly to remedy the apparent lack of logic in the structure of the code, we propose to take next Appendix B.

As we have mentioned, conventional titles have not been included in examples showing composers and titles. This, and the inclusion of conventional titles as an appendix, infers that such titles are not viewed as particularly important in this code. Yet elsewhere their need seems to become manifest.

Conventional titles are not regarded as necessary for compositions having a distinctive title. The section on title transcription, however, does not establish any rules to ensure that entries for all works with distinctive titles are brought together; we are told to give all languages of titles as they appear on the title page for each document.

For musical forms, we are given the following citation order

medium
serial number
opus, or thematic index number
key
date of first publication or composition
arr. (for arrangements)

This comprehensiveness is not demonstrated in one example, at least:
BEETHOVEN (Ludwig van).—[Symphony, no. 5; arr.]
In addition an example indicates that excerpt titles follow 'parent' titles, as in AACR.

eg WAGNER (Richard).—[Lohengrin. Prelude, Act I; arr.]

Appendix A Manuscripts is particularly useful in our context, since it brings together two aspects of special cataloguing.

Understandably, we are told to transcribe titles 'scrupulously' (p 43) and fully. Any additions are given in brackets, after the whole of the title as given in the document. Imprint equivalent consists of 'Ms.' followed by an abbreviation for country of origin, and then the date as on the manuscript or as ascertained by the cataloguer. Collation gives the height then the width in millimetres, followed by the number of pages or folios. If pages are unnumbered, the cataloguer is allowed to number them in pencil.

Further, it should be remembered that any other parts of the code should be applied to the cataloguing of music manuscripts where relevant. However, mention is not made of any difficulties arising from cataloguing facsimile reproductions of autograph scores, although these are fairly common now, and possibly certain representative examples may be found in quite small non-research libraries, *eg* a school or children's library may stock some for display or interest purposes.

A full example is given as follows (p 44):

CHAUSSON (Amédie-Ernest).—L'Albatros. Paroles
de Baudelaire (Fleurs du mal). [Song for contralto
and piano. Music by E. Chausson.]—Ms., autogr.,
1879. 358 × 270 mm, 5 unnumbered p.
(Ms. initialled and dated in pencil: *Cannes Octobre* 79)

The final section of the code, Appendix C, outlines the systematic arrangement of music used in Hofmeister's *Jahresverzeichnis*.

We are told that a 'miscellaneous' section will be needed if the scheme is used for shelf arrangement, but not why: *eg* that a document could be entered in a variety of places in a bibliography, according to its contents, but that in a library a physical place must be found for locating the document itself. We are also told that a library may need such a system for shelf classification if the library has no subject catalogue, inferring, strangely, that if the library has a subject catalogue, it does not need to classify on the shelves.

The system mentioned has no notation, such as any shelf or catalogue classification needs: this vital fact is either overlooked or ignored in the code. While not criticising the arrangement used by Hofmeister, for it is indeed very comprehensive, we wonder why this system was chosen for full reproduction in the code, with no mention of systems normally used for library classification, *eg* Dewey decimal, or Library of Congress, or British catalogue of music. These are especially designed for libraries; and whatever their faults, at least they include the notation so essential for 'mechanising' the arrangement of documents on shelves or entries in a classified catalogue. Each, in its own way, also has an alphabetical index, another vital accessory ignored by the code.

It is most difficult to sum up this code-within-a-code. On the face of it, it should present a distillation of all that is important in the organisation of music in libraries. It is part of a monumental work, sponsored by the most authoritative international organisation of music libraries, and being issued after a period of ferment followed by crystallisation of principles in the world of cataloguing. Yet the cataloguing events of the past two decades seem to have passed it by. The only sign of current thought worthy of note would appear to be the Appendix on conventional titles, yet even this seems to have been included almost as an afterthought.

The code is of value for librarians compiling a bibliographic-oriented catalogue. Yet even that purpose seems to have been overtaken by AACR, published six years later; it was also pre-empted by the LCRDC and ALA rules, out for some twenty years before the publication of this code.

The code seems barely to touch the fringe of the problems of the subject/form approach. It does nothing substantial to resolve many problems in this sphere, whether concerned with the classified arrangement on the shelves or in the catalogue, or with the alphabetical catalogue.

We have covered this code in detail, in an effort to substantiate a fair assessment. We regret having to conclude that it does not seem to have made a substantial contribution to the organisation of music in libraries.

IAML v III Rules for full cataloguing

Volume III contains ten main sections. First: the Introduction. Then follow Chapters labelled 1 to 5 containing the actual rules, respectively: Choice of entry; Filing titles; Elements of description; Added entries; and Cross references. There follow 3 Appendices: I Examples; II Glossary of terms; and III Abbreviations used in filing titles for thematic indexes. Finally is the Index.

This, the middle volume of the projected five of the whole code, may be regarded as a corner stone, or central tent pole, so to speak, helping to support, but supplemented by, the two volumes either side of it.

From the current English-speaking librarian's point of view, it appears to be the most conformist of the three volumes to appear to date, in that it derives avowedly from ICCP and so for the most part is, we suggest, compatible with AACR.

Before examining it in detail, it should be pointed out that the volume is deliberately self-limiting, despite its rather omnivorous title. As the outline of its contents above infers, it is confined to author-type headings, with relevant supporting added entries and references, and description. The rest of the contents support these objectives fully. However, there is no attempt to include classification and subject/form headings, as volume II the Limited code attempted. Further, this volume deliberately excludes *form* of headings, it being assumed that libraries will use local codes or practices, or perhaps basic reference works, for this purpose: in particular, reference is made to ICCP (p 10). We are not finding fault with this volume in this respect, except to comment that its title is misleading in using the word 'full': an explanatory sub-title might have helped. However, the author makes fully clear her objectives and the coverage of the volume in the valuable Introduction.

Concerning presentation: as one might expect, most of the work consists of parallel texts in English, French and German, so the pagination of 116 must be divided by three if one is looking for quantity. An exception to the parallel text arrangement, understandably, is the Glossary which has a separate section for each language. However, notably, the Index is in interfiled trilingual form.

The work quite early on states the Purposes and Principles of the IAML Cataloguing Code Commission. These are summarised here, but librarians contemplating use of the code may wish to consult this section in detail (p 9). Purposes include a mention not only of the catalogues of individual libraries, but, as one might expect, an emphasis on cooperation between libraries at an international level and the production of international and national bibliographies and catalogues. Principles infer the need for compatibility between the cataloguing of music and that of other materials, also an inference that detail recommended would cater for bibliographic-oriented catalogues, and further that all types of users should be catered for, whether musician, performer, scholar or amateur. We feel that these hopes are very ambitious, but we hope to demonstrate that, within the limits of the volume already mentioned, they are, within reason, realised.

The objects of the volume are further crystallised in the section on the scope of the work (p 9). In particular, a distinction is made between: (a) international bibliographies and union catalogues; and (b) local libraries use, with the need for added entries and references, as opposed to (a) which need only one entry per item. Lubetzky-type principles are adhered to in the declared intention to identify and describe an edition of a work. It is further emphasised that the volume tries to cater for both international interfiling of entries and local libraries' needs for alternative rules in certain instances and local libraries' adaptations. We suggest that in the latter may be included the possibility of limiting the amount of detail in a unit entry. The work is also as specific as possible in the types of work to be covered. Basically this amounts to 'performable music' works (p 10), with explanation further defining and exemplifying this term. Justifiably, the prime consideration has to be music itself, not works about it, so instruction books for instruments and voice are included, since, presumably, these are aimed directly at performance. However, examples given are confined to actual scores (or librettos), and do not include tutors, for example.

As already mentioned, this volume seems compatible with AACR. But for the most part it understandably derives its warrant direct from ICCP, in effect short-circuiting individual codes whether AACR or from countries which are not English-speaking. Therefore, in the code a summary is conveniently given of the parts of ICCP used as a foundation.

Entry (*ie* choice, not form of entry) is dealt with concisely. This aspect need not be dealt with here, since the essence of the conclusions of the rules is covered by AACR itself and is commented upon in its relevant place in this book. However, some useful discussion of difficulties peculiar to music is brought in. As stated or inferred in other parts of this book, we do not concur with the assumption that non-book materials are as similar to normal book forms as some codifiers and commentators have happily assumed. Therefore, the discussions in the code should prove useful. One example is that of pasticcios as described in the code, with the contention that 'Such problems seem to present complexities which cannot be resolved by the basic statements of ICCP' (p 11).

This volume then deals with the so-called Filing title, and one is referred back to volume II of the Limited code, but with, also, reference to ICCP again, and with the affirmation that 'The need for filing titles is much greater for publications of music than for other materials' (p 12).

The basic principles outlined in construction of filing title are: (a) choice of original language of first edition of work; and (b) use of the minimum number of elements for identification purposes. (a) applies to 'non-form' works. Works in a particular form can have their entries interfiled since 'names of musical forms are similar in most languages', and most language forms can be 'arbitrarily filed together' (p 12). This is an understandable recommendation since the code is intended for international use, although it disagrees with AACR which for the most part recommends English-language form.

An alternative rule caters for libraries which wish to use their local language. Since the code asserts that there is little difference between names of forms in most languages, we suggest that it would therefore not matter if the alternative rules were followed or not.

A more important difference emerges in the code's dealing with later components of its filing title, in that the next item recommended is opus or thematic index number. The argument supporting this, that in effect collocation is aided (p 13), is not so convincing when one compares the ruling with AACR's recommendation of medium performance, which we find more self-explanatory and likely to be of use to all types of library and bibliography users. In this code medium of performance is added 'when it is the only such element available (p 13). Such a ruling could lead to inconsistency in interfiling entries for works depending on whether or not the cataloguer regards the medium as the only further identifying element. An alternative rule allows for use of medium, rather like AACR, but it obviously receives only a very reluctant inclusion. The code supports the exclusion of medium with three reasons: (a) it constitutes a subject or classified approach; (b) it manifests an alphabetico-classed catalogue 'destroying the alphabetical character of the catalog'; (c) it causes filing complexities in an international list (p 13). We feel we can readily accept only (c), because of the different names given to, say, instruments, *eg* 'piano' as opposed to 'Klavier'. However, not all instruments and voices are as dissimilar as in that example. Could we not hope that an internationally accepted vocabulary could be suggested, possibly Italian? (a) and (b) seem to us to display a lack of appreciation of the differences between 'classified', 'alphabetico-classed', and 'alphabetical' (inferring

HARALD SÆVERUD

Twelve
pieces for orchestra
from the music to

Tolv
orkesterstykker
fra musikken til

Zwölf
Stücke für Orchester
aus der Musik zu

Henrik Ibsens „Peer Gynt"

Opus 28

Concert edition — Konsertutgave — Konzertausgabe

PARTITURA

COPYRIGHT 1950 FOR ALL COUNTRIES

MUSIKK-HUSET A/S — OSLO

NOREG-EDITION NR. 48

Eneret for Danmark
IMUDICO A/S — København.

Ensamrätt för Sverige
GEHRMAN — Stockholm.

Figure 1(a)

Typical title-page facsimile from IAML v III

APPENDIX I / APPENDICE I / ANHANG I

EXAMPLES

The numbers of the rules illustrated are given at the left. Examples illustrating two or more rules are filed under the first number. An index of the further rules is given at the end of appendix I.

1.111 GAGNEBIN, Henri.
4.14 Chant pour le Jour des morts et la Toussaint; cantate pour soprano et baryton soli, chœur mixte, orchestre à cordes et orgue. Texte de Jules Baillods. Réduction pour chant et piano par l'auteur. Genève, Edition Henn. cop. 1950. 52 p. 30 cm.

I. Baillods, Jules. Chant pour le Jour des morts et Toussaint. II. Title.

1.111 BOND, Capel.
2.441 [Concertos in seven parts. No. 6]
Concerto no. 6 in B^b for bassoon, string orchestra, and continuo. Edited and arranged by Gerald Finzi. London [etc.] Hawkes & Son (London); sole selling agents: Boosey & Hawkes [cop. 1957] Score (18 p.) 31 cm.

Duration: about 7 min.

I. Finzi, Gerald, ed.

1.113 BEETHOVEN, Ludwig van.
4.16 Beethoven for the young musician: dances, sonatinas, variations. Compiled and edited by Poldi Zeitlin, with a foreword by Sister Alice Marie. New York, Edward B. Marks Music Corp., cop. 1955. 32 p. 29 cm.

For piano.

I. Zeitlin, Poldi, ed. II. Title.

EXEMPLES

Les numéros des règles illustrées par ces exemples sont donnés à gauche. Les exemples qui se rapportent à plusieurs règles sont classés au numéro de la première de ces règles, mais on trouvera une liste des autres numéros à la fin de l'Appendice I.

1.111 GAGNEBIN, Henri.
4.14 Chant pour le Jour des morts et la Toussaint; cantate pour soprano et baryton soli, chœur mixte, orchestre à cordes et orgue. Texte de Jules Baillods. Réduction pour chant et piano par l'auteur. – Genève, Edition Henn. cop. 1950. – 52 30 cm.

I. Baillods, Jules. Chant pour le Jour des morts et la Toussaint. II. Titre.

1.111 BOND, Capel.
2.441 [Concertos in seven parts. No. 6]
Concerto no. 6 in B^b for bassoon, string orchestra, and continuo. Edited and arranged by Gerald Finzi. – London [etc.], Hawkes & Son (London); sole selling agents: Boosey & Hawkes [cop. 1957] – Partition (18 p.) 31 cm.

Durée: environ 7 minutes

I. Finzi, Gerald, éd.

1.113 BEETHOVEN, Ludwig van.
4.16 Beethoven for the young musician: dances, sonatinas, variations. Compiled and edited by Poldi Zeitlin, with a foreword by Sister Alice Marie. – New York, Edward B. Marks Music Corp, cop. 1955. – 32 p. 29 cm.

Pour piano.

I. Zeitlin, Poldi, éd. II. Titre.

BEISPIELE

Die Nummern der entsprechenden Regeln stehen am linken Rand. Beispiele, die sich auf zwei oder mehr Regeln beziehen, sind unter der ersten Nummer eingeordnet. Ein Nummernverzeichnis der weiteren Regeln folgt am Schluss von Anh. I.

1.111 GAGNEBIN, Henri.
4.14 Chant pour le Jour des morts et la Toussaint; cantate pour soprano et baryton soli, chœur mixte, orchestre à cordes et orgue. Texte de Jules Baillods. Réduction pour chant et piano par l'auteur. Genève, Edition Henn. cop. 1950. 52 S. 30 cm.

I. Baillods, Jules. Chant pour le Jour des morts et la Toussaint. II. Titel.

1.111 BOND, Capel.
2.441 [Concertos in seven parts. No. 6]
Concerto no. 6 in B^b for bassoon, string orchestra, and continuo. Edited and arranged by Gerald Finzi. London [u.a.] Hawkes & Son (London); sole selling agents: Boosey & Hawkes [cop. 1957]. Partitur (18 S.) 31 cm.

Dauer ca. 7 Min.

I. Finzi, Gerald, Hrsg.

1.113 BEETHOVEN, Ludwig van.
4.16 Beethoven for the young musician: dances, sonatinas, variations. Compiled and edited by Poldi Zeitlin, with a foreword by Sister Alice Marie. New York, Edward B. Marks Music Corp., cop. 1955. 32 S. 29 cm.

Für Klavier.

I. Zeitlin, Poldi, Hrsg. II. Titel.

Figure 1(b)
Excerpt from Appendix I of IAML v III

'alphabetical-specific'). An alphabetical-specific heading is no less specific because it is a compound heading, and 'form' plus 'medium' is a really basic example of such a heading. An alphabetico-classed heading surely consists of, in effect, a genus, followed by a species, the latter inferring by *its* own term alone that it is part of the relevant genus. The term 'piano', say, does not infer 'Sonata', so the compound term 'Sonatas. Piano' is no more alphabetico-classed than, say, 'Schools—Organization': each word is needed in conjunction with its companion word to make up the whole, single concept of either 'Piano sonatas' or 'Organization of schools'. This situation is different from such a heading as, say, 'Instruments—Piano', since a piano is *inherently* an instrument and so 'instruments' is superfluous —unless of course one wishes in fact to alphabetico-class. The same comment can be extended to the defence against alleged 'classification'. Once one accepts that a certain heading must be compound to be specific, inevitably there is a form of grouping, because all second-cited terms are sub-arranged under the first-cited term. In this case, the first-cited is form, which would then be sub-divided by medium. Over this misunderstood topic, we recall criticisms that the *British technology index*, when it was started, was alphabetico-classed, simply because it attempted to be really specific. Whatever objections may be made of such long specific headings, surely one cannot accurately accuse them of being either 'classified' or 'alphabetico-classed'. Some critics may feel that this point has been rather drawn out, but we feel it is important that students, especially, should not be misled by the code's reasoning here, particularly since so much else of the volume will, we feel, stand up to detailed investigation.

Description is explained on p 13ff. Most of it does not excite comment, except concerning its longevity. As we have tried to pinpoint elsewhere in this book, detailed description of whatever form of document is fully justified only with bibliographic-oriented records—applicable in only a few catalogues and bibliographies—rather than in retrieval-oriented records. Alternative rules are not given in detail as in the rules for heading and filing titles. It seems to be assumed that local libraries will initiate whatever variations they need (p 13). However, a movement towards simplified cataloguing is allowed at the start, when only certain data is specified as essential. This includes: title in first language; edition statement; first-named place and publisher; and collation. The rules themselves cater for such additional elements as a second title and distributing agent.

One unfortunate but apparently necessary aspect of these rules is that additions to the information derived from a document itself are specifically relegated to the notes, *ie* at the end of the entry. The reason given is that these would be in the language of the library and —it is inferred—would therefore cause inconvenience in using an internationally compiled list (p 14). However, the title of a work would be given in the language used in the edition being catalogued, and AACR's general rules for description state that additions may be made if desired in the language of the title (R 133D), so we do not fully accept this reasoning.

There is a short section discussing two particular problems in the cataloguing of music. The first deals with the entry of librettos (p 14). The three rival solutions are mentioned: composer of music; author of words; title when neither composer nor librettist is known, as may happen with some seventeenth and eighteenth century works. Unlike AACR's recommended rule, the final decision goes to composer, because, in effect, use of a libretto is dependent on use of the score of the work and because of soughtness. Again, contrary to AACR, an alternative rule surprisingly—to us—allows *title* entry for all librettos, which surely contravenes ICCP, AACR and all other codes based where possible on an intellectual responsibility principle.

The second problem is that of language, understandable in an international code (p 15). Emphasis is naturally placed on heading, filing title, and 'recorded' title, *ie* title as given in the document, presumably since these determine the arrangement of entries in a catalogue, and the information given in effect summarises the relevant parts of actual rules. It is assumed, although not specifically ruled, that entry names will be constructed according to usage of the country of composer. Form titles are in the language of the library. Significantly the compiler specifically rejects the possibility of a 'standard language', as we have already suggested, though without sufficient reason, we feel. 'Non-form' titles are to be given in the vernacular, according to ICCP; sometimes, as in AACR, we feel this principle is applied rather too strictly, although we acknowledge the difficulty of deciding what may be 'best known' to a library's clientele, and in any case we have to remember that the code is intended to be international.

As a basis for discussing the code, we have used the compiler's Introduction, rather than the rules themselves, since she gives background explanation, discussion and reasons for her rules, and these coincide with the objects of this book. The rules themselves occupy pages 19 to 61, and obviously these latter must be read carefully and understood by librarians contemplating application of the code. The rules are well demonstrated by examples giving actual solutions verbatim and not 'generalised' answers as in AACR. We prefer this code's method to AACR—like it or not, cataloguers tend to follow precedents, and actual entries are therefore likely to strike them more than, say, a mere 'main entry under Gagnebin'. Furthermore, examples are consolidated in full in Appendix I, giving the numbers of the rules used. What is more, several facsimiles of actual title pages are also included. We suggest then that AACR's precedent of giving title page transcriptions is carried to a logical and most helpful conclusion. As it happens, we do not agree with the typographical layout given to actual solutions, since these do not seem to make sufficient use of indentation and spacing. Also, it will be noticed that, where relevant, designations such as 'ed.' are included in headings; these are mandatory only in the North American text of AACR, and are omitted in, for example, BNB entries. (See examples, p 132 and between p 132 and 133.)

To sum up this volume: we feel it is far more to be recommended than v II Limited code. Admittedly, this is mainly because it corresponds more with accepted modern principles of cataloguing, with which we happen to agree. This is not merely a matter of subjective preference. We suggest that ICCP principles should be adhered to in the interest of: (a) international cooperation; and (b) generally sensible cataloguing from the user's point of view. However, it further discusses and exemplifies fully, so that the practising cataloguer can feel he knows where he stands. We hope that volumes IV and V, to come, will continue and consolidate the tradition which volume III attempts to establish in the cataloguing of music.

Readings

Checklist of works cited in or relevant to this chapter. General works included in the checklist with the first chapter of this book (p 28-29) also include information on the topics covered by this chapter. Full bibliographic citations are given in the consolidated Bibliography, p 304-312. A list of abbreviations is given on p 7. The titles of periodical articles are given within quotation marks.

AA 1908

AACR 1967

ALA 1949

ANDERSON 'Cataloging the contents of certain recordings'

ASLIB (Includes section on sound effects)

BM

BAKEWELL 'Cataloguing and indexing activities'

BARNES 'Classification and cataloging of spoken records in academic libraries'

BRYANT *Music librarianship . . .*

CCR

COATES *British catalogue of music classification*

CUNNINGHAM 'From Schmidt-Phiseldeck to Zanetti' (on IAML v III)

CURRALL *Gramophone record libraries . . .*

CUTTER

DOVE *Music libraries . . .*

GARRICK 'A tape library index system for language laboratories'

HORNER (p 386-387 on RILM [Music] abstracts; computer-compiled)

IAML

LC *Music and phonorecords*

LC *Subject headings . . .*

LCRDC

MLA

NEW YORK PUBLIC LIBRARY *Music subject headings . . .*

NOVIKOVA 'Actual problems of contemporary music cataloging'

REDFERN *Organizing music in libraries*

SCHOLZ *A manual for the cataloging of recordings in public libraries*

SOMERVILLE 'Cataloguing of gramophone records'

TREZISE 'Gramophone record libraries in Australia'

UNIVERSITY OF BRITISH COLUMBIA *A computer-based catalog system for phono-disc and tape recordings*

CHAPTER THREE

Films

THE MOVING film is probably the most complex medium of all. Technically it is the most difficult to make, and it is the hardest to use in the sense of needing the most complex and expensive equipment, as well as needing a special environment of its own for satisfactory receipt of its message, and requiring the exercise of two senses: sight and hearing.

It is applied, further, in a variety of ways mechanically, ranging from the 'home movie' set-up to expensive cinemas and television as a medium. In various ways, it also embraces other media: the sound recording, which can be complex enough on its own; the filmstrip; the transparency or slide; and its principles extend to take in electronic (EVR) or magnetic tape audio-visual recording as used on television. To take one example, the ordinary documentary for instruction purposes, which is normally run straight through, thereby encouraging the criticism that the film gives but a transient fleeting image, is now being supplemented by videotaped lectures and demonstrations. These are projected on closed circuit television and controlled by a tutor, with both knowledge and accompanying printed material, who is able to stop the show at both planned and spontaneously required intervals for discussion to take place, and to play back—and even to stop the projection at a certain shot on demand or need.

Films fulfil a variety of purposes, embracing all those offered by just about all other media added together, and automatically taking in the standard trinity of library services: information, education, recreation; with the possibility of cornering the market in the fourth '-tion'—inspiration. Films comprise various categories, which unavoidably involve some cross classification: so-called documentaries (non-fiction); fiction, sometimes partly inaccurately called 'imaginative films'; newsreels; cinemagazines (the very term implies encroachment into the world of print and journalism); stock shots or 'picture material'—short shots which may never have been used, or which may have been used in one or several films; sound effects; and dubbing tracks. Cataloguing rules which can cover all of these applications of film more or less automatically take in the slide—in effect one form of a film but physically a unit record; and the filmstrip—physically the same as a section of film or a series of slides joined together. The last two mentioned require different projectors from moving films, although their principle of operation is subsumed by the movie projector. However, when these two media have to be synchronised with accompanying sound—the whole producing a result approaching that of a sound film—their operation, and catalogue description, may become more complicated and detailed. Apart from this, most of this chapter may be taken as applying to filmstrips and slides where relevant, while unique needs outstanding will be summed up at the end.

If the uniqueness of films has still not been brought home, it might be remembered that moving films are the only library material the entry of which in catalogues cannot be made intellectually compatible with the entry of other materials in 'general' catalogues. Other materials, albeit sometimes with a stretch of the imagination, can be said to have an author-equivalent: not so films, generally, despite some efforts to regard a director as an author-equivalent, or the author of an original literary work as the overall 'author'. The description aspect, however, can be said to have imprint and collation equivalents, although various components may warrant extra, or diminished, detail, and some film codes recommend a sequence of description components different from that of printed books. However, it should be mentioned that one does not necessarily agree that the detail and sequence of description of books is necessarily ideal for all circumstances.

The heading and description of a typical film may not ideally be identical in all libraries, despite some successful and praiseworthy efforts to introduce central catalogue services. Types of libraries range from national or state film 'archives' to those of small primary schools. A parallel may be drawn with maps. Some libraries, by their nature and objectives, must concentrate on the identification and detailed 'bibliographic' description of a very large number of items for posterity (whenever he or she comes along and whoever he or she transpires to be). A small educational institution is much more interested in a subject approach, the emphasis being on accuracy and up-to-dateness of the film, a clear statement of its subject(s) and emphases, its intellectual level, its running time, and any special information needed by an amateur projectionist. There are various degrees throughout the spectrum of libraries and users. A noteworthy one is the large public, or state, library which is attempting to fulfil both an archive and an immediate information retrieval role.

A factor which applies in all cases is that a film must as far as possible be selected through surrogates, *ie* catalogue and similar entries, without actually being handled. All films are fragile by nature and wear out positively with each successive use. A book can be handled gingerly, but a film must go through a machine if it is to be sampled; however clean the machine may be, its sprockets still yank the film physically between spools at a rapid rate. A film may in fact be both very rare and well worn. Admittedly, libraries can have new prints made—but at a cost. Another simple fact is that the running time of a film is set (unless the operator delinquently speeds it up a lot during what he considers to be less interesting shots). It is better to spend a few minutes reading a detailed summary of a film in a catalogue, than waste an hour on what transpires to be an unwanted document. In any case, a film loan service may depend on a central depository, with a postal loan system to distant areas. Even in a physically integrated collection, the prospective user cannot 'browse' a film, in the same way that he can, say, slides or most other pictorial representations.

What all this amounts to is that descriptive detail of a film may have to be far greater than that for an equivalent book; and, as has already been inferred, the detail may have to be tailormade for a particular type and location of library and its users. Inevitably, we must face the problem of local needs possibly at variance with central catalogue services, and the main medium, MARC, comes to mind. So, 'it [MARC] will be developed to include . . . audio-visual material', according to a statement by BNB in its first volume of MARC Documentation. The time should eventually come, therefore, when cataloguers of films are saved at least some of the repetitive bibliographic work to which they are subjected at present. As to whether MARC will ultimately work with films—assuming it can get a worthwhile proportion of the total output of films upon which to work—will probably depend upon two factors: (a) the length and detail possible in 'Summaries' (corresponding to annotation for books) and (b) the number and variety of approaches made possible. This vital question, with recent developments, is enlarged upon in the last chapter of this book.

Because of the unusually large number of approaches likely to be needed, and also because of the great detail in a catalogue main entry—possibly running to several cards in a card catalogue—it may be decided to depart from the now quite widely accepted principle of the unit entry. Instead, only the main entry will include all the detail recorded about a film in the catalogue, and there may be an index, or several indexes, referring to the main entry, and to the location of the film, to cater for other approaches. Even a computer-compiled catalogue, with its ease of multiple approach, may have just one full entry, with other approaches entered and detailed in a 'stripped down' form to obviate bulk in the resultant printed catalogue.

As we have decided, demands on a film catalogue may be many and various. Taking into account all likely needs, then, a main entry may include the following, though not necessarily in the order given:

Heading
Title transcript [which may be identical with the Heading]
Alternative title
Subtitle
Other release titles

Studio
Sponsor
Production company
Distributor
Donor or source of supply
Production staff, including director, producer, and writers and editors of dialogue, and composers of music
Cast
Country of origin

Date

Gauge
Length
Physical type, *eg* sound; colour
Intellectual type, *eg* newsreel
Running time
Series
Certification

Summary [annotation]
Contents

Review sources

Notes

eg Other versions

Literary source [though there is a case for featuring this higher in the entry]

Related material and variations

Accompanying material

Source, if stock shot or from a ' serial '

Copyright details

Technical details, *eg* if a film loop [though again there is a strong case for featuring this higher in the entry]

Physical condition

Availability

Tracings of added or index entries: title, collaborator, subject, etc

Location in collection [often at the top of the entry]

It may be that all or most of the data mentioned above may be needed, *eg* for a full length sound film with many noteworthy contributors, and with world-wide distribution. On the other hand, for, say, a locally produced film, perhaps for a local television station, there may be far fewer contributors, and the main detail and approaches may be for subject needs. This, too, may apply for a newsreel or ' commercial '.

In any case, a reminder may be necessary, that, even for full bibliographic cataloguing, not all of the data named above may be needed.

HEADING

Films are the supreme example of ' diffuse authorship ', meaning that it is impossible usually to name one person or body who is individually most responsible for the intellectual content of a film. In some fiction examples, the connoisseur may identify a film with its director: people talk of a David Machem film or a Godard film. In some other examples, the author of a literary work on which a film is based may be regarded as the most sought approach. Normally, however, the title is regarded as the main approach term, since the most sought. Intellectual responsibility usually has to give way here, despite the principles emerging from ALA 1949 and implicit in AACR 1967. If any searcher is interested in the ' author unit ' as represented by an individual or body, he is catered for by the index(es) or added entries supporting the main entry, as recommended by all codes. Such added entries/index entries are dealt with later. However, we admit that a real problem exists with films based on an established literary work, *eg* Shakespeare's *Macbeth*, as inferred above.

It is not enough to decide on title as main approach term: the question then arises as to which title. There are two chief occasions for a film having two or more titles: (a) a film, say, made and released in the United States under a title, in English of course, may possibly be released in another English-speaking country, say, Britain, under another (English) title; and (b) a film made and released in a non-English-speaking country will usually have a title in the language of the country, say Swedish, while the same film may be released in, say, Britain with an English title. However, it is not sufficient to use only the English language form in an English speaking country. The vernacular title may be used by some people, and the English by another. Again, for various reasons, it may so happen that the vernacular title 'sticks' in some cases, *eg La notte* and *Mon oncle*, but not in others, *eg Bicycle thieves* and *The seventh seal*: Italian and Swedish respectively in origin. On top of capricious user demand, librarians must also decide on the breadth of bibliographic unit to be needed in a catalogue. A decision has to be made as to: (a) whether all entries for one particular film are to be collocated at one entry point in the catalogue; or (b) whether entries are to be scattered under the titles used for various releases. If (a) is chosen, the further decision has to be made as to the form of title to be used at which to collocate all the entries for one film, with different titles, usually either the original (vernacular) or the 'home' library's language version. If (b) is chosen, and if main entries are given for each version, there will need to be references all ways between the various titles catalogued. This may depend on whether more than one release is in stock in the library concerned, although more than one release will usually be stocked only in large collections. The main codes differ on the problem: their solutions are given in the later subsection on Codes. One suggests that, whichever is chosen as the entry term, both titles should feature prominently at the top of the entry. This suggestion is best implemented by the use of a uniform title, if different from the title in hand, this having immediately beneath it the title of the release in hand,

eg [TIRER sur le pianist]
Shoot the pianist

or vice versa, for a variation between countries having different languages;

and [WHISKY galore]

Tight little island

manifesting a variation between two English-speaking countries.

TITLE TRANSCRIPTION

As shown above, the filing title will be followed in the entry by the title in hand, if different. The latter should be given exactly as given in the 'titles' of the copy in hand, not, *eg*, as given on the censorship certificate if any, or as on the containing can or box, or as possibly written on the 'headout', or leader of the film which is used for lacing up in the projector. These may vary, and the object of the title transcript is positively to identify the copy in hand. In this respect, the 'titles' of a film may be regarded, in toto, as the film's 'title-page substitute'. Just as a title page of a book may have at its head the author's name, or the title of a series of which the book in hand forms a part, it is possible that the early frame or frames of a film may include information other than the actual title of the film. So, as with cataloguing a printed book, the cataloguer is allowed to manipulate and transpose the order in which information is given in a film. Also, just as a book may have a title page or title pages in different languages, a film may have titles in either various languages or in a language other than that of the 'title-page' (chosen) title. In such a case it seems resonable to select the 'home' language version, or to add a translation into the home language if this is not chosen (touched on further below). One suggests that to do otherwise would savour of pedantry on the part of the cataloguer. It is surely too much to expect the average user to have a reading command of such languages as Russian, Hungarian, Polish, Czech, and so on, even if he does know the rather more common languages like French and Italian.

As with normal book cataloguing, the title will be followed, running on, by any alternative title or sub-title. Construction of these subsidiary elements is substantially the same as in cataloguing book-form material with title pages. With films, the subsidiaries are taken from frames at the start of the film, either the title frame itself or those immediately following it.

Contrary to some film codes' decisions, we suggest that at this point there should be included other titles by which a film may be known, as these may help to identify a particular film. Also, since other title approaches are likely to be covered by title added entries and references, and since these are probably more sought than, say, names of producers—hence the basic principle of title as main entry—these tags should be high up in the entry.

Not many books have a title lacking, since it is not all that common for books to be published without either a title page or a cover bearing the title of the work. Because of the physical form of films, the leading frames may possibly have become detached, or even, with older films or uncompleted films, there possibly may never have been a title-page equivalent. Sometimes a film's original title may be worked out by (arduously!) comparing the film and its remaining credits with external sources, and so its original title may be divined. This situation is called by one code (BFI) 'missing title', and the title arrived at is given with a suitable typographical indication that it was not actually given in the film itself. Another situation exists when, as mentioned above, and as far as can be ascertained, the film never had a title. In such a case, a 'supplied title' (BFI term) is given, from internal evidence usually relating to the subject matter of the film. Again, a suitable typographical device is recommended to indicate that the title is 'supplied'. It is suggested here that, in such cases, the 'missing' or 'supplied' title should not be given in the authoritative position of the Heading, but on the next line down (on a card). A more accurate form may turn up later, and this can then be inserted in the Heading space in the entry, above the information previously put in by the cataloguer. However, the latter may have come to be accepted by habit, and it should be retained in a fairly prominent position in the entry, *ie* in the 'transcribed title' position.

CREDITS

In book cataloguing, the title transcript is traditionally followed by the author statement. The 'author-equivalent' in a film may consist of any person or organisation responsible in some way—intellectual, technical or financial—for the film's having come into existence. It may be remembered that any of the people or bodies mentioned here would be on the short list if one were forced to conduct an enquiry as to who should be appointed for main entry heading, if films have to receive author entries, and not title entries as is customary. Here, the literary purist may well seek to include the author of a novel or play upon which the film is based, although (unfortunately, one feels) codes tend not to give original sources so high a place in the entry. So, if one wishes to implement a pointer towards a broad intellectual approach, there is a case for including at this point a mention of the author and title of a literary work from which a film is derived, however indirectly. Even if the author and/or title bear little resemblance to the resulting film, the name and title may prove to be likely approaches to the film. We have already established that the intellectual responsibility principle has given way to the sought tag, with the acceptance of entering films under title, and we are not betraying any cataloguing ethic by suggesting putting these tags high in the entry, rather than relegating them to the notes, at the bottom of the entry, as is the custom in most codes. It might be mentioned that literary source often appears early on in the credits, and this may be a further reason for suggesting that it should appear high in the entry. In the case of printed materials, say a play based on a novel, it would be expected that information about the source of the final work would be given in the title transcript if stated on the title page, but brought out in the form of a note way down the entry if not. We suggest that the same principle, or practice, be applied to books: if the information is not given on the title page it could still be inserted immediately after the title, within brackets, by the cataloguer, as nominally allowed by AACR, for example. This practice is not necessarily incompatible with MARC format, for those librarians who hope eventually to take part in central computer cataloguing. Customarily, in film codes, the managerial side of a film's production is given precedence over the intellectual side of production, *eg* scenario writers and directors—the nearest approach to an 'author' of a film—give way to the people who in effect correspond to the publisher, bookseller, etc of a printed work. As with normal printed works, there is a point in suggesting that those with an intellectual, as differentiated from a financial, interest in a document, should receive prominence high in an entry for a film. Intellectual contributors include those having to do with a film's dialogue, *eg* scenario writer(s), editors, and director and co-director or assistant director if any, as well as musical composers and arrangers.

Managerial participants include the studio at which the film was made, the sponsor responsible for having the film initiated or who put up the money to have it made, and the production company responsible for organising the personnel and materials used in the film. Also relevant here may be a distributor who, in effect, controls the outlets through which the film is screened, *eg* via various chains and circuits. As mentioned above, these firms or people correspond to the publisher, wholesaler, and retailer of a book. Yet the publisher of a book is noted quite low in a book entry, although we admit that, if it were not for his capital investment, the book might never see the light of day.

All in all, we suggest that there is an unnecessary inconsistency here between book and film cataloguing. The book catalogue rules possibly unfairly play down the publisher's part in the coming into existence of a book, while the film cataloguer possibly unfairly enhances the publisher-equivalents of a film.

Other data of relevance in the description of a film include the country of origin, and the date of original release. The country is of potential importance in assessing the slant or emphasis of a film, and for this reason is evidently valuable. If it is included to show the language of a film, or indirectly to indicate the address to which an aspirant screening organisation should apply, we suggest that merely naming the country of origin may not be directly helpful. In the first instance, the original language used, or subsequent dubbing or subtitling, could be given explicitly preferably nearer the top of the entry, as this information may be vital in deciding whether or not to show a film. In the second instance, it seems reasonable to relegate this information to a lower place in the entry, since it is likely not to be among the most sought information about a film. If the country is named to show location of the making of a film, it would surely be more explicit simply to name location as part of the notes on a film. The date serves two main purposes: (a) the identification of a film, *ie* bibliographic information; and (b) the up-to-dateness of a film, or the style or mode of its presentation, assuming that fashions in film making at a particular time tend to be followed by directors. (b) may probably be better expressed in the form of a verbal annotation, since a date may be indefinite—one may find a ' conventional ' film in the style of the 1940's made in the 1960's or 1970's. If the main object of the catalogue is ' bibliographic ' the date is obviously necessary, and should be given early in the entry just as date of publication of a book appears quite high in the traditional catalogue entry—though, one suggests, possibly not high enough, since books are often cited and identified by author, title, edition and date.

The importance of the cast depends usually on the type of film, being usually more important in fiction films. However, in films coming under the heading of documentary, a commentator, especially if he features in the film, may be a sought tag: Johnny Morris and his television films about countries and animals is an outstanding example in Britain and in countries importing British television films. So, then, a leading personality appearing in a film should be cited in the cast list, of course. Commentator is not always cited as a member of ' cast ', but we suggest that, since well-known personalities including actors and actresses may be used as commentators, they should be included in this category, *eg* Henry Fonda (as we say, a well-known actor—to the older reader at least) is the commentator in *The impressionable years,* a film about the children's library of New York Public Library. Nowadays, it is sometimes difficult to decide who are the ' stars ' of films and therefore to be named. It is not uncommon to find the really leading actors and actresses named before the title is given; after the title we are notified of several people billed as ' starring ', then we find many frames devoted to ' co-stars ' and so on, and finally one or more people are ' featured ' or ' introduced '. After all this, the viewer can take breath while two or three dozen people are listed as ' with '. A film catalogue entry exists either to identify a film, or to indicate to a potential user whether or not he will find it useful for his purpose, and not to publicise extras, whether or not they are Hamlets manqués. Therefore, we suggest that the naming of members of the cast of present day fiction films may be cut down as far as possible: ' if in doubt, leave it out ' is a valid maxim here. This is particularly the case if there is a tendency towards the practice of making added or index entries for all people named in the main entry. For the cataloguer who wants an arbitrary decision, we suggest that not more than the leading two or three of the cast should be cited.

The judgement of the censoring authority is sometimes taken seriously by the potential user, *eg* a teacher or youth club leader who may be held responsible for ' exposing ' young people to a film. As it happens, standards and codings vary between countries, *eg* an Australian perusing a British list of films should ascertain the equivalents of British standards compared with current Australian practice. At the moment, in the throes of the ' permissive society ', censorship categories may not correspond with decisions made even in the recent past. So, the category allocated by a particular authority, *eg* the British Board of Film Censors, has to be considered in relation to the date of release of a film in the country concerned. Sometimes relevant here may be a statement as to whether either whole sections of visuals or perhaps original dialogue has been deleted on the ' advice ' of the censoring authority. One remembers seeing a Scandinavian film in Hobart in the 1960's in which the original dialogue happened not to be represented fully in the English subtitles presented with the film. In such a case, the rigorous cataloguer may wish to indicate, say in the Notes, that certain excisions were made in the copy made available in a particular country.

It may be felt useful to give details of dubbing and subtitles fairly high in the entry; or else, this information may be given in the Notes.

COLLATION

This includes physical information about the film. Corresponding approximately with book cataloguing, it includes the quantity, the type, and the size of the film. If one wished it to correspond as near as possible, it would give (a) number of reels; (b) whether colour or black and white, and whether silent or sound; and (c) size of reels as to diameter and gauge of film, or number of frames for filmstrips. In fact, these items are not usually given in this order. A more common method is to name the gauge of the film in millimeters; then the 'material' of the film (BFI), *ie* presentation, somewhat as mentioned above; and (c) length in feet (or number of frames for filmstrips, if relevant). We acknowledge that (a) and (b) are likely to be useful to the prospective user, but as to (c), in relation to films, he is more likely to be interested in the running time, *eg* in minutes. Films present an ideal opportunity for the cataloguer to indicate how much time a 'reading' of the document will take. After all, presumably with books, size and number of pages attempt, however crudely, to indicate how long it will take to read a given book, by trying to present a picture of the bulk of the document. A user may need to know how long a film is so that he can use a take-up reel of the correct size. But this is not a significant fact for a catalogue to record, unlike the gauge of a film, knowledge of which at the start may well decide whether a prospective user pursues his request. In any case, as far as length of film is concerned, hence the diameter of a reel needed to contain it, many film libraries use a diameter characteristic for storage purposes, which may be indicated by simple literal notation, *eg* S for small—400 feet, M for medium—800 feet, L for large—over 800 feet. This location letter precedes the number indicating fixed location within the respective sequence. Just as with books, then, length is not likely to be of considerable relevant significance. However, it is of potential value, at least, for bibliographic purposes, to indicate quantitatively if a film has been edited, provided the research worker involved knows the length of a perfect copy.

As with books, there seems to be a confusion, in collating films, between the bibliographic and retrieval objects of the catalogue. Apart from the evidence suggested above (and subject to criticism by experts in the area of film alone) the sequence of data given seems to be illogical. Books' collation is given in the order of (a) number of pages (or volumes for multi-volumed works); (b) details of illustrative material; and (c) spine height. (a) and (c) are mainly of bibliographic use and their retrieval purpose can be subsumed and improved upon by a simple symbol at the start of the call number indicating sequence according to size, *eg* Q for quarto, F for folio (and even E for 'elephants'—elephant folio—in one library at least!), along with P for pamphlet indicating approximately that the work has few pages, and even VF for vertical file indicating very few pages indeed. A detailed statement of illustrations can be of direct value for retrieval purposes, as well as for bibliographic purposes, especially for certain subjects and treatments of subjects. To take but one example, it may be helpful to the historian to know that a book on charters includes so many facsimiles. So with films, then, statement of 'material' or type of film can be very relevant to the potential user, helping him decide whether to initiate a request for a film. Examples are whether the film is sound, silent or mute, and whether there is a separate equivalent of a sound track, on disc or tape; also whether black and white (monochrome as it is sometimes called) or colour, and even the type of colour—though unhelpfully the latter, while it can be expressed concisely, is at present taken down to Notes in some codes, so separating it from the obviously connected information that the film is in colour. In fact, a simple statement of 'Technicolor' obviates the need to use the simple word 'colour' at all. Another useful, and possibly critical, item of information is whether the film is 'wide screen' or equivalent in trade names.

In sum we would suggest that film libraries used mainly for retrieval purposes need Collation only for two types of information: (a) type of film; and (b) running time, or number of frames for film strips. Libraries serving mainly a bibliographic and conservation purpose, and whose catalogues may be used as source material by film research workers and 'filmographers' will need to continue to give all the data recommended in the codes, and possibly even more if they have time.

Perhaps an apology is needed at this point for the apparent assumption that a catalogue serves two mutually exclusive purposes: bibliographic; and what we call retrieval, meaning largely as a finding guide, often for subject purposes, and selection from a range of possible films with a view to suitability for audiences and the needs of, shall we say, either the group organiser or the personal enquirer. (Some libraries will lend projectors as well as films, in the way that libraries expect to supply suitable 'readers' for microforms.) We acknowledge that any one catalogue's objects are not necessarily 'either/or', and that it may be attempting to serve both objects. However, in such a case, it may still be possible to reorganise all the data in an entry so as to try to serve each need in a more mutually distinctive way than demonstrated by some prominent codes.

Finally, it may be worth pointing out that if a library stocks only films of a certain type or size, then the indication of this, say 16 mm for gauge, need not be repeated in each and every catalogue entry. In a printed list-form catalogue, it would be clearly stated in the introduction to the catalogue as a whole.

SERIES

Traditionally, in catalogue entries, the series statement (or 'note' as it used to be called) follows the Collation, but precedes the Notes. We suggest that if it is one of the factors used in selecting a film from a range of films, then there is a case for putting it higher in the entry, nearer the title, above the credits. It can usually be expressed succinctly in a few words, and so it should not be unduly obtrusive. However, it is admitted that series may possibly not be as important in helping a user to decide on a film as is the case with many series, at least, of books.

NOTES, ETC

In a catalogue of books the omnibus Notes takes in what may be regarded as three separate items as applied in film cataloguing: (a) summary; (b) contents; and (c) other notes. The order of these items varies between some codes. There are two conflicting factors here. The cataloguer may be tempted to put short items first, followed by the longer items, because a user can readily scan the shorter ones before coming to the more expansive parts. On the other hand, the more expansive parts may possibly be more useful to the average enquirer. Customarily, in book cataloguing, we have first brief items expanding on items already dealt with cryptically higher in the entry, *eg* Imprint, Collation and so on, the information being given in the same order as the parts of the entry expanded on. This would then be followed by possibly more expansive information, *eg* explanation of the subject or author's approach to subject, and then Contents or Partial contents. Film codes also tend to give information in this order.

The Summary in a film catalogue entry gives in effect what was called an annotation in past catalogue practice, more honoured in the breach in these hurried days—regrettably, we suggest. So, here is definitely an instance in which book cataloguers can learn from film cataloguers. Of course, the detail in a film catalogue is needed because we cannot conveniently turn over the frames of a film in the way that we might flip through the pages of a book. The summary of a film may incorporate almost a contents-equivalent, a calendar, or even a running commentary on the detail of a film, reel by reel. We are not suggesting that a book annotation should work through a book chapter by chapter or even page by page. The book-equivalent for a film is needed because films do not have chapters (except for so-called 'serials'), and a user may need to select a particular part of a particular reel. In a book catalogue entry, a contents list is usually sufficient, as long as each chapter title is self-explanatory. Details of the varied approaches to 'Summary' as recommended by codes are given in the subsection on Codes, later.

Another item of information recommended in some quarters is a citation of one or more reviews of a film, preferably contemporary rather than retrospective. This practice, we feel, could be used more in catalogues of books. Possibly the need is more acute in the case of fiction and other pure literature because of the nebulous nature of the forms represented by such works. It should be possible to turn up readily the reviews cited; this might involve the maintenance of a special file of cuttings, or facsimile copies, of reviews filed by form of film title employed in the catalogue. Some codes recommend that the entry for each film should include an extra card, say, giving summaries and similar information. It might be possible to include in the catalogue itself copies or partial copies of reviews themselves. This could apply especially when a code allows that the subjective views of the cataloguer or others on the quality and presentation of the film may be included in an entry.

More terse notes usually follow the expansive Summary. These include both physical details, *eg* that the film is in loop or cassette form, and intellectual details such as the literary source of a film. As already mentioned, we suggest that such information, which may well be regarded as worthy of an approach to a film, should appear higher in the entry. It is likely to be of more value than, say, certain aspects of Collation, which at the moment precede it in the entry. Such information as ‘ film loop ’ or ‘ cassette ’ might well appear immediately after the title. An item worth pinpointing, and again possibly the cause for an added/index entry, is accompanying material. In the case of an instructional film, this may take the form of a summary of the film, and information expanding on the content of a film. Very important too, it may include a select bibliography of further sources of information, in whatever physical form that information may be presented. This should, we suggest, be mentioned in the entry, just as the presence of a bibliography in a book is mentioned in many library catalogue entries.

In at least one code, Tracings are listed before Notes, and this we find inexplicable. Tracings are usually advice to library staff rather than to the library's patrons. However, unconventional as the suggestion may be, we feel that if tracings are given prominently enough, they can serve the dual purpose of information needed for catalogue maintenance, and as sources of information for catalogue users, *eg* a subject heading may possibly obviate the need for a note on the subject content of a film. It is just possible that tracings as such might be eliminated. Information to the user could be: (a) presented in the form actually used as a heading in an added/index entry; and (b) distinguished typographically, say by underlining or capitalisation, so that catalogue maintenance staff readily see that, in fact, it represents a tracing for an added or index entry heading. Naturally, whatever device is adopted should not be used for parts of the entry nor used as tracings. It might even be possible to amend the conventional physical layout of the entry, with, say, tracings appearing down the right hand side of an entry in a prominent position. For catalogue departments which are severely short of clerical staff for typing in added entry filing headings, but which like to use unit entries, the filing term for a particular copy of the card could be underlined in red. However, there is a lot to be said against underlining as indication of filing headings of tracings dotted about throughout an entry, because of very likely confusion on the part of the untutored user.

LOCATION IN COLLECTION

As with any catalogue entry, the actual location of a film should be clearly indicated, for the information of staff dealing with requests, and so that a user may give the required information clearly on a request or call slip to obviate double checking by staff, or for location by user if films are on open access. Films are usually shelved or filed in some form of (a) size, and (b) accession number or chronological order, often by fixed location, since they are rarely kept on open access and it is regarded as pointless therefore to keep them in classified order. There may be a further symbol, perhaps as the initial part of the shelving code, to indicate type of film. This may apply especially for newsreels because it may be an important retrieval factor to have these in a separate sequence arranged chronologically. Where there is a subject approach in systematic classified order, say by UDC, it is important to ensure that there cannot be confusion between such notation and the notation used for actual physical shelving or filing of films.

Filmstrips

Where entries for both moving films and filmstrips are interfiled, both author/title type of entries, and subject entries, there should be a clear statement in the heading of the form. In Britain and British-oriented countries, one can follow the author-title heading by the words ' Film ' or ' Filmstrip ' in parenthesis. In America and American-influenced English-speaking countries the term ' Moving film ' or ' Motion picture ' would probably be preferred to ' Film '. We doubt very much if there is much need for separate ' form ' files listing all the films and filmstrips under such added entries as FILMS and FILMSTRIPS. However, if computer storage is practicable, this can be conveniently achieved, as expanded on further in the last chapter of this book.

Title headings themselves need not be substantially different from those for films. The number of credits and cast (if any) will be substantially smaller than for films, and the retrieval oriented librarian may cut them down even further without loss. However, the publisher-equivalent may be an indication of authority as with books and should be retained.

There is a case for author-type main entry, again as mentioned further in the last chapter of this book. Collation will be significantly different from films and will usually require only gauge, number of frames and whether colour or black and white. In addition, if there is a sound track to be synchronised this will need to be detailed: whether disc or tape, as an indication of reproducing apparatus required, with revolutions per minute for discs and inches per second for tapes. Diameter of tape may be useful as an indication of suitability or not for the prospective user's machine. We doubt whether it is worth giving such details as number of discs or tapes and playing time, except for bibliographic record purposes on the comparatively rare occasions where relevant. Accompanying material, *eg* speaker's or lecturer's notes, should also be mentioned.

Subject transparencies and slides

Perhaps people in general tend to think of slides as being 35 mm cardboard or plastic-framed products arising from tourism, whether taken by the traveller or bought ready-made and slyly slipped into the amateur slide evening of 'my trip around the world'.

In addition, however, we must bear in mind transparencies designed for use with overhead projectors, especially in education, and more particularly home-made ones, or transparencies produced by educationists for limited circulation. An example, of interest to librarians and students of library science, might be a series of transparencies which portrays the build-up of a catalogue entry, successive parts of the entry being demonstrated by transparencies intended to be overlaid as instruction proceeds on those already being projected.

Strictly, the author of a transparency is the original photographer, or the person responsible for making a non-photographic transparency. The authorship of a slide or other transparency taken from a book or other medium is the original author or artist, as featured in the book, etc. The bibliographic cataloguer will no doubt make an entry under the intellectually responsible author or author-type individual or body. In such case, AACR gives rules which may be followed, *eg* author and title followed by statement of medium.

However, it is possible that many prospective users will not know of, or be interested in, the name of, say, an obscure cataloguing lecturer slaving over sheets of plastic in Western Australia. If they are interested at all, they are most likely to be stimulated into demanding such a document, usually via their libraries, according to the subject covered. There is not necessarily a contradiction here. Many users of any form of document, whether a book on cataloguing or a map of dams in Western Australia, are probably primarily interested in the subject. The author is often of relevance only as a further means of sifting documents as to authority or value to the user in his particular context. Much of this applies also to filmstrips, as is evidenced by the fact that a filmstrip is virtually a series of slides physically attached to each other in a logical sequence, *eg* to revert to the example cited, the build up of a catalogue entry can be shown either by a series of 'flip-over' transparencies for use on an overhead projector, or by a filmstrip, whose components severally represent the 'build up' demonstrated physically on the flip-over transparencies.

This amounts to a restatement of the situation existing with many maps—among other media, and including books—that the topic or subject of the document may be asked for more often than the author-equivalent, but that there is a need for both approaches. However, if extremely limited cataloguing has to be practised for reasons of economy (time, space, expense of records), one definitely recommends that subject should take priority.

Whether or not a subject (only) entry is made, it is likely that, under basic cataloguing rules, this will be followed by name of author, and then by title of the document in question. Statement of medium should follow the title, as with filmstrips. The use of 'Transparency' as a generic term may be considered, on the grounds that the user will have access to either a slide projector or an overhead projector if he is a teacher in an institution whose library stocks both forms. However, we recommend specific statement of type of form, using the conventionally accepted even if semantically unsound 'Transparency' and 'Slide'.

The usual catalogue details will follow, corresponding mainly to those used for films, *eg* production company, etc.

The collation, as with filmstrips, will be different from that of films. Number of transparencies and size of transparencies (if applicable) must be given; also a statement as to whether they are colour or black and white may be needed. Size could give a ready indication of type of apparatus needed for projection, if specific terms are not used high in the entry as recommended above.

Fewer notes as to content and intellectual quality may be needed, since transparencies can be viewed quite conveniently 'by hand'. However, if the librarian wishes to make it possible for a selection to be made by the prospective viewer from the catalogue, or if the prospective user is not at the service point where the items are kept, more detail will be needed. An annotation (or ‘ summary ’) should be included, then, with a note of intellectual level if relevant. Slant, or aspect, may well be mentioned. In the example mentioned above on the catalogue entry, a mention would be made if the catalogue entry is a reproduction of Library of Congress practice: ‘ L. C. practice ’ is all that is required for the teacher or reasonably knowledgeable student. We suggest it is not usually necessary to give some form of Contents stating the coverage of each item in the series.

Codes

FILMS

There are several noteworthy and well-known codes for films, in addition to a considerable number of articles by individual librarians. One authority states ‘ Rules for cataloguing film are very few and far between when compared with the rules in existence for cataloguing books . . .’. We suggest, however, that, at least now, there may be too many alternatives from which to choose. But, at least two of the codes currently available were produced after the above-cited quotation was published: these are ASLIB and AACR. Inevitably, with several codes to choose from, there will be some, even if slight, divergencies of practice and advice, for both major and minor decisions.

A plea has been made for standardisation in film cataloguing, especially in the use of terminology and abbreviations (GREENFELL *J doc*). This article is worth following up, unless one has decided already which code to follow on setting up or recataloguing a film collection.

A likely choice may be AACR, produced some eight years after the article was published. But AACR as brought out in 1967 is far from being a sacred tablet and unchangeable. As explained in rather more detail in the last chapter of this book, some influential librarians, though possibly few in number, have registered a considerable volume of complaint about the treatment of special materials in general in AACR. Our reading of the published accounts of the criticism suggests that film cataloguing is a major target for criticism. So a librarian adopting AACR as issued in 1967 may fairly soon find himself facing a choice between the older and the newer versions. However, some indications are that many changes will not conflict substantially with the 1967 edition, but will rather expand upon and explain it. Notwithstanding, we would suggest adopting AACR, because this is most likely to be MARC-compatible, *ie* to be adopted by BNB and LC in their computer tape-recorded data, and to be used in their hard copy bibliographies and catalogues. This is amplified in the section on AACR.

Another factor is the potential use of catalogue substitutes. Of all special materials, films probably need most detail. Therefore, there is a particular need for taking advantage of bibliographic research and recording of data done by external agencies. However, deriving from the variety of codes, and because of the variety of subject approaches possible, it may prove difficult, though not insurmountable, to use several published lists in conjunction with, say, a local card index leading to them for additional detail if required. Nevertheless, the experiments conducted by BNB in producing computer versions of the *British national film catalogue* within the MARC format are an indication of the type of useful uniformity and consistency which is possible. The use of MARC-oriented computer cataloguing is dealt with more fully in the last chapter of this work. At this stage we suggest merely the relevant heading, title, location of film in the library, and of course location in the relevant printed catalogue, all catalogues referred to being kept at the catalogue. Of course, there would need to be fuller entries for items not covered by the catalogue substitutes stocked. This method would not be economical or worthwhile with very small film collections. At the other extreme, if a collection were large enough, and its stock were mainly American and British in origin, it might be possible to consider having the relevant LC catalogues and the *British national film catalogues* with locations of items actually in stock suitably marked in the catalogues themselves. This method could stimulate the broadening of the use of film, since items relevant to a request but not in stock would automatically be brought to both the enquirer's and the librarian's notice.

Concerning the actual codes: CUTTER (4th ed), AA 1908 and BM (1936) do not mention films, although the form had been invented before these editions of the codes were published. By way of an example, the first moving film made in Australia was one of the Melbourne Cup in 1896. (The uninitiated may need to be told that this is a famous horse race, and the event appositely fits the myth of Australia being a nation of gamblers.)

ALA 1949

This does not deal with the form as such, but R 15 deals with 'Scenarios (Motion picture)' in three lines. They are to be entered under title in the form: Elephant boy (*Motion picture*). By contrast, interestingly, radio scripts (R 14) are entered under author when known, and if anonymous under broadcasting company or station. Collections of scripts go under editor or title. We have here a nice example of confusion which the student may wish to sort out and comment upon, bearing in mind the principles crystallised later by Lubetzky.

LC

LCRDC strangely does not cater for films. The omission is remedied in LC's *Motion pictures and filmstrips*. The edition used for comment here is the 2nd preliminary ed, 1958. Much of this code was transferred bodily into AACR, and for the most part, apart from exceptions noted briefly here, AACR decisions may be taken as embracing the LC code. The code was endorsed by the ALA and obviously was intended to be used in conjunction with ALA 1949. Like AACR, entry is under release title. Non-Americans reading this book will have to bear in mind that a release title in the US may be different from that used in, say, Australia or Britain, with any ensuing complications, including the use of LC published catalogues as catalogue substitutes. As we suggest elsewhere in this book, there is a case for entering certain films (and many filmstrips) under an author equivalent. Qualifiers after the title are (Motion picture) or (Filmstrip), as in AACR.

A minor difference from AACR are the examples given in the 'change of title' note. Another is that LC gives fewer examples of credits than does AACR, though we suggest that the difference is not very significant. Another mildly interesting example of a difference is that, under 'serials', LC's example is *Batman and Robin*, while AACR's is *Zombies of the stratosphere*. A sign of the times? Another understandable difference is that, under added entries, LC cites 'releasing agent in the US', while AACR British text names 'distributor in the United Kingdom'. The obvious moral here is that each country must adapt whatever code it uses to genuine local needs.

Finally, the LC code has a useful short list of abbreviations intended as an addendum to Appendix III of LCRDC. The industrious student may wish to compare these with those given in GRENFELL *J doc*.

There are three specifically film codes which we propose to deal with now. They are given in chronological order, as each succeeding code overtly or covertly seems, quite justifiably, to have drawn upon what went before it.

UNESCO International rules for the cataloguing of educational, scientific and cultural films and filmstrips . . . 1956

In theory, this internationally compiled code should be used as a standard for all future practice, but, understandably, some well-established institutions have continued their past, nationally-oriented, practices.

It is confirmed at the outset (p 3) that 'underdeveloped' countries may well need to catalogue films produced by other countries, and the code, again understandably, tries to cater for all countries by adopting a neutral stance. This situation does not apply only to 'underdeveloped' countries, of course. There is other introductory material which should be followed up by those wishing to study in depth the problems of international cataloguing of films. Here, we should point out that the countries chiefly contributing to UNESCO were Britain and the US, respectively LC and the British Film Institute (BFI). (A reminder may be needed that BM's legal deposit rights do not embrace such special materials as films and sound recordings.) Also called upon was the International Scientific Film Association.

The card form is assumed—acceptable at the time, but, we suggest, subject to revision in the light of computer developments since 1956. But an obvious advantage of the card form is its flexibility for manual manipulation, such that entries from a variety of sources may be interfiled, assuming the 3″ × 5″ (7·5 cm × 12·5 cm) as conventionally accepted.

An elaborate system is outlined, and here we wonder at the number of cards which may have to be reproduced and filed. However, this may be a western-oriented judgement, and there may well be enough willing labour available in some other countries at salaries which make such processes feasible and economic.

Three basic operations are outlined: (a) to describe a film, (b) to evaluate a film; and (c) to indicate its availability. It is envisaged that each film will have, in effect, four main entry cards: (a) basic heading/description; (b) evaluation; (c) international availability; and (d) national availability. In effect, the result envisaged by UNESCO emerges as a combination of a local-holdings catalogue and a union catalogue: an admirable ideal—if only it can be realised. There would be a need for a total of at least six cards per film, since a further two may be needed for a foreign language version and a series entry in certain cases.

Four types of information are contemplated: (a) title, leading to further information, in effect description; (b) foreign language versions available; (c) others in the same series; and (d) subject approach to films and filmstrips.

It is envisaged that, in effect, there will be three approaches: (a) a reference number file, *eg* UK 54-93, indicating country, year, and accession number respectively; (b) title; and (c) subject. This system if adopted could be helped by the equivalent of an International Standard Book Number for each film.

The code then goes into descriptive cataloguing, the term being taken to include heading. It draws upon LC 1958, already mentioned, and British Film Institute (BFI) 2nd rev ed 1952.

Heading decisions involve a choice between the academic accuracy of the original title and the possibly more sought release title of copy in hand. The latter is chosen. The title is followed by 'Film' (or 'Motion picture' depending on national preference), or 'Filmstrip'. An appropriate title is supplied within square brackets by the cataloguer if the copy in hand has no title, and it describes briefly the subject of the document, *eg* [Studies of children at play in organised groups].

The title is transcribed as given in the film, including alternative title or sub-title. Detailed instructions on capitalisation and punctuation are given. The heading includes reference number for the film.

There next follows production agency, then Imprint-type information including date, then 'maker' if different from production agency, in the form:

DRILLING AND TAPPING CAST STEEL (Film) US-52-17-a
U.S. Office of Education, Washington, U.S.A., 1942. Made by Emerson Yorke Studio.

The date is the operative one, *ie* that of original release, and not, say, that of copy in hand. This is the best choice, as with all library materials, as it is an obvious indication of how up-to-date the document may be. Usefully, too, date of making is also given if different from date of release. Because of its salient importance, we agree that it should appear high in the entry—book cataloguers can learn a lesson here—but we do not agree with its being insignificantly sandwiched between items of verbal information which may be quite long.

Physical description includes a lot of what we would call bibliographic rather than retrieval data. Running time is given when available. Where this is given, we wonder what purpose is served by including also number of reels. Again, running speeds are established now, and projectors are equipped to give the different speeds needed for silent films as opposed to sound films. Yet we are told to include running speeds in the form of metres per minute and feet per minute. We think that this topic need be touched upon only in exceptional circumstances, such as a silent film running at sound film speed. For filmstrips, statement of number of frames is given and is usually needed for planning a 'running-time equivalent' on the part of the prospective user. Other necessary information catered for includes details of accompanying material. For filmstrips, if accompanying material is a sound recording, running time is usefully catered for. We are also told, usefully, to state physical form of accompanying sound material for filmstrips—disc, tape, wire—but we doubt the need for giving information like number and diameter of discs or its equivalent for tapes and wires, as prescribed by the code.

Other necessary information includes statement of whether colour or black and white, and of gauge, both of which may be needed to help selection by a potential user. The gauge is particularly important, since it indicates whether a document can be used at all depending on machinery available. The same applies to film loops, which the code, in its exhaustive way, caters for.

Notes cater for a variety of information, much of which may be more useful than production-type data which the code places higher in the entry. For example, change of title comes here. This could be vital in identifying a film and so should come immediately after the title of the copy in hand at the top of the entry. It could be given in the form (Previous title: I was a fireman). The Related material notes sometimes clash with some parts of Physical description (Collation-equivalent), and this aspect could cause confusion in both cataloguing decisions and use by clientele. Another important part of Notes is Credits and Cast. We agree that much of this information is rightly given low in the entry. But director may well be more important than production companies, as this is the nearest approach to 'author' in many films, and so should be named higher in the entry, especially in the case of 'imaginative' productions, such as those by Ken Russell. Summary comes next, and we recommend this as one of the last items to go if limited cataloguing has to be practised. We agree that the

Summary should be objective, especially since in this code criticism can be quoted on the Evaluation card—if only the hard-pressed cataloguer has time to round up such opinions. Perhaps there would be time to include under Evaluation opinions of local users, *eg* teachers in an educational library, although this useful aspect is not specified in the code. The Continuations element could be useful, although examples in the code seem to confuse some basic collation-type information and Contents with the sequels-type information inferred by Continuations.

There is a special section on cataloguing foreign language versions, which could have been subsumed under such topics as choice and form of title, previously covered.

At this point in the code comes Evaluation data. We have already commented upon this, but, to sum up this important topic, we suggest that this section should be implemented in as much detail as possible.

We feel that the subject approach, whether UDC or DC with attendant indexes, should have received more attention, since we are convinced that an adequate subject approach is more important than a lot of the descriptive detail dealt with at great and inordinate length. Samples of UNESCO cards, which show their derivation from BFI, appear below.

```
The CATHODE RAY OSCILLOGRAPH (Film)                    U.K.53-93-a
  Radio Research Board, London, U.K., 1952.  Made by Gaumont
  British Instructional

  32 min., sd., b&w, 35mm., 16mm.  (History of engineering
  series, No.3)

  Related filmstrip:  Cathode rays
  Credits:  Technical adviser:  Sir Robert Watson-Watt
  Summary:  Construction and application of the oscillograph
  in radio research

  U.D.C. 621.317.755.  Series:  History of
  engineering No.3

  British Film
  Institute
```

Figure 2

Set of cards from UNESCO (p 8 ff) (drawn from BFI)
(Reduced by about one-third)
(a) Original version of film

It is assumed that the film "The Cathode Ray Oscillograph" has two foreign language versions: a German dubbed version and a French sub-titled version. Sample cards for each of these are illustrated below:

Der KATHODENSTRAHL- OSZILLOGRAPH (Film)   U.K.53-93-a1
German dubbed version of: The Cathode Ray Oscillograph.
Radio Research Board, London. U.K. 1952 Made by
Gaumont British Instructional

32 min.. sd., b&w 35mm., 16mm. (Serie: Die Geschichte der
Ingenieurswissenschaft)

Related filmstrip: Kathodenstrahle.
Credits: Commentary writer Prof. P. Schultz.

British Film
Institute

(b) German version

L'OSCILLOGRAPHE A RAYONS CATHODIQUES (Film) U.K.53-93-a2
French sub-titled version of: The Cathode Ray Oscillograph.
Radio Research Board, London, U.K. 1952. Made by Gaumont
British Instructional.

32 min , sd , b&w, 35mm., 16mm. (Série: L'Histoire des
sciences techniques)

Related filmstrip: Les rayons cathodiques.
Credits: Sub-titles by Dr. A. Dumesnil.

British Film
Institute

(c) French version

The CATHODE RAY OSCILLOGRAPH (Film) U.K.53-93-b

Contents: The necessity for a new instrument for radio research is demonstrated by showing the failure of needle and mirror voltmeters at frequencies much below those found in radio research. The construction of the cathode oscillograph is clearly explained and the function of each part demonstrated. The use of the time base and the application of the oscillograph, the determination of the height of the ionosphere and the degree of ionisation of the upper atmosphere are also shown.

Comments: Authoritative and convincing. Photography excellent throughout and commentary to the point. Apart from the application of the general theory of the compounding of the wave forms and simple periodic vibrations the electrical aspect of the film is valuable in the hands of lecturers appreciating the full implication of the production.

Type: Instructional

Grading: Higher and technical teaching: highly recommended.

Evaluator: S.F.A. Panel for Technical Films

British Film Institute

(d) Evaluation card

The CATHODE RAY OSCILLOGRAPH (Film) U.K.53-93-c

Versions: 1 English; 2 German; 3 French (sub-titles)

Owner of rights: Radio Research Board, 3 Brompton Lane, London, W.C.2.

Comm. distr.: Gaumont British Instructional, Film House, Wardour Street. London W.1; 35mm.: B; C

Non-comm. distr.: Alpha Productions, 217 Belmont Lane, London, W.C.1; 16mm.: Aa; C; E educational inst.

TV distr.: Television International, 31 Burton Avenue. London, W.2; Clearance image: all countries; sound: countries Bern Conv.; 35 & 16mm.: Ab

Certified for purpose Unesco A.V. Agreement; Certificate U.K. Ministry of Education

British Film
Institute

(e) Availability card for international use

Key to Symbols

A: outright purchase per copy
B: outright purchase of duplicating rights
C: rental
D: long term lease
E: free loan

These rules are particularly important because of their influence via the published *British national film catalogues* which are available as catalogue substitutes and as a cataloguing authority all over the world. There are also several significant published articles on BFI practice, *eg* FANNING *LA record,* FANNING *Lib world,* and GRENFELL *Librarian*; also relevant is GRENFELL *J doc,* already mentioned. Fuller citations of these articles are given in the bibliography starting on p 304. The edition of BFI commented upon here is the 5th rev. ed, 1960.

BFI has considerable literary warrant. By 1962 it had a stock of 19,000, dating from 1889 (FANNING *LA record*), and of course it is still growing. Its great variety of stock includes many newsreels, a particularly significant form in these days of extensive television libraries. Television companies' librarians would be advised to consider carefully the relevant part of this code. Again, BFI has paid considerable attention to the subject approach, using UDC, with which we concur because of its manifest universality, its flexibility, and the possibility of its being accepted as a truly international index language in the future, even if meanwhile it undergoes radical revision.

The code is bibliographic-oriented by its very nature as a master code for the recording of film archives, resulting in its catalogues being used as an authority, as mentioned above. But, even if local librarians decide to simplify the description used in their catalogues, we recommend serious consideration of the many approaches catered for, including those for subject, which can help in the compilation of a retrieval-oriented catalogue.

The code is divided into the following parts: Title catalogue; News film catalogue; Indexes; Style. Also there are three Appendices: Designation of credits; Classification and headings; Sample cards. Finally there is a detailed Index. The work opens with a very useful Preface by David Grenfell.

Main entry heading (within UDC number in published catalogues) is by title—although, as we mention elsewhere, there may be a case in some instances for entry under either director or author of a notable literary work from which a film is made. In accordance with an academically-conscious film archive collection, form of title used is that of the original release in the vernacular language. Bibliographic searching may well be needed if the copy in hand is not an original issue, and local librarians may decide to revert early on to the sub-section of the rule which allows entry under the title of the copy in hand; the code prescribes that in such a case the title shall be preceded by an asterisk. Perhaps the convention of putting various forms of supplied title in square brackets might have been more useful, although this code, in its examples, uses square brackets to give original release title when different from copy in hand, *eg* [GASLIGHT] with a reference from * MURDER IN THORNTON SQUARE.

A useful 'retrieval' rule which follows deals with different films which are derived from the same film sources. Each film is entered separately, but with connecting references. A popular example is given of films relating to Scott of the Antarctic (if we may quote a popular fiction film title made after the code was compiled). Examples of titles are 90° SOUTH; the GREAT WHITE SILENCE; and the STORY OF CAPTAIN SCOTT.

A 'missing' title, in this code, is one which is known, but is not on the film. This is given in square brackets. A 'supplied' title is one which is constructed by the cataloguer when the title is not on the copy and cannot be found. This is given in parenthesis. This distinction is necessary for BFI and it may well be useful in a retrieval catalogue to obviate errors in identification.

As with other codes, a sub-title or alternative title is transcribed. What is more unusual, and likely to be very useful, is a recommendation not only to give references from sub-title or alternative title but also from a significant part of the title after the first word.

eg *the* ADVENTURES OF ROBIN HOOD
Refer from... ROBIN HOOD

This catchword approach is not of course a substitute for subject entry, but it may help supplement the subject approach and obviate indirect approach to an imperfectly remembered title via the subject indexing and UDC notation.

High in the entry there now appears the location symbol, including where necessary a particular reel within a work. This information is relevant only in BFI itself, but it points the useful moral, if such be necessary, that any library must name location of document high in the entry and clearly, especially if material is open access, although in fact this does not apply in BFI.

Credits are led by names of studios and production and sponsoring companies, then followed by names of ' all individuals who participate in the production of a film '. As already mentioned, the director at least is likely to be more sought than corporate bodies and should feature higher in the entry. We further query the needs to name all individuals; some selection guidance would have been useful, whether on production staff or on cast, as demonstrated by AACR, which we consider later.

So-called ' Source material ' appears, rightly, reasonably high in the entry, although we feel that in certain cases it may be more important than corporate bodies associated with a film, such as when a well known literary work or composer are involved.

There follow country of origin, more useful than local town, etc given in most codes; and date, which, as mentioned elsewhere, is worthy of a higher place. Types of date are detailed. A complaint here is that ' c ' is used for approximate date, which could be confused with ' copyright '; the conventional ' ca ', for ' circa ', would have been preferred, or the English abbreviation ' approx '. More minute information may be given for television productions, down to day and month of transmission: we agree that this information may be of value in identifying a document and pinpointing the occasion of its being broadcast.

Collation gives basic ' physical properties ', as might be expected. Bearing in mind the bibliographic-oriented nature of the code, more than enough detail is given from which a librarian may select his requirements. The detail includes, as well as ' sound ' and ' silent ', the intermediate ' mute ' for silent films intended to be used with (external) sound. The detail on sound itself, for synchronised recordings, is itself more than enough from which to choose in cataloguing sound recordings as such. A final example of the minute detail is that length has to exclude blank film (presumably a ' head-out '), and if actual film footage has been removed the length of the original has to be given within parentheses. Needless to say, we feel sure that this type of detail would not be necessary in the average local library. Perhaps, in any library, actual details of a scene which has been cut might be more useful, especially since many films are censored to varying degrees in various countries. However, such information would be best covered in Notes. In relation to censorship, we are told to give certification by the British Board of Censors. This could easily be adapted to suit the home country, and Australian libraries, for example, would substitute relevant Australian certifications. In a MARC format, provision should be made at this point for a field to cover locally inserted data, while the British data could be suppressed if not required.

Various items of local information follow, such as donor and reason for acquiring a film.

Next comes the Summary, a ' descriptive précis of the action and content of the film '. Considerable detail is expected, including, in effect, contents statements naming reel numbers. Such information may be most useful to users and, as previously stated, we recommend inclusion of this type of information in preference to some items of physical description. In addition, there is provision for Notes.

Provision is also made for a statement of review sources, even with specific recommendations on how to cite a review article. Such information is likely to be very useful, if only the actual articles are readily available. Treatment of a fiction film is shown in the sample cards reproduced on p 170-171.

Information follows on how to record Continuations and ' Serials', the latter being defined as ' prepared for release in chapters '. There appears to be some havering between entry of separate chapters or episodes under the parent title or that of the individual items, since parts of serials go under the former and parts of so-called cinemagazines go under the latter. But this practice can be justified on the grounds of subject integrity. Television programmes like the BBC's *Panorama* are included under ' cinemagazines '.

Finally, even trailers are catered for.

Newsreels are very important, whether at the time or as used later in documentaries or fiction films. But they are stocked by few libraries, mainly film archives and television libraries, and interested film librarians are recommended to study the relevant BFI rules in detail. But it is a fact that newsreels of today can be the source material of tomorrow's history, so we shall deal briefly here with BFI's short but excellent guidance in dealing with this unique form.

Each item should be entered individually, that is, ' continuations ' treatment is not applied. Entries include subject-type titles and dates, particular attention being justifiably paid to the latter. Source, in the form of a production credit, *eg* Pathé gazette, follows date. Detailed summaries are given, including ' script of the action ' with a blow-by-blow account of footages, with a total footage at the end. Subtitles given in the film are also to be included; supplied titles are underlined.

Collation includes the usual physical detail required for projection. Inevitably there have to be detailed subject, including biographical, approaches.

As already indicated, a special section of the code is devoted to indexes. It will be remembered that the *British national film catalogue* uses one long main entry for each item, entries being in UDC order, with plentiful indexing to the UDC notation. Incidentally, it is noteworthy that the classified entries employ feature headings, giving the verbal equivalents of the—sometimes complex—UDC notation. We recommend this intellectual structure, especially since UDC seems likely to become the most generally accepted general index language and because it is the most flexible and hospitable general classification scheme available at present and in the foreseeable future. It is understandable then that BFI's indexes are particularly important; our only basic complaint is that they could have been dealt with in more detail in the code.

Index entries are recommended for personal and corporate author-type contributors to a film. We query whether dates of birth and death are needed for personal authors, when available; we prefer the AACR ruling for using them only when essential to differentiate between otherwise identical headings. The ruling for corporate entries seems happily to anticipate AACR British text. An additional example of BFI's exhaustivity is that references are prescribed, for corporate names starting with initials, to the used form, *eg* from D. W. GRIFFITH PRODUCTIONS to GRIFFITH PRODUCTIONS. AACR is departed from in that British Government departments are entered directly under their names, *eg* MINISTRY OF INFORMATION, with a reference from GREAT BRITAIN. *Ministry of Information.* This principle could conveniently be applied to other countries without, we hope, contradicting MARC format. Hence 'home' government departments could be entered directly, and foreign departments could be entered initially under name of country. However, a problem could be encountered with federally constituted countries. If BFI's principle is followed, we recommend treating both state, or provincial, and federal departments as 'home', with additional qualifiers for 'state' or 'federal' as apposite. Local areas are entered directly, with a reference from parent country, *eg* TOKYO MUNICIPALITY, with a *see* reference from JAPAN. Tokyo Municipality. We recommend this advice, as is made evident in the chapter of this book on maps. However, if a library preferred indirect entry via larger area for maps, as quite widely practised, and

TITLE **BLACKMAIL** LOCATION NO. 198 I

STUDIO: Elstree Studios, Herts.
PRODUCTION CO.:
British International Pictures (B.I.P.)
PRODUCER: [John Maxwell]
DIRECTOR: Alfred Hitchcock
ASSISTANT DIRECTOR: Frank Mills
SCRIPT: from the play by Charles Bennett, adapted by Alfred Hitchcock
DIALOGUE: Benn Levy
PHOTOGRAPHY: Jack Cox
CAMERA ASSISTANT: [Derick Williams]
[Michael Powell]
ART DIRECTION: W. C. Arnold (*sic.*)
[Norman Arnold]
FILM EDITOR: Emile de Ruelle
MUSIC: Hubert Bath
Harry Stafford
British International Symphony Orchestra
CONDUCTOR: John Reynders
SOUND SYSTEM: R.C.A. Photophone
[The song *Miss Up-to-Date* by Billy Mayerl & Frank Eyton
Musical score by Campbell & Connelly

CAST

Alice White	Anny Ondra
Mrs. White	Sara Allgood
Mr. White	Charles Paton
Det. Frank Webber	John Longden
Tracy	Donald Calthrop
The artist	Cyril Ritchard
The landlady	Hannah Jones
The Chief Inspector	Harvey Braban
Det. Sgt.	Ex-Det. Sgt. Bishop (late C.I.D., Scotland Yard)
The charlady	Phyllis Monkman

[Joan Barry was Anny Ondra's vocal double]

COUNTRY:
Great Britain
DATE: 1929
WIDTH: 35mm.
COMB./POS.
FEET: 7,[illegible]98
CERT.: A
REG. NO. Br.2739
DISTR.
Wardour Films
DONOR:
Mr. John Maxwell
DATE RECD. 1936

SELECTION COMM. REF.
AE 185 (1584)
24.11.54

2. Obverse of main entry for a FICTION FILM (8″ × 5″)

Figure 3

Part of a BFI entry for a fiction film (*p* 37) (*actual size*)
(*a*)

SUMMARY: **DETECTIVE AND THRILLER.** A story of murder and subsequent blackmail. R1.1 Scotland Yard's flying squad arrest a criminal; after he has been subjected to an interrogation, identification parade, charged, fingerprinted and put in the cells the men in charge of the case, including Detective Frank Webber, prepare to leave (787). R1.2 Alice White, Frank's girl friend, is peeved at being kept waiting; he takes her to a Lyon's Corner House; they quarrel and Frank leaves her, but subsequently observes Alice leaving the cafe in the company of another man with whom she has made an assignation (1468). R1.3 The man, an artist, invites Alice into his studio; they are observed by Tracy, a furtive character not unknown to the artist (2272). R1.4 The artist offers to paint Alice; whilst she is changing . . .

REVIEW REFS., ETC.

Bioscope, 79 (1186), June 26, 1929, p. 31

Close up, 5 (2), August 1929, pp. 131–135

Kinematograph weekly, 148 (1158), June 27, 1929, p. 43

Noble, Peter. Index to the work of Alfred Hitchcock. Spec. suppl. to *Sight and Sound*, May 1949 (Index series, no. 18), pp. 12–14

REASON FOR ACQUN.

As a pioneer sound film; for its dubbing technique and as an important Hitchcock film.

NOTE:

The song *Miss Up-to-Date* was written for the musical play "Love Lies", produced at the Gaiety in March 1929, and in which Cyril Ritchard appeared.

SUBJECT REFS.

343.713	Blackmail
942.12[1]: 727.6	Holborn – British Museum
942.13[1]: 725.71	Westminster – Lyon's Corner House, Coventry Street
351.741: 942.13[1]: 725.188	Flying Squad – Scotland Yard, Westminster

3. Reverse of main entry for a FICTION FILM (8″ × 5″)
(*The summary continued on another card*)

(*b*)

if an integrated catalogue of all media were compiled, inconsistency could result. It is unlikely that references from larger to smallar area would be needed if a multiple-entry classified catalogue were used. However, it would be necessary to clarify the difference between place of origin of a film and place as subject of a film. In general, librarians who cater for all possible author-type approaches to films are advised to study this part of BFI carefully, even though they may decide to reject the claims of some rather remote approaches as exemplified by say, CINEPHONE SOUND (U.S.A.).

The precise subject approach of BFI is evidenced by the published *British national film catalogue*. As already mentioned, the basic catalogue has its main entries in UDC order. The verbal approach to UDC notation is catered for by chain indexing. Later, we hope that PRECIS (PREserved Context Indexing System) might be used generally for films as it is at present used for monographic books in BNB, especially bearing in mind the BNB experiments at present being made (late 1972) with MARC oriented BNFC computer-printed catalogues. Our latest information, from Mr John Linford of BNB in September 1972, is that computerisation of BNFC is well under way, and that BNFC programs will be used for the production of the catalogue of the British Universities Film Council in 1973. We may well hope, then, that BNB's PRECIS indexing may become more widely accepted in the near future, in this case as applied to films.

BFI caters for analytical indexing of all films whether or not in newsreel form. We feel this is necessary and to be recommended.

Biographical entries feature largely and justifiably in BFI's indexing. However, we doubt if such minute details are needed for each individual as are exemplified by, say

> KITCHENER, Horatio Herbert, *1st Earl Kitchener of Khartoum and Broome*—British Field Marshal 1850-1916

Form entry is also catered for. Fiction examples are DRAMA: historical; COMEDY; MUSICAL. Non-fiction examples are ACTUALITY; DOCUMENTARY; PROPAGANDA. An element of subjective judgement cannot help but be brought into the last-named, but this does not necessarily detract from the value of such valid minuteness. Further, 'treatment' is catered for by terms such as CARTOON; COMPILATION; TELEVISION. Cross-classification is evidenced here, but we consider that these approaches are likely to be useful in a local retrieval-oriented library, and we commend consideration of them to librarians who take film cataloguing seriously and whose stock is extensive enough to defeat the human memory.

The section of the code on Style incorporates useful filing rules, which often, interestingly, antedate the ALA filing rules of 1968. Our experience with students gives the impression that at least some librarians of tomorrow favour more literally alphabetical filing. Therefore, it is gratifying that BFI seems to cater for this attitude.

To attempt to sum up BFI. We feel that this code caters adequately for both bibliographic-oriented and retrieval-oriented catalogues. Therefore, it should be a useful source of help for any librarian in whatever capacity he finds himself. The art of using BFI is that of selection and not of changing of rules. We feel this can be accomplished, and such a situation is the more gratifying since BNFC is being computerised within the MARC format, as already mentioned, and as further commented upon in the final chapter of this book. If asked for the 'best buy' in film cataloguing codes, we would recommend BFI.

ASLIB Film cataloguing rules

These came out in 1963, and an obvious debt to previous codes is manifested and acknowledged. The Preface is interesting academically and useful to the lecturer, student and practitioner in, perhaps unconsciously, pinpointing both the bibliographic-oriented and retrieval-oriented attitudes which have emerged to the present writer in compiling this book. The code, like BFI, attempts to cater for both traditional film librarians and television librarians. As it states explicitly, it attempts to cater for 'all types of film libraries', which it details. Its outline of the basic principles of film cataloguing usefully crystallises topics in a way which can be particularly useful to lecturers and students, and, if sensibly applied, can be of practical value to the film librarian in the field. A trenchant comment by our old friend Cutter is quoted: 'No rules can take the place of experience and good judgement, but some of the results of experience may be best indicated by rules'. This may in fact be a restatement of the fact that any book is merely a substitute for experience, but we feel that such a reminder is worth the space given to it.

This code draws a great deal on, especially, BFI, including actual examples, and so we need not devote as much space to it as in our treatment of previous codes. There are some minor typographical variations which do not affect the basic philosophy of the code itself; our main comment on these is that they may be slightly less fussy, or non-self-explanatory than in, say, BFI. One example, is that original release title is given in plain upper case, 'missing' titles are given in square brackets, and 'supplied' titles are given in parentheses. Choice and form of entry are virtually the same as in BFI, but such typographical and arbitrary idiosyncrasies as the asterisk are not used.

It is interesting to note that the uniform title principle of AACR is not anticipated; hence the bibliographic unit, as assumed by AACR, is narrower. Perhaps we should indulge an aside at this point. A bibliographic unit can be: (a) a basic, say, literary, work on which a film is based; (b) an actual film, irrespective of various releases in various countries and with dialogue and/or subtitles in various languages; or (c) one particular copy or issue of a film under, possibly, a title in the 'home' language of the country concerned. ASLIB chooses (b). Hence it would enter a particular film under The PERSONAL HISTORY, ADVENTURES, EXPERIENCES, AND OBSERVATIONS OF DAVID COPPERFIELD, THE YOUNGER, with just a *see* reference from DAVID COPPERFIELD, the latter being the form of title likely to be adopted under condition (a). Whether or not the main entry itself should be under title, in whatever form, or author—or even director—is mentioned elsewhere in this book.

Order of supporting data may best be demonstrated briefly by an example from the code. Our comments on order of description have already been outlined in our treatment of BFI, and we prefer ASLIB's in general.

> BLACKMAIL
>
> *p.c*: BIP *p*: John Maxwell *d*: Alfred Hitchcock *s.c.*: Alfred Hitchcock, from the play by Charles Bennett ph: Jack Cox *ed.* Emile de Ruelle *m.*: Hubert Bath, Harry Stafford *cast*: Anny Oudra, Sara Allgood, Charles Paton, John Longden, Donald Calthrop, Cyril Ritchard.
>
> [There would follow further data such as country of origin, date, collation, etc]

In the example given no punctuation is shown between items. The abbreviations may seem rather cryptic; the user could get used to them, but a general key on the catalogue would not come amiss. It may be noted that the code assumes selection 'for certain individuals', but the code itself gives an exhaustive list of participants which might be included. Not shown in the above example is *Sp.* for sponsor, which (unusefully we feel) comes before individuals, with production company where relevant.

The rest of the description is substantially the same as BFI.

Liberal added entries are prescribed, corresponding largely with BFI's author-type entries. It is up to the local librarian to decide to what extent these are implemented. We suspect that in many cases, *eg* cast, considerable selection would be needed.

Newsfilms cause an offer of treatment either as continuations or in effect BFI-type treatment. Apart from this alternative, treatment and detail are similar to BFI. Geographical location is specifically mentioned under subject approach, but this would automatically be catered for by BFI's chain indexing of UDC. The samples reproduced on p 176-179 give an indication of the code's detailed recording of a television newsreel.

'Picture material' receives a section to itself in ASLIB, and in this respect the code can be particularly useful to the—possibly few—librarians dealing with what are more generally referred to as 'stock shots'. Main entry is under subject, whether verbal or classification notation. Considerable useful detail is prescribed for each shot which should obviate a lot of screening only to reject items. Camera treatment and type of shot (medium, short, etc) are prescribed, as well as a precise description of each shot, with date, source of material, etc. This section of the code could be particularly useful to television librarians who inevitably cannot anticipate what news will break and must rely on detailed indexing to produce specific material at extremely short notice, possibly within a few minutes, to back up a news item.

A most useful section follows, dealing with Sound material, divided into two parts: Sound effects; and Dubbing tracks. The first part is of just as much value to sound recording librarians as to film librarians, and so is commended for their attention. Many general libraries have, or should have, records of sound effects, not only for professional use in, say, film production, but also for, say, amateur theatricals directors, who may naturally turn to public libraries for sound effects just as they hope to get texts of plays from public libraries. As with stock shots, main entry is by subject. An example given is

Serial No. 324/60

Saturday, 19th November, 1960

	Neg. rl. no.	Source	Footage	Gauge	LOCATION nos. (pos.)
FORD HEADLINE	1		6'	16 mm.	40725
XMAS LIGHTS	1		25'	16 mm.	40726
MOBUTO PARADE, CONGO	1	BCINA	30'	16 mm.	40727
GUATEMALA	1	BCINA	35'	16 mm.	40728
CHURCHILL HOME	1		9'	16 mm.	40729
TANGANYIKA WEDDING	1		27'	16 mm.	40730
PRESSED STEEL MARCH	1		20'	16 mm.	40731
TRAFALGAR SQ. RALLY	2		23'	16 mm.	40732
ALFRED HINDS, LAP	2		14'	16 mm.	40733
ESCAPED PRISONER SEARCH	2		23'	16 mm.	40734

8. Main Entry for a TELEVISION NEWSREEL (Filed by Serial number) (8" × 5")

Figure 4

Set of newsreel entries from ASLIB (p 59 ff). ASLIB's captions are self-explanatory

(a)

PROGRAMME AS BROADCAST

NEWS SUMMARY No. 324/60

Transmitted from A.P.

Saturday, 19th November, 1960
5.50 p.m.
Duration: 2'35"

NEWS READER: Richard Baker (SNF)

FILM DETAILS

Story no.		Source	Mute/Comb.	Gauge	Footage
	Ford Headline (LONDON)	BBC (Av)	mute	16 pos.	6
24301	Xmas Lights (LONDON)	BBC (Av)	sep. mag.	16 neg.	25

STUDIO: Richard Baker reporting on: Fords; Sir Winston Churchill; Congo; Foot and mouth disease; Alfred George Hinds; By-elections; Anti-Polaris protest march, Glasgow; Dartmoor prisoner search.

CAPTIONS: BBC TV - THE NEWS

MAPS AND CHARTS
None used.

STILLS: Mr. Henry Ford - Reuter.

MUSIC DUBBED ON TRACK
Xmas Lights.
BELLS ON HER TOES
(Cecil Angel)
CONWAY B.M. 200A (39")

9. TELEVISION NEWSREEL CONTENTS SHEET (Filed by serial number)

(*b*)

ISSUE NO: 324/60
SOURCE: BBC — ORIGINAL FOOTAGE: 150 — GAUGE: 16 neg. mute
EDITED BY: J. Smith — DATE: 19.11.60.

TITLE: XMAS LIGHTS	STORY NO: 24301	FT.	SECS.
Angel aloft		2	3
L.S. Angel aloft pan to men working		5	$7\frac{1}{2}$
Angel on ground		7	$10\frac{1}{2}$
C.U. Angel face blowing trumpet		8	$12\frac{1}{2}$
Crowd		9	15
Angel going up		12	20
People looking up		13	22
G.V. Angels over Regent Street		15	24
Oxford Street "snow flake" on ground		17	28
C.U. men working on "snow flake" on ground		18	30
Snow flake going up		21	34
Man watching		22	34
G.V. flakes going up		23	39

10. TELEVISION NEWSREEL SHOT LIST (Filed by serial number)

(*c*)

ISSUE NO: 324/60 5.50 p.m.	TITLE: XMAS LIGHTS story no: 24301	CRE/LR	10.11.60.

BAKER IN VISION:	Thirty shopping days to Christmas
FILM:	and up go the decorations in London's West End . . . over Regent Street . . . angels.
CUE 62"	Forty-six of them . . . some ten feet tall get ready to take off with their golden trumpets.
CUE 14"	They may not look it, but they each weigh seventy-five pounds.
CUE 22"	And for Oxford Street . . . giant snow-flakes made of plastic and wire . . . one-hundred-and-fifty are going up. Inside are hundreds of lamps, but the Christmas lights won't be switched on until next Thursday. 2' 9"

11. TELEVISION NEWSREEL COMMENTARY CUE SHEET (Filed by serial number)

(*d*)

637.133
MILK pasteurization plant working

or

MILK: Pasteurization: Plant

It will be noted that the latter structured heading follows the formula of Thing: Operation: Agent. Librarians wishing to decide on a citation order may wish to turn to E J Coates' *Subject catalogues* for more information on citation orders for compound subject headings; however ASLIB itself does not go into such fine detail. Description of sound includes considerable useful detail, including, *eg*, the actual object emitting a sound which simulates a completely different situation, an example being a carpet sweeper simulating movement of waves on a sandy beach. Apart from subject information, considerable information is given on Collation-type information for physical description of optical film, magnetic film, tape, and disc. Some representative full entries are shown on p 181.

A similar degree of detail is given for dubbing tracks. Although specifically designed for film librarians, and although the originals may be of limited availability, these rules could also be of use to a 'popular' librarian for sound effects requests—if only the originals could be obtained. We cannot go into great detail here, but a reminder may be useful that a lot of this section deals with music, whether instrumental or vocal. Reference is made at this point to MLA, dealt with in detail in the chapter of this book on Music.

The next section of ASLIB deals with added entries. Most of this is devoted to choice and construction of headings, a topic which has since been subsumed by AACR. However, it is reassuring that many of the decisions forecast those of AACR. There are exceptions, however, and we propose to leave it to the industrious student to ferret out AA 1908 influences.

The remaining sections of ASLIB deal with typographic style, definitions, and abbreviations, culminating in some very useful specimen entries.

All of the ASLIB code is interesting for the teacher and student, although, as we have said, it derives considerably from previous noteworthy codes, especially ASLIB. But its essential value to the practising librarian is its dealing with sound effects and, indirectly, stock shots and dubbing tracks. To date, we have not found a better code covering these aspects of special cataloguing, and these parts at least are firmly recommended to the do-it-yourself librarian with a retrieval-oriented service in mind.

OPTICAL * 35 mm.
RCA
VA

SUBJECT HEADING: FOOTSTEPS

DESCRIPTION OF SOUND: Footsteps—walking on iron up to and past microphone and then up and down iron steps. Exterior.

PRODUCTION: SAN DEMETRIO, LONDON (1943)
COPYRIGHT: Ealing Studios.

FX no. 2057 neg./pos. Key nos. 25Z E 75538-902 (364 ft.)

5. Entry for SOUND EFFECTS Film (optical) (5" × 3")

629.111.31 LOCATION NO: MT 584

Wheelbarrow over cobblestones. Low-pitched rumble. Constant.

35 mm. fully coated. (27 ft.)

PRODUCTION: HANDLE WITH CARE (1952)

COPYRIGHT: Shell Film Unit.

6. Entry for SOUND EFFECTS Film (magnetic) (5" × 3")

Figure 5

ASLIB sound effects entries (p 58)

AACR

Chapter 12 of this general code deals with 'Motion pictures and filmstrips'. As we infer elsewhere in this book, we doubt whether the two forms can be considered together, although in fact, the two forms are dealt with together in some other codes. However, a code dealing with only films, with filmstrips as a subsidiary topic, is different from a multi-media code, namely for an integrated catalogue of all media, as is the case with AACR. In this code, it might have been more apposite to deal with filmstrips in Chapter 15 'Pictures, designs, and other two-dimensional reproductions'. For a slide, say, has more in common with a filmstrip than the latter has with an essentially moving image. A filmstrip, after all, is virtually a series of slides fixed together in a particular sequence, which is how slides are often used. Further, a slide projector often has an accessory attachment enabling it to be used for projecting filmstrips. Also, a series of slides may be synchronised with a sound recording, including automatic changing at a signal from the sound recording; this makes a series of slides virtually the same in its result as a filmstrip. We feel, then, that filmstrips—a far more commonly, economically and conveniently used medium than moving films—tend to be overshadowed in AACR by the more dramatic, expensive and complicated medium of moving films themselves.

In this code, the term 'motion picture' is used in both the British and the North American texts, although this term is rarely used outside North America. Certainly in British-oriented countries, just 'film' or even 'cinema' may be a more commonly used term. The main reason for the uniformity between the two texts is not governed by the advantages of uniformity—considerable as they may be—but to obviate redrafting of the basic text. This is an unfortunate symptom of haste in getting out the part of the code dealing with special cataloguing, and in turn may partly account for the current moves towards revising these chapters of the code.

As we have already stated, much of the LC rules of 1958 were transferred bodily into AACR, and we have to remember that these rules were drafted some twenty years ago and represent the first widely accepted code for cataloguing films. Hence their wide acceptance. For example, AACR automatically accepts the concept of title main entry for films, including filmstrips, although as we substantiate elsewhere, there is some reason for doubting this assumption.

This part of the code starts by limiting its bibliographic unit, possibly contradicting the basic principle of the code as a whole, by entering a film in hand under its release, and not its original, title. The title is followed by 'Motion picture' or 'Filmstrip', in the form Shoe-shine (*Motion picture*), for a film originally released in Italy under the title *Sciuscia*. A subject-type title is supplied in square brackets where 'a film lacks a title or if its title cannot be ascertained', following the basic rule for monographic works with no title pages (R 132 B2): Newsreels do not receive the minute treatment recommended in, say, the ASLIB rules, but are simply entered under latest title. A form of 'bound with' note is included for two films on the same reel, in the form

The Truman story (*Motion picture*)
on reel with They're in the Army now.

and vice versa. However, two films 'that can be considered parts of a whole' receive a two-part heading, which seems to contradict the essence of the general rule for monographic works which enters books of multiple authorship under one author only.

eg Emperor waltz [and] You and you (*Motion picture*).

Added entries are prescribed for almost any author-type and title approach which may be needed. Significantly, variant titles are included, and not represented in the form of references. Similarly, the next rule, dealing with title transcription, has examples which show added entries, not references, for alternative titles and catchwords in titles.

In common with other codes, title is usually followed by production company, and sponsor where relevant, then distributor; and only then by release date. Again, as in previous codes, date of manufacture is usefully given when different from date of release. We reiterate that a production company or sponsor is no more (or less) significant than a commercial publisher of a book, and we doubt whether it should come so high in the entry, taking priority over date and such an individual author-equivalent as director.

Physical description includes the same type and length of information as given in earlier codes, already commented upon. Accompanying sound material, for filmstrips, is fully exemplified, possibly with too much detail, as mentioned in relation to other codes. After the collation-equivalent comes the series statement, in accordance with book cataloguing practice.

The Notes and following parts are vital in many cases, in our opinion, and rightly they receive considerable attention. We need not detail AACR's treatment since we have covered it in relation to other codes, but we particularly commend this part of the code in two respects. Instructions are clearly expressed, with any exceptions and qualifications (such as limiting the number of credits and cast); and examples are useful and plentiful. We need not reiterate our complaint that some Notes, etc are important enough to come higher in the entry, while AACR follows well-established conventions. It is disappointing that a new code does not manifest a fresh look at detail like this. However, as we mention elsewhere in this book in more detail, there is substantial activity at the moment, on both sides of the Atlantic, towards revision of the special cataloguing parts of the code. One example of an admittedly small aspect calling for attention is that in Collation we have to state 'colour' where relevant; then in Notes we have to give, say, 'Technicolor'. Surely these two items could have been elided by merely giving the latter term in Collation.

The Summary rule is to be recommended for its careful, concise explanation, and examples which in effect round up whole entries showing the Summary in its context. (See examples on p 185.) These examples could be used in classes and in practice as a basis for comment on the code's treatment of films as a whole. We mention this because the code usually gives in its examples only the data relevant to the specific rule. For example, these full examples show the production company's name running straight on after the title heading, making it seem even more prominent than the personal authorship-type collaborators given much lower in the entry. AACR does not cater for critical comments as does UNESCO. Newsreels generally are treated as continuations, and 'collected series' of filmstrips are entered whole, as multi-volumed monographic works would be. However, Contents are expected, giving number of frames for each part in the form: 1. Two to make friends. 29 fr.—[etc etc]. Rule 33M could be invoked for analytical entries, although we are not reminded of this. While we realise that the compilers of the code expect an understanding of it as a whole, by its very nature, reminders of basic rules are sometimes given under later rules, and one here would not have come amiss.

In summing up AACR, we admit that it is manifestly a bibliographic-oriented code and not retrieval-oriented, so we should not criticise it for not being what it did not set out to be. The treatment of newsreels is an example. Generally, it is a convenient round up of rules from

The Medical effects of the atomic bomb. Part 2: Pathology and the clinical problem (*Motion picture*). U. S. Dept of the Army, 1950.

37 min. sd. colour. 16 mm.

Summary: Explains the thermal, traumatic, and radiation effects of atomic bombing; and includes clinical observations, medical diagnosis and prognosis, and pathological materials for illustrative purposes. For medical personnel only.

Red Nichols and his Five Pennies (*Motion picture*). Universal Pictures Co., New York, 1950.

15 min. sd. b&w. 35 mm.

Musical short.

Fort Algiers (*Motion picture*). Erco Pictures Corp. Released by United Artists Corp., 1953.

78 min. sd. b&w. 35 mm.

Based on a story by Frederick Stephani.

Credits: Producer, Joseph N. Ermolieff; director, Lesley Selander; screenplay, Theodore St John; music director, Michel Michelet. *Cast:* Yvonne De Carlo, Carlos Thompson, Raymond Burr, Leif Erickson, Anthony Caruso.

Summary: An adventure melodrama. A young girl who is sent to Algiers by the French Military Intelligence exposes the leader of a series of Arab uprisings and aids the French Foreign Legion in a battle to protect the oil fields from Arab attackers.

Modernism (*Filmstrip*). Encyclopaedia Britannica Films, Chicago, 1950.

60 fr. colour. 35 mm. (Contemporary American painting)

Credits: Collaborator, Daniel Catton Rich.

Summary: Defines and illustrates trends of various modernistic art styles in American painting. Explains how these are accomplished largely by the use of colour and form, disregarding recognizable subject matter.

Figure 6

Complete examples from AACR (p 226) including Summaries (slightly reduced)

earlier codes, and it is intended for what we now call the multi-media catalogue, a concept which we firmly recommend. Also, and this will become of increasing importance, it is MARC-compatible. Therefore in general we would recommend its adoption by librarians, especially those embarking on the cataloguing of audio-visual materials for the first time. As explained elsewhere, BNB is now using MARC format in the production of film catalogues, and librarians would be well advised to try to conform, in the interests of future central cataloguing. It is assumed here that BNB's computer-produced film catalogues, although directly derived from BFI, are AACR-oriented. MARC format is very flexible, and it is likely that most variations genuinely needed locally could be made within the MARC format. The librarian who takes this

—as we regard it—vital aspect of special cataloguing seriously should keep track of BNB's MARC manuals. *Eg* HALL caters for special materials (full bibliographic citation is given in the Bibliography).

Even though Part III of AACR (special materials) is being revised, we still think it advisable at the present to try to conform to it as it is now. When the revision is finally published, we believe that entries according to the first edition will largely be compatible with the new edition.

SLIDES, etc

LC's Pictures, designs and other two-dimensional representations, 1959

This may be regarded as a source code for still illustrations, especially since quite a lot of it, including some examples, was incorporated into AACR, as happened with other special materials. Its content derived from a preliminary draft of 1954, which attempted to reconcile the practices of some seventy five libraries. To this extent, it tended to conform to the pragmatic codification of ALA 1949, rather than to the more radical, principles-based, AACR. However, and despite what we have said, reference is made to the 'relatively untried nature of the rules'.

Types of works covered include prints, paintings, drawings including architectural drawings, photographs, transparencies and slides. Some further information is given on relevant terms, but suffice it to say here that 'photomechanical processes' are also named. Terms are not defined adequately, for some cataloguers at least, as happens with AACR. However, cataloguers may find useful the naming at least of such terms as 'daguerrotype' and 'photocopy (positive)'. In defence of LC's apparent lack of coverage and definitions, we suggest that some cataloguers are still bedevilled by a certain supineness, and that some still expect to find a rule or precedent at every turn, instead of expecting to apply basic knowledge and commonsense to slightly differing forms or manifestations of various forms as they crop up.

We need not go into detail here in relation to specific rules for entry as far as they reflect emergent AACR practice. Perhaps a reminder is needed, however, that LC caters only for author-type headings and description, and that—as the code says—a predominant choice may well be made for subject entry only.

In choice of heading, the usual personal and corporate authors are mentioned, with entry under personal author in cases of conflict. Where relevant, such a qualifier following heading as '*Attributed works*' is recommended. But if several artists are 'attributed' in relation to a work, entry is to be under title. Photographs of works of art go under the heading for the original artist, generally. Exceptions include—strangely—photographs of three dimensional works, and—understandably—copies of art works using a different medium from that of the original. There is a parallel here with the spectrum of transcriptions, adaptations, etc which applies with music.

Sets are to be catalogued as such, *ie* not individually or analytically.

Added entries are prescribed—justifiably for those libraries which can afford the time and space—for all 'authors' associated with a work, and—especially useful we feel—for titles.

Description tends to follow book-type form, but adapted to the form of material in hand, *eg* physical description may include such a statement as 'oil painting on wood.' In particular, mention is usefully prescribed for accompanying material, though possibly with too much detail. A further noteworthy type of information to be included is location of original, where some form of reproduction is being catalogued. Rather surprisingly, little detail seems to be laid down for sets, such as Contents where relevant.

AACR

The relevant part of AACR is Ch 15, which, for no apparent reason, is separated from Ch 12 Motion pictures and filmstrips by Ch 13 Music and Ch 14 Phonorecords. Ch 15 is entitled Pictures, designs, and other two-dimensional reproductions, and is in fact identical with the LC code dealt with above. As just mentioned, there is a lot in common between the two as well as their titles.

Entry is dealt with in two main sections: R 260, 261, 262 on Single works and sets of works; and R 263, 264 on Collections. There is also a Description section: R 265 to R 272.

The Introductory notes divide the objects of the chapter into four main types: (a) individual pictorial works; (b) sets of such works; (c) reproductions of such works, whether single or in sets, and (d) collections as assembled by various types of owners. It is acknowledged in effect that the subject approach may be regarded as paramount, although reference is not made to other sources of information as happens in the chapter on Maps. The introduction also, and we feel necessarily, reminds cataloguers of the possible need to reduce or expand the detail as prescribed by the code. We emphasise the need for such 'permission' because some cataloguers persist in acting as though a catalogue code were handed down on sacred tablets. As usual, we feel that the detail prescribed is more than enough for almost all libraries, and that commonsense simplification should be carefully applied throughout.

As we might expect, in general an author-equivalent is established, according to the basic principles of the code, and contrasting with the title entry assumed for not only films but filmstrips despite some literary warrant, as we pursue elsewhere in this book. Therefore, entry for individual works or sets is decided according to the cataloguer's estimate of in effect intellectual responsibility, whether personal or corporate. However, a footnote (p 255) implies that the basic rule may be liable to further examination. Possibly this rule and its implications may be the subject of attention in the current re-examination of AACR's treatment of special materials. The part of the rule allowing entry under copyright owner or printer, etc is, we suggest, in need of attention. Title entry may be considered more useful in some such instances. We agree in general with R 260 B which, in case of conflict between corporate and personal entry, favours the latter, as does LC. R 260 C allows the use of 'supposed artist', etc in a heading, about which we have doubts, since such designations can cause confusion in filing and use. This is one instance where an attempt at academic accuracy seems to take undue preference over utility, especially since it may be invoked quite a lot in art works. Useful reminders are given concerning occasions when added entries may need to be invoked.

Unlike the rules for films and filmstrips and those for recordings, there is no provision for explicit designation of form following the title of documents dealt with in this chapter. Not only is this simply inconsistent with the entries for the forms mentioned above, but it does not conform with the concept of the integrated catalogue assumed for the code as a whole and about which we are reminded in the Introductory notes to this chapter. This point—and the contradiction between entry for pictorial works under author and entry for filmstrips under title—is demonstrated on p 256. A set of slides entitled *Trickling filter process* goes under U.S. *Public Health Services*; yet the filmstrip would go under title immediately followed, on the same line, by 'Filmstrip'.

The rules for collections need not detain us long. We would just like to emphasise the need in some libraries for analytical entries.

Despite the reminder earlier in the chapter, Description seems on the whole to be reasonably economical. Some detail is given on uncertain dates, but such information is likely to be needed for the type of work dealt with here, whether for direct subject value of an illustration of a particular event or person or for a work of art. A very detailed alphabetico-classed list of art media is included for those who may wish to designate if, say, a document is a photographic colour separation negative. However, the number of libraries needing such detail in their catalogues may be few. The rest of the Description, as already inferred, gives a great deal of information, following the precedent established for books and as interpreted into terms relevant to special materials, and as exemplified in other sections on this code in this book.

Readings

Checklist of works cited in or relevant to this chapter. General works in the checklist with the first chapter of this book (p 28-29) also include information on the topics covered by this chapter. Full bibliographical citations are given in the consolidated Bibliography, p 304-312. A list of abbreviations is given on p 7. The titles of periodical articles are given within quotation marks.

AACR 1967

ALA 1949

ASLIB

BFI

BAKEWELL 'Cataloguing and indexing activities'

BIRD 'The cataloguing, classification and indexing of a collection of slides'

CHIBNALL 'The National Film Library and its cataloguing rules'

CROZET 'Cataloguing a photograph library'

CUMMINGS 'The art reference library'

FANNING 'The cataloguing of film material in the National Film Archive' (Lib world)

FANNING 'The National Film Archive' (LA record)

GRAHAM *The cataloguing and classification of cine film at the Royal Aircraft Establishment*

GRENFELL 'The cataloguing of films' (Librarian)

GRENFELL 'The cataloguing of newsfilm in the National Film Library' (Univ film journal)

GRENFELL 'Standardisation in film cataloguing' (J doc)

GUNTHER 'Slides in documentation'

HAVARD-WILLIAMS 'The slide collection at Liverpool School of Architecture'

HALL *Potential use of* MARC *records in three libraries.*

HILL 'Photographs: cataloguing and classification'

KULA *Bibliography of film librarianship* (p 33-43)

LC *Motion pictures and filmstrips*

LC *Pictures, designs and other two-dimensional representations*

ROGERS 'Works of art'

STEELE *The cataloguing and classification of cinema literature*

UNESCO

WASSERMAN 'A computer-prepared book catalog for engineering transparencies'

WHITE *Slide collections . . .*

CHAPTER FOUR

Maps and atlases

THIS CATEGORY of special material is often dealt with by writers under the omnibus heading 'Audio-visual materials'. In fact, although no doubt maps and atlases are 'visual' in the sense of being mainly graphic rather than textual, we should remember that they have been in existence for thousands of years, and have been seriously written on as a library material for some 100 years; there are substantial published accounts of the cataloguing of maps from the turn of the century. This latter may possibly account for the apparent confusion between the various types of approach needed, since many rules still in use or under discussion antedate the academic distinction between the author-type and the subject-type approach. This important aspect is explored later, but here we might mention CUTTER as being, as so often, ahead of his time in forming such a distinction.

Apart from its historical significance in library science, we should emphasise that this category forms a very important component of the stock of just about all types of libraries; it is a significant medium for information to users at all intellectual levels and states of knowledge or ignorance. So, we feel that no apology is needed for the considerable space devoted to this category of special physical form in this work. From their use for military and para-military purposes, witness the sponsoring of maps by such organisations as the UK Ordnance Survey, we have now reached the point, when, for example, one US school library survey—chosen at random—shows that from forty six questionnaires received, it emerged that thirty four schools thought maps worth serious attention as an item of library stocks (HICKS, p 64). We should further remember that maps are often used, *eg* in education at all levels, whether or not the examples used actually receive catalogue treatment.

Stemming from these observations it is apparent that a great variety of types of cataloguing of maps and atlases may be required, if a library is to cater directly and fully for its clientele, with no required information lacking, but without a mass of data—even if clear to the professional cataloguer—which is not required by the user. Perhaps the latter can learn, despite himself, from some of the ' how I done it good ' published information and unpublished advice from colleagues. Therefore, although we shall give here some examples of minute detail as expounded in some codes and accounts, it is appreciated that many librarians require practical advice and guidance, and some samples will tend towards various highly limited forms of map and atlas cataloguing. On the other hand, some of the pragmatists may be made aware of some approaches, and some description detail, which may in fact prove of practical application.

A question which seems always to have been a source of discussion as to what extent rules for a printed book catalogue can be applied to maps and atlases. An ancillary problem is the difference between maps and atlases as such. Here, an attempt is made to try to dispense with the latter comparatively briefly with the obvious—but apparently necessary—reminder that an atlas is but a collection of maps presented in conventional codex form. However, acknowledgement is necessary that, though nowadays an atlas is usually planned and prepared as a whole, *eg* current street atlases of towns, some atlases, especially in the past, may have comprised a fairly motley collection of previously existing separate bibliographic units. We suggest that some current tendencies to catalogue atlases differently from collections, series, etc of sheet maps stems from the purely accidental nature of their physical format and therefore of their shelving in most libraries, whether in an oversize sequence or in an atlas case. The latter may even lead to, say, an economics atlas being shelved with other atlases, because of its physical format and because of the presentation form ' atlas ' which will separate it on the shelves from, say, a large format tabulated economic survey which will be shelved with ' normal ' oversize works. Such practices, if persisted in, point up the increased need, not only for catalogues tying up the subject value of such works, but also for them to be actually used. So, in this field, possibly above some others, one pleads the need for extra attention to the recording of such works, *ie* atlases of all sorts—under various approaches. In support of our claim that maps and atlases are virtually the same, it is proposed hereafter to use ' maps ' as embracing both physically separate maps and maps bound and integrated into atlas form. An obvious exception must be made when dealing with codes' differential treatment of the different forms of physical presentation.

To return to the basic problem of maps in relation to textual works, it may be that the first controversial assertion came from Cutter's own code, but penned in fact by P Lee Phillips: ' The cataloging of maps and atlases differs very little from the cataloging of ordinary books ' (CUTTER, p 140). This opening statement, in his appendix to CUTTER, has been quoted ever since by both protagonists and antagonists. Partly belying this statement is the very fact that Cutter felt it necessary to have this appendix in his code, and that Phillips not only spent some seven pages on map cataloguing, but also he felt the need to refer to other publications on the subject published at the turn of the century. In support of Phillips' claim one might note that few libraries use special cataloguers for map cataloguing, *eg* one UK survey states that of fifty one UK university libraries, only one, apparently, turned to extra-departmental help in map cataloguing (FRIEDMAN). And of course, in school and many public libraries the librarian (possibly the only staff) inevitably deals with all forms, physical form being—rightly in such contexts—subservient to the integration of use of all forms of material.

As in so many other instances, we might turn to BOGGS & LEWIS for a contribution to, and even tentative conclusion on, this topic, although if we can ourselves draw a conclusion from the various and varied statements in BOGGS, the answer is still indeterminate. The principal author, apparently, familiarised himself with practices in Washington, New York, and London, and concluded ' It is clear . . . that general objectives in the classification [one suggests this infers all retrieval techniques here] of books and maps are the same ' (BOGGS, Preface). This attitude is consolidated by the statement ' rules herein being meant to be an extension of, rather than a divergence from, book cataloging practice ' (BOGGS, p 4). This compromise, then, is the nearest we can get to a conclusion, and we tentatively support it here. However, evidently both Boggs and the present writer consider there is enough difference between normal and special cataloguing to warrant the compilation of special codes. Yet, whenever a topic is not catered for, or when one feels it is not catered for satisfactorily, in special works, one suggests a return to basic principles, and that rare commodity—commonsense.

A directly related question is whether maps are to be recorded in a special catalogue, or whether their records are to be integrated into the ' general ' catalogue of the library, or at least in a union catalogue version of it even if this is not on public display. A further inevitably contributory factor is whether there is a separate map department. 'Department' itself may have varying meanings. There is no doubt that national and state libraries usually have a wholly self-contained map department or division, examples being the British Museum and Library of Congress at national level, and the (Public) Library of New South Wales at state level. Examples of special libraries (of varying origin) having separate and significant map sections are the Royal Geographical Society in London, and the US Department of State (*ie* foreign affiairs).

At the other end of the spectrum we have the school library, sponsoring actively the use of all media, and the small local public library, whose map provision is quite sketchy (whether we like it or not) beyond works of exclusively local interest. In the latter case, may we issue a plea for the establishment of some form at least of record beyond the memory of the local history/information enthusiast on the staff. People *do* die, retire, leave; and to leave a vacuum in stock records does not prove that a member of staff is indispensable—if anything it shows that such a member of staff suffered delusions of grandeur. In short, even the smallest map collection needs some record, even if only a check list. One suggests that local maps should be recorded, along with other sources of information, in a local information index. This might be an alphabetical-specific card index including: (a) actual items of information; (b) directions to class/shelf numbers (or in a subject index to a classified catalogue); and (c) records, under alphabetical-subject headings, of actual items in stock (as in the conventional dictionary catalogue).

As to integration or not in a general information index or catalogue of stock, one suggests that these attitudes offer themselves: (a) lack of records of maps at all, in the general catalogue, reliance being placed on users themselves knowing if they want a map, and staff always being on the alert as to the possible need for passing an enquiry to the map collection; (b) occasional reminder-entries in the catalogue that maps exist in stock on topics for which maps are likely to be useful, *eg* geology, history, economics, demography, and of course topography; and (c) entries for all maps in the catalogue, the fact that the document is a map being shown in the subject heading, *eg* GEOLOGY—AUSTRALIA—MAPS, and/or in the location symbol for documents, *eg* MAP 330:994. (c) is recommended in BOGGS (p 73 ff), *eg* using such a heading as MEXICO—MAPS—1941. Other writers, of several, advocating this treatment are JOHNSON (p 102) and HICKS (p 43). One would not advocate (a) at all, except when one were absolutely sure that there were always on public duty or wholly accessible an aware readers' advisor who had time to conduct a reference interview with every enquirer to ascertain that a subject request might need to be turned into a map request. Perhaps it should be reiterated that an enquirer, especially in a general library, may have a request, *eg* concerning population- or resources-distribution, which, as it happens, could best be answered by the use of maps. One does not have faith that everyone needing a map will ask clearly and articulately for 'a map on . . .'. (b) will serve for the librarian-in-a-hurry, providing practice, staff selection, or inservice training ensure that the staff on duty, or the catalogue guiding, make certain that eventually the enquirer arrives at the reminder of maps via the catalogue. Needless to say, one would prefer, in general libraries at least, method (c).

Possible approaches, and their construction

Some approaches to maps may be similar to those to letterpress books. For the sake of completeness, the many possible approaches are named and commented upon here and—possibly rash—conclusions are reached as to which are most likely to be needed in many libraries. Whether a specific librarian, in haste, and under pressure of the potential use of other materials, and even of other activities, has time to utilise them, may unfortunately be another matter.

AREA covered by map: from world—even extra-world—coverage to a very local district, *eg* township.

It may be an area defined purely geographically, *eg* Australia, the Americas or all of the British Isles. It may be a geo-political unit, *eg*: the Commonwealth of Australia, including at the moment Papua-New Guinea and various Pacific islands; or the United Kingdom of Great Britain and Northern Ireland; or the United States including Alaska. It may further be an area given a name for administration purposes in relation to a specific subject activity, *eg*: in Australia the Orde River area; in Britain the area covered by the London Metropolitan Police Force; in USA the Tennessee Valley area made a 'unit' by F D Roosevelt's New Deal in the 1930's.

In constructing an alphabetical catalogue, one inevitably must decide on the form of entry for place names. (An attendant problem—to some people—of place *versus* author will be dealt with under the subsection on Author, below.) Basically, there is a choice between direct and indirect entry: this, one suggests, is virtually the same problem as direct or indirect subject entry in cataloguing any other form of material. It comes down to what is often referred to as 'specific' versus 'alphabetico-classed' although, strangely, writers do not seem to have lit upon these standard, even if slightly ambiguous, terms in relation to maps. The topic is usually introduced by saying that an enquirer may be interested not solely in a specific area, but also in the larger area of which it forms a part. The writer then enlarges on the theme and feels that the user may be interested not only in the larger area mentioned above, but also in the even larger area which contains that. Thus we would have, not just LONDON but ENGLAND—LONDON, then GREAT BRITAIN—ENGLAND—LONDON, and even EUROPE, NORTHERN—GREAT BRITAIN—ENGLAND—LONDON. People seem to have stopped short of putting WORLD before this type of construction! It is not felt to be necessary here to enlarge on the decline and fall of the alphabetico-classed catalogue, except to remind the reader that very few libraries have retained this form. If they use an alphabetical-subject catalogue they usually employ some type of specific entry combined with a network of references. One dares to suggest—despite the practice of the Library of Congress and that of the Royal Geographical Society—that the use of direct ('specific') entry can apply to maps with substantially no more inconvenience than when applied to other materials, but with the positive advantages of consistently chosen specific/direct headings which have been demonstrated over nearly a century since Billings and Cutter lighted upon them.

A further problem is that of language of heading. Maps, rather like music, can be international in use and understanding, so it is very likely that even small libraries will acquire some maps in languages other than the home one. In many cases, especially countries, states and large towns or cities, there is likely to be a home-language version of many place names of the world; this applies particularly to a language like English. Writers usually advocate the use of the English form of, at least, states and countries. This rule corresponds approximately with current catalogue code practice, and one doubts if it would encounter much serious opposition (*eg* AACR Rule 72). In a dictionary catalogue, consistency between place as subject and place as author is an acknowledged necessity. Codes do not differentiate between 'large' and 'local' places, and similar rules apply to, say, names of countries, shires, towns and so on. However, in map cataloguing, one authority at least, BOGGS, recommends the vernacular for 'local' names. While acknowledging that SWEDEN is more acceptable than SVERIGE in general use in an English-speaking country, he advocates MÜNCHEN, rather than MUNICH, since the former is the local official form (BOGGS, p 67, 68). No real explanation is given for the difference in treatment. We might mention, for what the experience is worth, that English-speaking Germans whom we have met in Britain and Australia refer to their home towns in their English form if there is one. Of course, not all places have an accepted English form, and the only solution is to use the vernacular in such cases. Admittedly this recommendation leads to inconsistency between various countries' practices and this in turn would lead to difficulties if and when catalogues from various countries are integrated mechanically, without human editing.

A further problem is change of name—surprisingly this topic does not seem to be dealt with by BOGGS, the acknowledged authority on map cataloguing. This may possibly be because most significant changes of names of countries have come since 1945 when BOGGS was first published. A contributory factor to this apparent indecision may be that BOGGS tends to use geographical rather than political names. However, one still has to refer to a country in normal speech: one cannot imagine nowadays asking for maps of Nyasaland unless one were deliberately seeking information about Malawi at a particular point in its colonial development. A few years ago the BBC would only refer to 'self-styled Biafra', and with the defeat of 'Biafra' in the civil war one presumes that one would not refer to that particular area of Nigeria under that name for normal purposes. However, for maps, drafted during and around the Nigerian civil war, it would be possible to think of 'Biafra' as a place without taking sides—of course the librarian must not lay himself open to accusation of political partiality. A similar situation applies to what geographically is Western New Guinea. Whether one approves or not of allegedly democratic annexation of a territory, one should use the name given to it at such a time, and by which it has come to be known: 'West Irian'. At the moment of writing (1972) librarians all over the world may be busy inserting 'Bangladesh' into their catalogues and scratching their heads over what to do about 'East Pakistan'. Also, at the time of writing, it seems that the area which we have become used to as 'Cape Kennedy' may possibly revert to its original name of 'Cape Canaveral'.

In general, for political changes of name, one suggests following the principles put forward by AACR for parallel situations, *eg* with bodies (R 68) and serials (R 60), and using 'consecutive' entry with connecting explanatory *see also* references both ways. A class number is not likely to change much, if at all in some cases, and locating symbols therefore may not need to be amended, but serve rather to collocate, like classification should.

Where a map collection is being recatalogued or newly started, however, there is quite a lot to be said for using the most recent form of a territory's name, with of course *see* references from earlier forms, and a scope note at the used heading. One suggests that it would be rather pedantic in most libraries to have to read up the history, say, of the present day Irish Republic to establish accurately during which periods it was referred to as the Irish Free State and Eire. If, on reading this, the critic says, 'But this is being inconsistent. You are only doing this to save the trouble of changing headings or doing bibliographical research', we can only reply 'Yes', and leave final judgement to the day when we all face the Great Cataloguer.

SUBJECT dealt with in map.

It will be seen, from some of the examples previously mentioned, that there can be an inextricable overlap between subject and area. In some cases, the area can be denoted by a single term, but in others, two components of a compound heading would need to be used, *eg* either LONDON METROPOLITAN POLICE AREA or LONDON—POLICE. BOGG includes several enumerated examples of integrated headings, *eg* ALASKA HIGHWAY; GREAT WALL OF CHINA. The formula fanatic might eschew these and produce ALASKA—HIGHWAYS—and even CHINA—WALLS—GREAT, but one would not support these, needless to say . . .

Apart from such intrinsic cases, many maps deal with an area in relation to a particular subject. Examples are Transport, or more specific types such as Motor transport and Railways; Electoral areas; Geology; Economic products; Economic distribution; Demography; Flora and Fauna distribution; Climate; Planning; Industry; Historical periods; Archaeology. These are possibly among the more common, but as the subject classification scheme in BOGGS shows, almost any subject can be represented in map form. For this reason, there should be the possibility of at least simple synthesis—the combination of any subject with any area. As far as possible verbal representation, as in subject headings or indexing, should be consistent for a given topic, wherever the topic is represented, *eg* BOGGS uses at one point TERRITORIAL CHANGES, at another TERRITORIAL GAINS AND LOSSES, and at yet another TERRITORIAL EXPANSION. A scope note explains when to use the different terms but not (to this writer anyway) why there have to be such differences. Also, although there is a difference between TERRITORIAL EXPANSION and (a heading not yet mentioned here) POSSESSIONS, some over-nice differentiations can be drawn. One can imagine the many happy hours which cataloguers could spend on where one stops and the other starts, but, as we know, the first object of cataloguing is not to amuse cataloguers. One suggests that semantic subtlety should give way to positive terms which are obviously mutually exclusive.

As to citation order, most codes and writings assume or state that—in a classification scheme, or list of headings—area shall come first, and subject second. A noteworthy exception is the alphabetical list in BOGGS, though not the classification scheme which adheres to consistent convention. Examples will be given later in the subsection dealing with that work. Suffice it to say here that something akin to the practices of conventional subject headings are used. As in such lists, some oddities can occur, *eg* MANDATED TERRITORIES—AFRICA but GREAT BRITAIN—POSSESSIONS. One sympathises with BOGGS in trying to anticipate future users' demand, and no doubt past demand was taken into account in the conclusions reached. And one does not subscribe to the imposition of a rigid formula for the sake of consistency alone—consistency has to serve an ultimate purpose. However, we feel that, emerging from the extensive thought and experience which obviously went into BOGGS, there is a possible somewhat contradictory conclusion that a citation order of Place-Subject should be usual, and that this should be reversed only after careful thought. There would need to be sufficient and specific references the other way of course.

What has been said here applies to the construction of headings in their own right. If chain procedure is used deliberately in constructing an index to a classified catalogue, reverse order may emerge if so dictated by the scheme. However, even then, some exceptions, manipulation, and supplementing will be needed to make the system overall sensible, *eg* as we have written elsewhere one might have, in a UDC-based system:

MAPS: ECONOMICS	33(084.3)
MAPS: GEOLOGY	55(084.3)

For topographical maps see names of localities
eg AUSTRALIA: MAPS (HORNER, p 214)

We are accustomed to the term ' author-equivalent ' by now, implying the two characteristics of (a) Intellectual responsibility, and (b) a name which is sought in relation to a document. Sometimes these may seem to contradict each other in ' ordinary ' cataloguing, as in a Festschrift or a concordance.

Authorship or quasi-authorship of maps can sometimes be more diffuse than with certain other types of works, at least. People, or organisations in some cases, who may have had some part to play in determining the content of a map may be: sponsor, *eg* a geographical society, or publisher; a surveyor; cartographer; editor; engraver; or even a re-engraver if a different process is used in the republication or re-presentation of a map. Such a name as an explorer whose findings are given on a map is in rather the same position as that of an author whose written works are concordanced; we suggest that he should receive, in fact, a subject entry. A few maps, particularly some older ones, may be dedicated to a person, whose name therefore may appear prominently on the map, thereby becoming a sought approach. An added author-type heading should suffice, if really necessary, in such cases. Such a name on a map would probably be more memorable or striking, hence sought, than that of a person to whom a work in page form is dedicated.

In making both main and added author-type entries, practice will vary a great deal depending on the purpose of the library and the existence of relevant catalogue substitutes—bibliographies and lists giving an exhaustive coverage of approaches, and which are convenient for consultation before the library's own catalogue is used, the latter being more a finding device than a bibliographic record. A library used by map practitioners and bibliographic research workers will naturally try to practise exhaustivity in the hope of ' holing out in one '. Such a library might be, say, the Royal Geographical Society's, or that of a government department the work of whose clientele may have considerable influence on other people. At the other end of the spectrum is the popular library and school library with an avowedly immediate utilitarian need, and whose stock is likely to be sought under well-known tags which do not necessarily take into account academic principles like intellectual responsibility. Such a tag is likely to be any name featuring prominently on the title page of an atlas or on the face of a map. In such cases one would recommend simply the sought name, irrespective of academic accuracy. It is likely in some cases to be a publisher, whether commercial or other such as a motoring or travel organisation or government department. There seems to be some aversion, with some cataloguers, to using names of commercial publishers as an unashamed main 'author' heading—perhaps through the fear of being accused of advertising? A similar situation exists in series entries for any materials, *eg* AACR R 33N(1) which manifests an aversion for 'trade publishers'. Some codes have, seemingly, allowed publisher as main entry for maps as a last resort—why not a first resort if that is the name most commonly associated with the work? This applies especially with many current street atlases and sets of tourists' maps. Sometimes, librarians have, perhaps grudgingly, allowed a publisher as entry word when it is the first word of a title. Title entry as such is dealt with later.

In other cases a name more approaching a true author may be the most sought, *eg* in reprints of well-known older maps, such as Speed's and Saxton's maps of English counties. Here, the choice for author main entry is obvious. Incidentally, we suggest that there is no need in such cases for research in order to give an exhaustively complete heading, with full forenames and dates of birth and death. The approximate date of each map is usually fairly easily ascertainable, and will appear in the description, and possibly in the call number if this is the practice in the library. It may also be given in the 'subject' (area) heading for the map, as recommended by BOGGS.

AUTHOR VERSUS SUBJECT/AREA

The only likely reason for this ever becoming a problem at all seems to be in history. The assumption in the past may have been that usually only one entry per document would be made; therefore, it was natural to select the most sought or useful approach. With many maps, this is likely to be the 'subject' (*ie* usually area) as opposed to the author-type approach. One does not deny this. But a parallel situation can exist for other materials. An enquirer may want books on, say, do-it-yourself house or car repairs, or the maritime conflict between the English and the Dutch in the past, as often as he may request specifically a book by Abbey, or the *Cambridge history of the British Empire.*

Area may have been retreated to in the face of the diversity and differences of authorship or quasi-authorship of maps. As has already been pointed out, author-entry of maps is not a poor alternative to area entry, any more or less than in the case of other material. Author and area may both be vital coordinates in pinpointing the map required, *eg* in a request for Speed's map of Kent. On the other hand of course a librarian would be foolish to present Speed's map of Kent to the average presentday enquirer who asks for 'a map of Kent'. Nevertheless someone may be interested in Speed's representation of areas as a symptom of his time, whatever areas are dealt with. As with other materials, we repeat, maps may be approached either as to authorship, especially for a particular work known to the enquirer, or as to area covered—or of course as to subject matter, *eg* for comparing density of population in various parts of the world as part of an examination of social phenomena.

Apart from Cutter's own rules, the only code which seems explicitly to recognise the two types of approach, each in its own right, is AACR, commented on further under the subsection on Codes later.

It may be mentioned at this point that title and area/subject may be a more justifiable cause for confusion of principles, as with other materials. But, again, the distinction between these two should have been disentangled long since. This aspect of the title approach is dealt with now.

TITLE

Title may be chosen as main entry, as commented on further below. However, let it be suggested first that title added entries should be considered seriously in all types of libraries, even—and especially perhaps—in libraries practising severely limited cataloguing, and more especially in popular general libraries. One suspects an element of professional-cum-intellectual snobbery, or at least a state of being out of touch, in some librarians who persist in being almost exclusively author-minded. There may possibly be some excuse for not using title added entries for books, if suitable bibliographies are conveniently available as catalogue substitutes; although even then this practice seems to imply that the public will not normally use the catalogue as a comprehensive key to a library's stock. It is noteworthy that the dictionary catalogue more commonly caters for title approach than does the classified catalogue and that Cutter (father, or at least midwife, of the dictionary catalogue) said the catalogue should be compiled with democratic public use in mind.

The principle behind these comments applies of course to the consideration of title as main entry, *ie* if title is considered to be the chief sought approach for any document, map or other, then title has a considerable claim for consideration as the main heading for a work.

Normally the title should be considered (a) for anonymous maps, and (b) for maps of diffuse authorship, *ie* those of 'diverse hands' such as publisher, sponsor, editor, surveyor, engraver and re-engraver. As with other works, an exception to (a) would be instances where a standard map's authorship was generally recognised but happened not to be given on a particular edition or printing.

In some cases, it may be considered necessary to have entry (main or added) under catchword, a practice, incidentally, still used in some dealers' catalogues for main entry, but sometimes subsumed under a more general subject heading. It should not need emphasis that catchword, or keyword, entry is not an alternative for subject/area entry. A few years ago we were subjected to many published accounts by people, who had not apparently made any study of the history of subject cataloguing, and who joyfully had reinvented the wheel, by lighting upon KWIC (KeyWord In Context) and then KWOC (KeyWord Out of Context) as a form of multiple entry for titles by courtesy of the computer. All this despite Billings and Cutter, who, a hundred years ago established the principle of consistent entry terms for subjects, irrespective of such variations in titles as synonyms and parts of speech. We suggest that title-catchword, or inverted title, entry may be very useful for identifying, and then locating, a map known to the enquirer but whose exact author and first word of title are forgotten. However, such an enquiry could conceivably be solved, even if very indirectly, by using the subject/area approach with attendant (plentiful) references, if such exist in the catalogue.

SERIES

Series title does not call for great comment as an approach, since it may not necessarily differ much from that of other material. Commonly encountered examples are the series of various-scale maps issued by the British Ordnance Survey, *eg* the justifiably famous one-inch maps of Britain. The author of course is the Ordnance Survey itself. There is a choice between single entry as a series and multiple entry, one for each map. In the former case, what is in effect the series becomes the title part of the entry, while in the latter each map would have its own title, denoting area, and the series statement would include the series title and the number of the individual map in the series. In either case the author entry would not be affected. If a library has a complete series or a series in progress, we would recommend single (collective) entry with series as the title part of the entry. There would normally not need to be a contents list; citation of the index map and its location should suffice. The library's holdings, or lacks, could be given in the Notes, as with serials. These possible different treatments would reflect on the area (subject) entry. In one case, there would be several scores of individual subject entries, each as near as possible delineating in a concrete and approachable term the area covered by each unit. This is difficult in many cases in the example cited since areas are decided by the accident of the British national grid, and not by sought centres of population. *eg* Aberystwyth in Wales is the main population centre of one sheet, but does not occupy a central position on the sheet. A further complication is that the Ordnance Survey has in fact issued several sheets, not in the logical numbered sequence, combining halves of adjacent national grid sheets, to give a population-centred map. These may well qualify for individual entry, or at least a separate entry as a whole under some such uniform title as, say, [One-inch: special sheets]. Needless to say, Notes would include information on dates of surveys, as opposed to dates of publication. Many popular libraries may have few enough maps in stock to be able to shelve such maps in a special permanent semi-display, with an index map pinned on an adjacent notice board. For those not acquainted with national topography, the index sheet could be accompanied by, say, a typed list of noteworthy towns and areas, and naming the number of the relevant sheet in each case. If really necessary, as the area approach, there could be brief entries referring to the sheet number and location of items.

eg LONDON, SOUTHEAST O.S.1″ 171
Maps, 8

(8, say, being the number of the book case assigned to this set, and clearly marked as such.)

Less coherent series would receive individual entry for each map, with a series-title added entry in each case. As with other materials, there may be doubt as to whether a series editor, if named and if decided upon as a possible approach, need be given a single entry for each item. A library may decide to make one (only) reference from series editor to series title, thereby catering economically for this, possibly rare, approach.

FORM

In special collections' catalogues, there is no point in having a form approach for ordinary stock, *eg* MAPS; ATLASES. However, such collections may have form-entries for materials in forms unusual for that collection, if required, *eg* GLOBES. The entry word(s) would be followed in the heading by the term used for the chief area-entry, *eg* WORLD; MOON.

In general libraries which include maps in their main catalogue, there is some purpose in having added entries under form names, or at least general references, *eg*

MAPS

See also names of areas, subjects etc. followed by the subdivision MAPS, *e.g.* FRANCE—MAPS; FRANCE—HISTORY—MAPS

This reference would follow the entries for maps as a subject, *eg* how maps are made, the history of cartography. A full added entry would probably be given for works dealing both with maps themselves and with the area dealt with by maps in the work, *eg The world is round* by Frank Debenham. Virtually this is multiple entry for multiple subject coverage.

A school or similar library housing a number of wall maps may find it useful to have added entries for WALL MAPS followed by the area/subject heading. Or it may rely on separate, *eg* typed, lists. For the benefit of pupils who do not happen to know, and who happen to look up the form in the catalogue, there could be a brief *see* reference in the catalogue to the separate lists. The maps themselves would probably be filed in racks, and the lists could be attached to them, to serve as an inventory or shelf list for convenient scanning on the spot.

As already mentioned, in a classified catalogue using chain indexing, maps may become the entry term in classes where it is a distributed relative in the classification scheme used.

PROJECTION

In some libraries, an approach via type of projection may be required, sometimes often, sometimes occasionally. Such a need is likely to arise with cartographers and others who are dealing with the actual drafting of maps, or the detailed description of them, *eg* teachers. It seems worth risking the statement that almost all other librarians can afford to ignore this approach. In fact it may not seem worth catering, in the catalogue, for the occasional needs of school teachers, especially since a school's map stock will likely be limited, and since in any case a teacher may well have noted sample projections in text books, which theoretically would call for analytical-form entries for this. If slides, or similar forms, have been made of selected illustrations, embodying maps, it may be considered necessary to record these in the catalogue. Two alternatives are possible: either (a) 'added-references', *ie* very brief entries for actual documents in stock and giving location but referring the user to the main entry; or (b) brief check lists not filed in the catalogue but kept, say, in typed form and easily accessible to both users and readers' advisors. Where unit entries are used, these two methods have less to be said for them.

If normal added entries are used, the cataloguer has the basic problem of connecting the added entry heading with the information about the projection as given in the (say, unit) entry. There are two possibilities: either (a) inclusion of projection details in the main heading, which is nice and obvious when required, but may entail considerable waste of effort in the many cases when it is not called for; or (b) inclusion of projection details in the description, or body of entry; this would normally be the practice in many libraries—assuming the projection to be exceptional, that is. One possible way of pinpointing the relevant part of the description is to draw a line from the added entry heading itself (illustrated in AA 1908, and in HORNER, p 318). This practice entails a conflict between neatness, and ready and economic utility. If the catalogue already includes a variety of types of presentation and format, the neatness aspect may not seem so trenchant. And many catalogues do come into this category, it is readily admitted, especially since a variety of central catalogue agency cards may have been incorporated. BOGGS caters for this need by brief references which we consider not highly satisfactory—touched on again within the sub-section Codes dealing with that work.

CONTENT OF HEADINGS

As has already been stated or inferred, 'subject' heading will include of course the name of the area covered, preferably direct and specific, one suggests. The area will usually be followed by the name of the 'true' subject, if any, of the map. In addition, libraries with very large collections may wish to subdivide entries systematically to a greater extent, before the customary sub-arrangement by the chief author-type heading. It is suggested in such cases that date of content of map should follow. This, when ascertainable, may well be different from the imprint date. Some publishers kindly oblige by giving at the foot of the map date of the latest surveys taken into account in drafting the map. In some cases, individual parts of the map may be singled out, *eg* that the map as a whole is accurate to one date, but that roads, say, are revised to a later date. In such cases, it may be decided to give inclusive dates. (All of this will obviate some of the need for essential information in Notes lower down the entry.)

Where an unusual projection is used, or in libraries where projection is regarded as significant, this too may be added. If a librarian desires even further information, scale may possibly be given.

The above assumes an alphabetical-subject approach. In the classified file of the classified catalogue, some of the data would be expressed through classification notation, *eg* area, subject and possibly projection and date. If not, then verbal extension might be used, these components being arranged alphabetically. Scale could be added to most notations in a coherent way. The subject index would almost certainly not be a full ' mirror image ' of the full class number in its construction. Re-inversion would need to be practised, of course, to avoid having components such as scale becoming specific index entry terms.

As in other cataloguing, uniform titles may be needed, *eg* for maps whose verbal content is translated or is in two or more languages.

ANALYTICAL ENTRIES

These are likely to be of three types: (a) insets, usually in a sheet map; (b) individual entries for maps in atlases, possibly selective, and dependent on local needs; and (c) maps in non-map materials, usually printed but possibly manuscript books, also very likely selective.

(a) Insets in sheet maps, in collections which have individual entries for all maps as separate physical units, will probably be made automatically. The analytical entry has its own heading, as to area, subject and especially scale as this may be larger than that of the containing map. In unit entry catalogues this information is followed by ' Inset ' (corresponding with ' in ' with normal book-form materials) and then a copy of the main entry, including location of parent work. It may possibly be necessary in some cases to explain the inset in an additional note, although this would normally be given in the ' Contents ' or ' Partial contents ' element of notes in the unit entry.

(b) Individual map entries for atlases have their own heading, as to area, subject, with scale if used in the catalogue, and date if used in the catalogue and if different from that of the atlas as a whole.

(c) Maps, in non-map materials, may receive analyticals for the usual area/subject reasons, but likely also if they are examples of a special type of map, *eg* as to projection used. Again, if it is the practice to give projection in the heading in such cases, this would be included in the analytical.

In addition, author or author-type analyticals may possibly be required in any of the above-mentioned cases. Each would consist of author heading, title of map, followed by ' inset ' etc as above.

Description

As with the description of all library materials, that of maps serves the two interconnected purposes of: (a) helping the user select a suitable item from the range of items represented in the catalogue at point of entry; and (b) identifying an item which is known directly, or known of from other sources. There is some doubt about the type of information required, and the order in which it is given, in all cataloguing. To ensure that the information actually wanted in all conceivable circumstances is available, it is possible that many entries, for many purposes, are in fact overfull, with the consequence that the user may be put off—blinded by library science, in fact. Again, concerning the order in which information is given: we suggest that, if the description must be very full, the sequence in which it is given assumes considerable importance, in the hope that, of course, the most required information comes early in the entry to obviate the need to scan a great amount of unwanted cryptically expressed information. We would suggest that many users are more interested in the scale of a map than in, say, the surveyor or engraver—the latter is more likely to apply in identifying a known map, and an older one at that. Many users today have more of a subject-type need—what area is covered, does it have certain subject slant, what scale is it, how up to date is it? Unfortunately rules for map description seem still to be catering for the seeker after bibliographic detail, especially as for older maps, except that a concession may be made by promoting scale to a place higher in the entry than in the past. The description items are named and commented upon here in an order which is different from that in some codes. It is purely tentative, and of course subject to further criticism and comment. Readers who wish to adhere to the nearest we have to a standard recommendation may prefer to follow AACR, commented upon later.

For a start, in constructing description it is necessary to take into account information already given in the heading, as, we suggest, there is no need to repeat information lower down, in the body of the entry, which has already been pinpointed in the most ostentatious part of the entry as a whole. A hint is taken here from the idea of feature headings, made widely known by BNB practice in its published lists (cards have varied from time to time) in relation to mainly book-form material: as much information as possible about the coverage of a work is condensed into the verbal heading at the top, thus obviating the need for notes lower down the entry. The user may never reach them: if they are there—more likely a decision may have been made to include notes only exceptionally as being too time-consuming for the cataloguer. But, we repeat, the type of information given in notes (other than—dare we say—pedantic bibliographic data like 'vertical border kinked half-way up') is likely to prove more useful than some information traditionally given higher in the entry. So, a very full heading may include:

AREA—SUBJECT—DATE—SCALE—PROJECTION

Therefore none of this need be reproduced lower in the entry except as subsumed by the title of the map. In our suggested listing of description data we shall assume, therefore, that the (feature) heading will include this information once and for all. The heading itself may be a verbal entry in its own right (alphabetical-subject catalogues), or a complement/supplement to the class mark, which itself is the entry medium (classified file of classified catalogues).

Assuming the unit entry principle is used, there will be an author-type heading, or if title main entry applies, a short-title heading, below the feature heading given above. The author, or equivalent, will be an obvious filing medium 'within' either class mark/call number in a classified catalogue or verbal heading in an alphabetical catalogue. Where there is no author heading, the next filing medium after the feature heading is the title. We suggest that a shortened form of the title is given in the place of an author heading, even though this does entail a slight repetition when one reaches the title transcript. Despite the strictures on repetition mentioned above, we suggest that this type of repetition can be time-saving to the catalogue user, since the first few words of the title will readily spring to the eye, as well as being a definitive filing device. Where a uniform title is used this automatically becomes the filing medium of course.

So, we have *Title;* followed by *Alternative title* or *Sub-title.* Since maps do not have title pages, the title is drawn from any part of the whole map, but if in case of choice from within the borders. Contrary to tradition, the title from a firmly fixed cover should, we feel, receive more emphasis than it has often received. A folding map, with a cover clearly seen and used as a means of identification, has a great deal to be said for it as a source for a catalogue title, especially if this is shorter than that on the face of the map, but still just as explanatory.

If there is no title on the map at all, one may have to have recourse to bibliographic searching—and this is where other people's finicky work can be of value! A better way, if at all possible, is to compare the map with others in a well-catalogued collection and so to draw upon information already elucidated by a responsible cataloguer. At the least, another edition, with title on it, may be found. Failing all these, a short descriptive title will have to be devised by the cataloguer, and inserted between brackets.

Alternative and/or sub-title are given as with other materials, especially since they may include useful information which otherwise might have to be virtually repeated in the Notes.

EDITION STATEMENT; EDITION DATE

We suggest that edition statement and date tend to be associated in users' minds and speech and that people tend to couple them with the title. These, then, should come at this stage—with acknowledgements that such a concept cuts into the standard Imprint as established in all reputable codes.

If *scale* is not given in the heading, and since it is needed by many users, we suggest it be included here. There seems little point in repeating the word 'Scale', as some such device as 1:1,000,000 is obviously a scale. We suggest the ratio form as shown; but the scale statement could start with such a form as '1 inch to 1 mile' (possibly plus metric equivalent with the advent of this measure) if the map is well known as such, *eg* British Ordnance Survey's series; this should be followed by the ratio form to facilitate comparison between entries and so selection of the required item. An atlas whose maps vary in scale can be represented by a statement of inclusive scale range or if this is not helpful by just 'Scale varies'.

AUTHOR STATEMENT

This need not be repeated if it is virtually the same as that used in the heading. The librarian in a hurry, especially in a library using current maps for immediate subject information, may decide to omit most or all the names of collaborators which could possibly be given here.

SERIES

Series may be used as a means of recognising a work, especially in the case of a popular series issued by a well-known publisher, whether trade or government department. Therefore we suggest that the series statement should follow next, quite high up the entry. We suggest that there is little point in enclosing this information in parentheses, as dictated by tradition. Again unlike tradition, we suggest that it is worthy of a fresh paragraph in a card catalogue. Normally there is no need to include the word 'series', since the statement should be self-evident; however, it should be included if needed to make syntactical sense of the statement. To save three letters and use 'Ser' seems to have little point as well as risking confusion and exasperation on the part of the untutored user—who will be using the catalogue, we hope.

PLACE; PUBLISHER

Both of these can then be given, although in many cases the place need be included only if: (a) it is obscure; or (b) it is needed to qualify the publisher's name, especially if this is a government department or organisation whose location is not made clear by its name. There is a case for country of publisher and not town or similar location. It seems to be both pointless and pedantic to name 'Chessington, Surrey, England' for Ordnance Survey maps. What we are interested in is that the map comes from the British Ordnance Survey, and not, say, the Australian equivalent. The colon recommended by AACR has some purpose in clearly dividing the place from the publisher: the comma may be necessary to separate parts of the name of the publisher, and so to use it between place and publisher may cause a running together of the two. In card catalogues, we suggest that in most cases there should be room to award this part of the entry its own paragraph. If a book form of catalogue is used, all parts may run on.

COLLATION

This serves two main functions: (a) to name the number of maps in the equivalent of a multi-volumed work; and (b) to give the sizes of maps. In an exclusively map/atlas catalogue, there seems little point in repeating the word 'map 25×35 cm.': Surely 'map' here is not needed in the circumstances mentioned. In an integrated catalogue if MAP were given in the feature heading, again it surely need not be repeated here. Just as there is a good case for omitting number of pages and spine height in book cataloguing, so is there a case for omitting map sizes unless very exceptional. Once a user has got this far in an entry, he is not likely to be affected by a few centimetres one way or the other. If size is given, we suggest following the convention of vertical length first and horizontal length second. Since metric measure is being adopted or considered in most English-speaking countries, it is suggested that this one-time anomaly be retained; inch measurements might well be given also in popular and children's libraries. However, as already inferred, such libraries may decide usually not to give size at all: if the size is significant for filing purposes this will surely be given in symbolic form preceding the class number, for ready location of the item.

Where a 'multiple-volume' work is in progress, the space for number of maps can be left open, if required, and numbers pencilled in to indicate current holdings pending completion of the full set.

Another purpose of collation is to indicate whether a map is coloured, and such information may prove useful and so should be indicated, *eg* '3 col. maps', or, possibly on rare occasions in many libraries, 'hand-col.'. There is something to be said for spelling this information out in full. Depending on ready physical access to the maps themselves, it may be worth giving further detail here, *eg* 'Roads coloured red'.

NOTES

In some respects, and contrary to fairly common practice, notes can be more important than some other parts of the entry—surely many practical users would be much more interested in the fact that a map has an inset, perhaps giving a certain area on an enlarged scale, than that there are minor variations between cover title, margin title, and face-of-map title.

Notes can be of three basic types: (a) bibliographic or physical information on a map as a document; (b) explanatory information in the cataloguer's own words about subject coverage, treatment, even bias, etc; and (c) contents or (selected by cataloguer) partial contents.

Codes usually expect the Notes, in effect, to work in order through all preceding parts of the entry and qualify the formal information given in them. We suggest here that it is inconvenient to have to look in two parts of the body of the entry to find out about, say, variations in title and imprint date. As far as possible, qualifying information should be given in the entry following the 'basic' information given there. AACR has established a precedent, at last, by allowing imprint date as well as 'operative' date in the 'date' part of the entry in the form 1960 (1972 reprint), as opposed to earlier codes which prescribed just '1972' in Imprint, with, say, 'This edition first published 1960' in Notes—in fact the operative date is likely to be the more important to most users. To carry this principle further: to help in identification and recognition, a former title could surely be given in brackets at the title part of the description, and not relegated to Notes.

We propose not to spend much space on category (a) named above. The bibliographic-minded cataloguer can find instructions and examples in AACR R 212 J. One factor, however, deserves notice here: information on type of projection and of meridian may be of practical use. If already given in the feature heading, though, this information need not be repeated in Notes. Even if not in the heading, there may be doubt if some types of information need be given in the Notes, as they are readily ascertainable on consultation of the map itself, and they do not materially affect the value of a map, once the idiosyncrasy is pinpointed, *eg* 'Oriented with north to the right' (AACR R 212 J5).

Category (b) can be of more immediate use in helping to select a map from information given in the catalogue. It has to be emphasised that such information is given at the discretion of the cataloguer, and in the cataloguer's own words—giving rise to one student's statement that Notes represent 'the cataloguer's cadenza'. Such notes may include original source of data given in the map, and so pinpoint a vital fact: its authority, authenticity, or possibly bias (*eg* a map showing boundaries of disputed territory). Another example might be that the map emphasises a particular area or subject aspect which takes so many words to explain that the information cannot be given in the heading, *eg* in a map whose basic operative date is 1948: 'electoral boundaries revised 1956', or 'main roads revised 1956'. Another example, especially for popular use, would be a statement that a map includes (useful) pictorial additional information such as named ancient monuments; this could be useful for teaching purposes because it may arouse students' interest. Another important topic might be a clearer definition than given in heading of area covered. 'London'; 'Perth' and similar centres of population may well have varying boundaries depending on the principle used in defining the meaning of a place-name, and this can be explained in terms of official delineation: local government, police, etc areas, if not already given in the heading.

(c) Contents may apply especially with atlases, although even in such cases, an explanatory note on overall area coverage may be sufficient, following examples in (b). A cataloguer may give Partial contents, pinpointing maps of particular local interest. This type of note is vital for mentioning the existence of insets, giving their area coverage, scale, possibly size, and any subject characteristics. We can also mention here notes on information other than the map itself, whether printed on the map sheet or in a separate physical form, *eg* explanatory text or index. If separate material really has to be filed or shelved apart from the map, its location must be clearly noted. Some of this information might emerge in tracings of added entries, and if these happen to have sufficiently self-explanatory headings and if the tracings are obvious enough, a repetitious note may be obviated. Many codes put library holdings in the notes. We suggest that if this information can be expressed concisely it should go in Collation.

Codes

Some of the codes dealt with here may be regarded by some readers as of historical interest only. However, on comparing, say, CUTTER with AACR one is struck by the similarity between their basic principles, so differences in their practice—specific rules—are mainly in detail. If we can attempt to consolidate an admittedly crude distinction between 'catalogue philosophies' (to use rather a grand term but to keep oneself in the terminological ratrace), we may say there are three basic attitudes towards the purpose of a catalogue. These are: (a) the bibliographic catalogue; (b) the finding list catalogue; and (c) the information retrieval catalogue. Type (a) concentrates on the type of physical description needed for identification of a work, an attitude justifiably reflected in the current attempts (1972) to establish an international Standard Bibliographic Description. Type (b) is aimed at rapid document retrieval and includes the sparest of any sort of bibliographic information; the least information it could normally survive on its heading, title, edition and date of a document, plus of course a clear statement of the document's location on shelves, in files, etc. It normally caters in one way or another for the three traditional approaches of author, title and subject, usually only at complete bibliographic unit level. Type (c) is aimed primarily at retrieval of the information which a document contains, either as a whole or in part. Often, as in Calvin Mooers' original definition of 'information retrieval', the subject approach may be inferred as the sole purpose of this type of catalogue. The catalogue (or index, if the reader prefers—there is no essential difference for our purpose here) pinpoints not only the essential contribution to knowledge of the document as a whole, but also the contribution of various parts within the document. Contrary to some beliefs, we suggest that the 'IR' attitude is applicable to all types of information and document. An index of, say, plays in an anthology or collection, by author, title, and possibly even subject applied selectively, is just as much 'IR' as, say, *Index medicus* and the computerised MEDLARS.

This preamble is necessary in general, and in particular in its application to the retrieval of information within maps and for the whole document retrieval of maps, as differentiated from the bibliographic identification and study of maps. Noteworthy codes on maps, including AACR unfortunately, still seem to be designed on the assumption that the primary need of catalogue users is the bibliographic identification of maps, and especially old ones. Whether or not this situation applied in the past, we suggest firmly that need in most libraries today is not bibliographic-oriented but information-oriented—whether the supplicant is a research worker comparing economic situations, the child or student on a project or assignment, or the pleasure-seeking tourist planning a holiday. This suggestion may embody merely the predilections of this writer, who admits being wedded to the notion of 'applied research' in the expenditure of limited funds in libraries, as opposed to 'bibliography for bibliography's sake'. Readers may well disagree with this contention, and we would welcome substantiated criticism of the views given.

However, despite all the above, codes exist as they are, and we give our summaries of them here. We devote considerable attention to Boggs and Lewis' *Classification and cataloging of maps and atlases,* since this is still the major work in quantity of advice and reputation, while only brief information on AACR is given, despite its being the current code and in current use in such records as BNB and to a limited extent in LC's catalogues, because it is easily available, and is quite widely discussed at meetings and commented upon in the literature of library science.

BOGGS

The overall structure of the work may not be ideal, and in this commentary we have found it convenient to draw together elements which are scattered in the work itself.

This work, significantly, seems to us to some extent to be in advance of its time in its introduction of what retrospectively, we can call the 'IR philosophy'. This is manifested in the construction, content and citation order of its 'main' headings, with their detail of area, subject, operative date, scale, projection, and form of presentation. Although, perhaps inevitably, we cannot bring ourselves to agree in all respects with BOGGS' handling of this data, it is significant that these headings possibly point the way towards BNB's verbal extensions (of class numbers) and feature headings in general.

Although the work avowedly manifests the practice of the US Department of State's Division of Geography and Cartography, the authors took into account, apparently, the practices of libraries in Washington—Library of Congress; New York; and London—Royal Geographical Society and BM. Also, ALA 1941 was taken into account: unlike the final revised edition of 1949, this code included rules for description as well as headings. ALA 1941 assumed an integrated catalogue, while BOGGS caters mainly for a separate map catalogue but with additional information on integrating map entries into a general catalogue.

The chief parts of this omnibus work, of relevance in the present context, are: Part II The catalog card; Part III Organisation of the catalog; Part IV Technical notes concerning maps; Part VI Subject headings; and two paragraphs in Part I, 2 (b) Relation to subject headings, which state that classification notation 'must agree with, but need not be identical with, the subject heading of the main entry. To a limited extent the subject classification symbols which are inserted in the Subject Headings [p 138 *ff*] serve to index the Subject Classification' (p 24). The significance of these innocent statements, bearing in mind that the work was published in 1945, will not be lost on people who maintain that the alphabetical-subject approach is inherently classification-based or 'classificatory'. Readers who do not have ready or frequent access to the work are warned that the organisation of the work as a whole is not always self-explanatory, *eg* Part I, Classification and the filing of maps, includes a subsection, 'Material in exceptional physical form', dealing with suffixes in call numbers for wall maps, relief globes, and globes. Also cataloguers who wish to use chain procedure for the construction of the subject index element of a classified catalogue will need to use in some detail Part V, which comprises the systematic classification schedules.

The Introduction summarises the peculiar characteristics of maps: scale, projection, differences of maps' 'authors', the physical form of maps, and the fact that maps transcend language barriers—generally acknowledged in relation to music scores but not always explicitly stated in relation to maps. It is stated that 'Atlases are like maps in general characteristics' (p 2): this should be obvious, but as has been stated elsewhere (*eg* HORNER, p 213), the difference in physical appearance has sometimes been allowed to cloud the essential fact that both atlases and maps are used for similar information retrieval purposes. However, in some parts, the work seems to go too far in claiming that maps are different from books. We do not necessarily agree that the concept of Germany at various times in history is more important in a map than in a book (p 1). The political historian, who works mainly with letterpress or manuscripts, is only too well aware of the need to qualify 'Germany' whenever he uses it in relation to European, and even colonial, history.

The work attempts to reconcile three objectives: (a) the compilation of separate map catalogues; (b) the integration of map entries into general catalogues; and in particular, (c) to conform as far as possible with LC 'book' cards. The latter objective, though we fear it may have proved constricting in some parts, *eg* the vexed problem of place in relation to subjects in the citation order of alphabetical-subject headings, is obviously a valid objective in the US, where central catalogue cards from LC are part of the cataloguer's way of life. A factor today is the hope of reconciling local needs with the basic format of MARC, especially in relation to the many fields which are now feasible as approach terms, and so are appropriately tagged in MARC.

On p 5 it is claimed that the author entry is not the main, but an added, entry, presumably because in the American dictionary catalogue, the author entry had come to be regarded as the main entry. As we have already suggested, this apparently interminable argument between area and author entry for map cataloguing is virtually irrelevant except in libraries practising severely limited cataloguing and where the unit entry is not commonly accepted. It is made even less significant since BOGGS devised a detailed feature heading (in modern parlance) which largely supersedes the problem of arrangement 'within' a class number, although—just to confuse the issue—BOGGS' samples of entries seem to utilise author marks as the final element in call numbers.

There is a quite comprehensive list of definitions (p 4 to 20), which is still likely to be useful, especially in the description part of an entry, and also when some of the great detail in other parts of the work is taken into account, *eg* the extensive accounts of such items as projections and meridians.

HEADINGS: SYNTACTICAL CONSTRUCTION

The usual varieties of the 'conventional' dictionary catalogue are used, *ie*

(a) Single word, *eg*	Archeology
(b) Direct phrase, *eg*	Great Wall of China
	Migration of man
	Sykes-Picot Agreement, March 1916
	Human use regions [how sought is this, one wonders?]
	Reclamation of land
	Spheres of influence
(c) Inverted phrase *eg*	Globes, Physical
	History, Ancient
	Man, Prehistoric [cf direct entry in Migration of man, above]
	London, Treaty of, 1915 [cf direct entry in Great Wall of China, above]
(d) Structured, *eg*	France—Railroads
	US—Air mail routes
	Canada—Motor bus lines
	Oklahoma—Boundaries—Texas 1927
(e) Parenthetical qualifications *eg*	Folds (Geology)
	Missions (Christian)

Incidentally, it might be inferred that maps of only Christian missions exist, since there is no entry for non-Christian missions—haven't the Muslims in their spread eastwards ever established missions and therefore become the subject of maps?

HEADINGS: INTELLECTUAL CONSTRUCTION

The overall structure is approximately that of 'coventional' lists of subject headings, *eg* LC, Sears, New York Public Library's music headings.

(a) These are ‘ used ’ headings; examples are given above under ‘ Syntactical construction ’

(b) Unused headings are given with *see* references to the ‘ used ’ equivalent

eg Fauna. *See* Animal distribution; Palaeontology
Botany. *See* Plant distribution; Palaeobotany

These demonstrate, incidentally, map orientation in heading construction and use.

Brazil—Agriculture. *See* Agriculture—Brazil

(c) Used headings are connected by *see also* references, giving a syndetic structure to indicate relationships between subjects.

eg Rainfall
See also Climate [‘ upward ’]; Droughts [‘ sideways ’]; Snowfall [‘ sideways ’]; Weather maps [‘ upward ’]
Religions
See also religions by name, *eg* Mohammedanism [downward; ‘ blanket ’ reference]

(d) Multiple entry, occasionally

eg Oklahoma—Boundaries—Texas 1927
Texas—Boundaries—Oklahoma 1927

(e) Headings show some apparent inconsistency in construction

eg Territorial changes
but Turkey—Territorial gains and losses
and Territorial claims. *See* Subdivision Boundaries under names of countries, followed by word ‘ (Claims) ’.

There are some exceptions to ‘ conventional ’ heading list practice:

(a) Headings serve directly as an index to the classification scheme

eg Boundaries, Internal fac
Religions ek
See also religions by name, *eg* Mohammedanism

(It is admitted that the LC list of headings includes relevant LC Classification notation, and in the absence of an official cumulated index to the scheme, is generally used as such. However, the BOGGS list is specifically named as an index to the List. It is noteworthy that Sears List does not give DC numbers any more. BOGGS therefore shows an interesting prefiguration of what nowadays is called a ‘ thesaurofacet ’.)

(b) Tracings are not given for headings from which references are made to the heading in question.

eg Mohammedanism does not have, say, xx Religions or BT Religions (broader term) in modern thesaurus practice.

Arising from this, there are many ' orphans ' in the list, *ie* terms with no named connection with other terms, usually superordinate (' containing ') headings; *eg* on p 161-2, of 35 headings, 9 are orphans.
(c) An interesting typographical device is used in the list as an instruction to the cataloguer, and is not intended to be reproduced in the catalogue. Headings which are not subject to geographical subdivision are shown in capitals (upper case)

eg ALASKA HIGHWAY
and GLOBES, PHYSICAL
but Agriculture

Two further aspects on heading construction require comment, because both are ' hot ' topics in alphabetical subject cataloguing and indexing, and because both are very relevant to the treatment of maps. One is the directness, or specificity, of area heading construction; the other is citation order, particularly in relation to area/subject.

Let us reiterate then that a heading like ENGLAND—LONDON is just as specific as LONDON on its own, but it is indirect as compared with the latter, which is direct. Having established this, it is proposed not to use ' specific ' in the present context, but ' direct ' as in the LC List of headings for geographical subdivision under subjects. (Incidentally it may be worth noting that LC uses indirect and direct, depending, apparently, on the nature of the subject, though without giving reasons for the choice one way or the other.) Also, as is probably well known, conventional headings lists, like LC, seem to have a rather nebulous way of deciding on the basic problem of area/subject citation order. BOGGS tends to follow the ' conventional ' pattern—we dare not say ' principle ', although we sympathise with the dilemma confronting the cataloguer who is trying to establish a cut-and-dried formula. One of the more systematically-minded subject catalogue specialists is E J Coates, and it is noteworthy that even he has not been able to devise a foolproof abstract formula. Like others before him, he has been reduced to enumerating subjects which take place/subject, and others requiring subject/place. Place gets priority in geography, geology, history, social sciences, linguistics, literature, ecology, names of groups of natural organisms both plant and animal (HORNER, p 155).

To return to BOGGS' attitude towards the topic, it can be stated that a rigidly consistent citation order is given for the classification scheme and entries constructed from it, *eg* in the shelf list and in filing arrangement of documents, viz:

(1) Area
(2) Subject
(3) Date
(4) Author
(5) Title
(6) Physical form

(p 20), whether or not one likes the happy indifference to consistent application of characteristics of division. (The 'mechanistic' chain indexer can take it or leave it!)

As to citation order in the Subject headings list (the main verbal approach to the collection since BOGGS assumes the dictionary catalogue), BOGGS is not so consistent—and, we may plead, justifiably so. However, some—to us—specious reasoning is brought in to support the citation of area, whether or not area receives priority as entry term. For example, it is claimed that maps cover certain areas in a way that books cannot, that in fact one cannot have in a catalogue of books Religions—Europe, but that this is needed in a catalogue of maps. Much as we try, we cannot divine any system behind the decisions emerging from the Subject headings list. One comes across, *eg*

Mandated Territories—Africa
but Great Britain—Possessions

Other examples at random include

France—Railroads (*ie* communications second)
but Agriculture—Brazil (*ie* technology first)
also Projections—Aitoff—World (*ie* 'form' first)

Surprisingly, non-specific general references are given from place names in the last two cases:

eg North America—Projections. *See* Projections.

At 'Projections' we have to look through all entries, selecting 'North America' (place) as third-cited item. Since double entry is given for areas in relation to boundaries, we might have expected at least double entry for areas in relation to projections. Incidentally, it is noteworthy that types of projections are cited indirectly, *eg*—Projections—Aitoff, not directly as—Aitoff Projection.

On p 69 BOGGS states that if the citation order of subject/area is used 'where it would make a useful heading' (no reasons given), this order has the advantage of the catalogue supplementing the map arrangement, while the shelf list can be used for the area approach; also the specialist in a subject will be assisted. There is no mention of what happens to the subject specialist in entries where his subject is a distributive relative—if in these cases, the alphabetical approach, with its specific references, can be used, why can this not happen with all subjects? This page of BOGGS gives some interesting background data to librarians who wish to delve into citation orders, and the eternal problem of the classified file and subject index in relation to the alphabetical-subject catalogue.

The direct place practice of BOGGS simply exists, and possibly needs no further substantiation, except for the more publicised practice of indirect entry of LC and the Royal Geographical Society. Interestingly, this apparently hot topic of today, judging by popular textbooks, is, then, merely assumed by BOGGS in passing. One example emerges in its pronouncement on language of place names. We are told to use, say, MÜNCHEN, not MUNICH, for 'local' places: there is no mention of the possibility of, say, GERMANY—MUNICH or GERMANY—MÜNCHEN (already discussed on p 197).

Concerning place names, countries and states are given in their English form—an obvious contradiction compared with local names. As already mentioned, we would suggest English form whenever it exists in a catalogue used mainly by English-speaking users—there is surely a limit to academic accuracy. BOGGS makes the rather dubious assumption that 'the general public is becoming more familiar with place names in the local official form in preference to the so-called conventional English names . . .' (p 67). Further, it is doubtful if *see* references are needed in many cases. The hope and practicability of international cooperation, including possibly the merging of files by computer, is a broader subject than that of just map area entries.

A topic not directly covered by BOGGS, despite its great detail, is what one does about changes of name. Presumably we would have referred at the time to ALA 1941. We have given our own views on this essential topic earlier.

Finally, as to headings, BOGGS recommends bringing dates into headings.

eg California—Roads—1931

and in some cases, including Scale as a further component.

FILING

To summarise, and infer from, BOGGS, arrangement of entries at an entry words would be as follows:

(1) Area Alone
(2) Area Date—earlier

(3) Area Date—later
(4) Area Limiting adjective
(5) Area—Limiting adjective Date—earlier
(6) Area—Limiting adjective Date—later

Arrangement of entries at a heading is as follows:

(1) Heading
(2) Title
(3) Edition, or failing this Imprint date.

INCORPORATION OF BOGGS INTO A GENERAL CATALOGUE

There are two major alternatives: (a) establishment of a self-contained map section within the catalogue, or (b) dispersing all entries throughout the catalogue.

(a) is given as a possibility for small collections—one would qualify this with 'very small' and 'plus a very special type of "form" demand'. *If* practised, it consists of: (i) preceding all 'main' (*ie* area/subject) entries with MAPS and then inserting the entries at that point, sub-arranging by what was the original 'main' heading; and (ii) dispersing all other entries through the catalogue: these would be 'author'; collaborator, series, title, etc as with normal 'descriptive' catalogue (added) entries. As may be judged, we have our doubts about the ultimate value of (a) (i): to dump a great load of entries into the catalogue under one word seems pointless, and contradicts the concept of an integrated catalogue.

(b) is a more valid interpretation of 'integrated', but by its very nature it raises problems. Obviously MAPS must be inserted into 'main' map headings to clarify verbally the nature of the document represented. Presumably the class mark/call number would clarify physical location; in any case, a general instruction on top of the catalogue, relating to all non-book forms and their treatment and location, would prove useful. To pinpoint the form, BOGGS recommends insertion of MAPS in heading as a whole but preceding date,

eg Mexico—Maps—1941

There would need to be references in the cases where subject ('topic') headings for maps differed from conventional practice, in the form:

Airmail Service, for maps, *see* Airmail Routes

References the other way would have to be added to, *eg* 'For books, *see also* [etc etc]'.

DESCRIPTION

BOGGS gives considerable detail and explanation on description, supported by a wealth of information for the bibliographic cataloguer to ensure that he can, say, adequately describe types of projection and meridian. As we have already mentioned, we feel that this type of information is not generally needed nowadays, and it is not proposed to go into BOGGS' advice here, valid as it may be when required. Those cataloguers interested in such detail should acquire a copy of BOGGS, or alternatively they may prefer to rely on a more modern and easily obtained set of instructions: AACR. In BOGGS, Description of maps comes on p 27-46, and for atlases on p 48-50; old and rare items are dealt with on p 50-51; and there are many examples of what BOGGS regards as unit cards on p 51-64, covering many fairly esoteric problems. The content and order of description data is given as follows, after the Heading, though the latter appears on the main entry only (!):

Title
- Title proper
- Translation, or Transliteration
- Author, surveyor, engraver, etc
- Edition

Scale

Collation
- Number of sheets if more than one
- Dimensions
- Height
- Width

Projection

Prime meridian

Notes
- Relation to other work
- Content and description
- 'Carto-bibliographical'
- Material not a part of the map proper

List of entries (*ie* tracings)

Added copies.

Layout of an entry is as follows:

Call number Heading

Title; author. Edition. Place, Publisher, Date.

Scale. Number of sheets, measurements. Projection.

Prime meridian. Notes.

Series note.

List of entries

Added copies.

Two examples from BOGGS are reproduced on p 226.

Finally, although not directly relevant here, we cannot help pointing out a contribution in BOGGS to the eternal, and hoary, problem of dictionary versus classified catalogue. 'If one knows a little about many things, a Dictionary Catalogue is his best steering apparatus around a library. But if he knows much about one or more subjects in particular, a Classed [sic] Catalogue may lead him further and more quickly towards his goal' (p 76). Unfortunately, the narrative goes on to imply that a 'classed catalogue' (*ie* classified file of a classified catalogue) is in the same order as a shelf list. However, it does admit that the 'classed catalogue' can have multiple entry, unlike the shelf list.

PARSONS (UK Directorate of Military Survey)

We extract here only the parts relating to cataloguing. Several pages, however, are devoted to a classification scheme, which, we suggest, could feasibly be replaced by the relevant parts of UDC in the interests of international uniformity, and particularly if the concept of central computer stores of data for special materials is to be realised.

Verbal entry by area is what we might call semi-direct, in that, for provinces, towns etc, entry is indirect via name of country, in the form GERMANY dist. BAVARIA, GERMANY Is. BORKUM, and GERMANY tn. BRUHL (nr. COLOGNE). Known areas, not confined to a country, are entered indirectly under continent, in the form AFRICA dist. NILE VALLEY. We may get filing difficulties when we encounter such headings as GERMANY dist. RUHR and GERMANY—Western; this is dealt with later. Double entry is used for frontiers between countries, using the form GERMANY—Western and BELGIUM—Eastern. As with the traditional alphabetico-classed catalogue, of which the non-librarian compiler of these rules has probably not heard, there arise the usual difficulties of locating entries for specific areas which apparently are not considered viable enough to be entered directly under their own names, *eg* Nile Valley and Ruhr. At the risk of manifesting our bias against the alphabetico-classed principle, we cannot help suggesting that this code is not exemplary for structure of area headings.

Example 2.

Map has a cover with a title different from the title on the map. The one on the map is given as title, and the cover title put into a note.

211a
1911R

Rand McNally standard map of England and Wales. Chicago, Rand McNally & Company [191–]

1 : 1,025,000. 64 x 46^cm^.

Colored by counties.
Cover title: England and Wales. Rand McNally pocket map.
Insets: London and environs.—Scilly Islands and Land's end.—Channel Islands.
On verso: Index giving location on map and population in 1911 of countries and towns, and locations of islands, lakes, mountains, and rivers.

1. England—1911. 2. Wales—1911. I. Rand, McNally and company.

Example 7.

Map in a book. Map has publisher different from that of the book. *Cf.* example 3.

Lithuania-Poland frontier. Edinburgh, John Bartholomew and son [1930]

1 : 3,000,000. 15 x 16^cm^. (*In* Statesmen's year-book, 1939. London, Macmillan and co., 1930. following p. xxxii)

Map shows Lithuania, part of Poland, and area in dispute between them, in colors.

1. Lithuania—Bound.—Poland—1930. 2. Poland—Bound.—Lithuania—1930.

Figure 7

Two typical sample entries from BOGGS (p 52, 54)

Subject of an area is covered by added entries; it does not seem to be integrated into the area heading, being included in a 'Subject file'.

Scale is to be represented as a proportion, not say, so many inches to the mile or vice versa. We have already commented upon this situation in the general introduction for maps.

Usefully, date 'of situation' is to be included in the heading, meaning 'survey date or revision date'.

Conventional procedure is followed for much of description, including a cataloguer's made-up title within brackets where none is given on the map. Insets are identified in the description, and where necessary they may be given, in effect, analytical entries. Supplementary material, such as index or accompanying text, comes before what would, in most codes, be given in Notes.

Considerable detail is devoted to added entries. Apparently, three files are envisaged, by: (a) Main area; (b) Scale; and (c) Subject. Of these, possibly (c) is of most interest, and students may wish to follow it up. It caters for such approaches as Explorers; Boundaries; Communications sub-divided by type such as Air, Railways, Roads, and so on; Economics; Ethnography, and Geology. In the examples given, these are shown as subdivisions under names of countries, *eg* GERMANY—ECONOMIC; DENMARK—GEOLOGICAL.

References are prescribed in the form

SIAM
See THAILAND

and (to overcome the alphabetico-classing)

BORKUM
See GERMANY IS. BORKUM

A filing order is laid down. Area comes first, followed by Scale with the larger first, then Date. Under Continents, we are told to use the order: Series; General; Divisions; Books. Under Country we have: Series; General; Divisions; Districts; Islands; Towns; Books. The order is fairly self-explanatory when reference is made to the classification scheme.

A brief outline of this system has been given as representative of an important 'do-it-yourself' system. We do not necessarily recommend that the system should be followed nowadays. The system outlined is now over twenty five years old, and we suggest it has been overtaken by events in the form of, *eg* UDC and (suitably manipulated) chain procedure.

DRAZNIOWSKY (American Geographical Society)

This system embodies the practice of the American Geographical Society as expounded in 1969. The stock includes some 300,000 maps and 4,000 atlases, 'some of them very rare'.

Verbal area entry is indirect: 'The division begins with the largest unit and proceeds to the smallest.' Entry points start at names of countries or similar units, *eg* archipelagos, smaller areas being given as a sub-division in the form:

Austria, Section
Tirol, 1966

There are references from the specific names, following conventional construction, *eg*:

Truk I. *See*
Caroline Is.
Truk I.

(Actually in the example cited, the used heading is Caroline Is./Truk Is.—with a final 's'—while the reference gives Truk *I* and not *Is.*)
An area covering two or more countries is entered directly, *eg* Alps,
but an area, or part of it, wholly contained by a country goes under the name of the country. This is part of the penalty of alphabetico-classing!

A plentiful supply of added entries seems, usefully, to be given, covering subjects as well as areas. So, a main entry may be made under Antarctica, subdivided by name of exploring organisation, with additional approaches for Exploration, and names of countries initiating expeditions. Similarly, entries are given under names of countries, *eg*

Germany, Section
East, 1943
German—Polish Boundary Problems, 1945

with additional approaches under Boundaries, and Poland (with subdivisions like 'Germany' above).

An indirect form of types of local areas is used, as indicated by the use of 'Section', as exemplified above. A further example is shown in the form of:

France, Cities
Paris, 1968

However, we may encounter anomalies, as

England, Section
London Region, 1965

but Great Britain, Cities
London, 1965

Each of these entries refers to the detailed classification notation, reflecting the verbal structure of the headings, but the details of which do not concern us here.

The 'true' subject approach, as differentiated from area, is dealt with, justifiably, at length, and includes the types of subject which we have previously mentioned, such as Transport, Economics, and Geology. Other aspects, already mentioned in our general introduction, are catered for, *eg* date of situation, and—we are glad to say—publisher. Considerable detail is devoted to description, including some nine types of information for individual maps and seven for sets of maps. The citation order of such information seems useful, *eg* Scale appears high in the entry. Also, a 'short description' for individual maps is prescribed, which seems a most useful element if only the cataloguer has time to compile it.

A list of subject headings is given, including references where relevant, but not including tracings of such references. Inevitably, with alphabetical-subject headings, we cannot avoid disagreement over some sitation orders, *eg* a great number of sub-headings is given under RELIEF, such as RELIEF—Models, yet RELIEF—Submarine is manifested as a reference to SUBMARINE—Relief. Similarly, there is a *see* reference from CHRISTIANS to RELIGIONS—Christian, but not one to, say, RELIGIONS—Orthodox, while under RELIGIONS—Christian there are no references to Christian sects, such as, again, RELIGIONS—Orthodox. A justification of these lacks may be that one should simply get used to the structure of the list, and that, presumably the catalogue will normally be used by (knowledgeable) staff. As will be seen from the examples given above, the subject approach tends to be 'indirect-specific'. This applies to other headings used, such as PRECIPITATION—Rain. Yet, we find a direct entry under SNOW—but admittedly with some eight subdivisions of its own, *eg* SNOW—Line (although SNOWDRIFT is a heading in its own right). Whether or not a map cataloguer uses the exact form of headings given in this code, he might well study them as examples of literary warrant with a view to potential application in large map collections. Some of the syntactical inconsistencies may well stand up to scrutiny, *eg* the use of POWER—Tidal (with a reference from TIDAL ENERGY), compared with the use of TIDAL WAVES. We propose to leave the student to think about the syntactical inconsistency compared with the semantic consistency of such examples.

ROYAL GEOGRAPHICAL SOCIETY

It has been estimated that RGS acquires at least 10,000 maps a year, in addition to atlases (BURKETT & MORGAN p 89-90). Further, RGS aims at acquiring 'most British and foreign atlases' and 'all topographical map series on a scale of 1:50,000 or smaller' (BURKETT & MORGAN, p 90). RGS also acquires various other significant and relevant items, including literary warrant. We pursue with diffidence our previously described preference for direct-specific entry, because RGS uses, in effect, an alphabetico-classed system, having such a structure as Europe—England and Wales—Yorkshire. However, we can safely agree that—once decided on a topographical entry form—'true' subject should be a distributed relative. So 'geology of Yorkshire' comes as a division of the form of structure given above and not under 'Geology' primarily. Obviously, a citation order has to be established, with which we do not quarrel; the only remaining point at issue is that there should also be a 'true' subject approach to supplement the topographical approach.

CUTTER

Maps are dealt with in three places in this code: (a) a special appendix by P Lee Phillips; (b) within Cutter's own rules; and (c) as part of normal book description.

(a) is the Section normally quoted by textbooks; it is the longest, most coherent, and most conveniently accessible part of the code as a whole; so we deal with it here. It comprises Section 368, p 140–146. It should be noted that Phillips' rules, in fact, are supplementary to other contemporary published accounts of LC practice, but they are full enough to stand (or fall) on their own. His opening sentence has been quoted by both protagonists and antagonists ever since: 'The cataloguing of maps and atlases differs very little from the cataloguing of ordinary books' (p 140). As if to substantiate this, he follows with the innocuous statement that '. . . for cataloguing maps and atlases both author and subject cards are made . . .'

Geographical area is the primary 'subject' approach, and, although Phillips does not identify the term 'alphabetico-classed', this in fact is what he recommends. Entry term is continent ('largest geographical division') of the area mapped; this is followed by country, then locality.

eg South America. Brazil. Rio de Janeiro (City of).

It is acknowledged that the method ' necessitates occasional cross references ' for ' insignificant places '. This is indeed a mild recommendation when one bears in mind the complexity of the alphabetico-classed catalogue.

It is recommended that analytical entries, under similar headings, should be made for maps in books, periodicals or atlases.

Concerning atlases, the admittedly valid point is made that they, more often than books, may be ' compilations rather than original productions '. Publisher is allowed as author heading if no other author is ' responsible for the issue of the atlas '—a significant ruling, but one which may not go far enough. For ' important ' atlases, such as older ones with well-known cartographers, each map may be catalogued separately. Contents lists may be needed. Other details are given, with which we concur in the context of the code. However, we wonder whether, even at the time the code was compiled, an added (*ie* form) entry is needed under 'Atlas ' for each such work catalogued.

It is acknowledged that ' for cataloguing maps and atlases both author and subject cards are made ', as mentioned above. An apparently innocent, but, we feel, principle-based statement which cuts across the still-existing arguments on area versus author, which, as we have already said, seems largely irrelevant.

Considerable descriptive detail is prescribed for sheet maps, merely named here since its significance needs no further comment: Author, with full name; title; scale; edition; size in inches within borders; place; publisher; date of publication. As will have been gathered, we do not necessarily agree with the need for each item, or its position in the entry, but this summary is recorded for information.

As to subject entry, examples shown (p 232-234) have the subject on the top left and date on the top right of the entry. It is hard to appreciate why these items cannot have been brought together.

In sum, however, CUTTER, as usual, shows a pleasing insight into what is now regarded as useful in map cataloguing, allowance being made for the time at which the code was compiled.

AA 1908

One of the very few advantages, we suggest, of this code is its brevity. It is not surprising then that maps and atlases receive short shrift, especially as at that time there was still a confusion between subject-type and author-type entry. One of the notorious characteristics of

Arrowsmith (Aaron, 1750–1823).

A new general atlas, constructed from the latest authorities . . . Exhibiting the boundaries and divisions, also the chains of mountains and other geographical features of all the known countries in the world. Comprehended in fifty-three maps from original drawings. 2 p. l. 53 maps 1. l. at end. 4°. Edinburgh, A. Constable & co. 1817.

Note.—Verso of each map is blank.

The following maps relate to America:—

1. The world.
2. The world on Mercator's projection.
48. North America.
49. Canada.
50. United States.
51. Mexico.
52. West Indies.
53. South America.

Figure 8

Map cataloguing examples from CUTTER, p 145-146

(a)

World **1817.**

Arrowsmith (Aaron. 1750–1823). A new general atlas, constructed from the latest authorities . . . Exhibiting the boundaries and divisions, also the chains of mountains and other geographical features of all the known countries in the world. Comprehended in fifty-three maps from original drawings. 2 p. l. 53 maps. 1 l. at end 4° Edinburgh, A. Constable & co. 1817.

Note.—Verso of each map is blank.

The following maps relate to America:—

1. The world.
2. The world of Mercator's projection.
48. North America.
49. Canada.
50. United States.
51. Mexico.
52. West Indies.
53. South America.

(b)

Atlas. World. **1817.**

Arrowsmith (Aaron. 1750–1823). A new general atlas, constructed from the latest authorities . . . Exhibiting the boundaries and divisions, also the chains of mountains and other geographical features of all the known countries in the world. Comprehended in fifty-three maps from original drawings. 2 p. l. 53 maps. 1 l. at end. 4°. Edinburgh, A. Constable & co. 1817.

Note.—Verso of each map is blank.

The following maps relate to America:—

1. The world.
2. The world on Mercator's projection.
48. North America.
49. Canada.
50. United States.
51. Mexico.
52. West Indies.
53. South America.

(c)

this code in general is its rigid adherence to strict rules with virtually no allowance for the now much-vaunted autonomy of the cataloguer. It is pleasantly surprising then that in certain circumstances, such as the absence of any named person who can be identified as cartographer, the cataloguer may be allowed to enter a map under its publisher.

The main entry treatment is covered by R 6 Cartographers, which states that maps are to be entered under cartographer, but if the latter cannot be found, under publisher. One of the examples cited is a commercial publisher. Atlases are the subject of R 165, but only as accompanying material, within the rules for Collation. Generally, in such cases, there would be included, running on from collation, such a statement as '*and* atlas of 30 fold. p. $23\frac{1}{2}$ cm.' If the accompanying atlas has its own title it is preferably represented in the entry in the way 'usually adopted for indexes': under the part of the entry for the parent work there is a dash followed by a full description of the atlas itself. An added entry for cartographer is indicated if different from that for the main heading for the parent work. There is little to quarrel with over these basic decisions for an author and description code. Although not represented in the code's index, maps in a normal monographic work are covered by R 161 Illustrations, etc. A pecking order is laid down for types of illustrations, and maps lie sixth out of ten types categorised. We might note here the contrast with AACR, which has such items cited in alphabetical order, which we prefer. Also, the number of such illustrations, including maps, should be given when easily ascertainable. The latter, though possibly not always significant, might be queried, in that the number of maps may be useful information to the user whether or not easily ascertainable to the cataloguer. *If* such detail is required by users, perhaps it should be laid out clearly whether or not it is easy for the cataloguer to obtain it.

ALA 1949

R 10 deals with Maps and atlases. One footnote cites sources of further information on the topic. A second footnote says that, although author-type entry is consistent with book cataloguing, 'small libraries' may use an 'entry under subject (*ie* area mapped)'. The possibility of main entry under area is accompanied by a citation of BOGGS.

Section A deals with maps, and B with atlases, and, although the two sub-rules go into detail with examples for each form, not surprisingly the conclusions are the same in principle. R 10A gives explicitly an order of preference, with publisher lying fourth, and title an also ran. R 10B names intellectual authorities but without enumeration: in this case publisher is mentioned second. Title is not merely an also ran; it is allowed 'if the work is familiarly known by title'. The usual added entries are allowed. B also recommends 'form subject entry under the form heading ATLASES'. One cannot help suspecting that the latter single-word heading, in a large collection, presumably sub-arranged by main (author) heading, would get so crowded as to cause more exasperation than document retrieval.

LCRCD 1949

As pre-AACR cataloguers will know, ALA 1949 (the 'red rules'), for headings only, is a near-Siamese twin of LCRDC (the 'green rules'), the latter dealing with 'descriptive' cataloguing in the broadest meaning of the term, which, we are told 'is commonly understood to apply not only to the description of an item but also to the choice and determination of the form of the headings' (p 1). Despite this bold assertion, in fact the code deals substantially with the 'body of entry' type of description, as confirmed by both AA 1908 and AACR.

Chapter 8 is concerned with 'Maps, Relief Models, Globes, and Atlases', significantly an identical title to the relevant part of AACR. As indicated above, the prickly topic of headings does not have to be dealt with. Much of the detail in AACR is very similar to that in LCRDC, and in fact is drawn almost directly from LCRDC. However, the sequence of items is slightly different: *ie* Scale comes after Series 'note' (*ie* statement), and not immediately after author statement as in AACR. As will have been gathered, we think that Scale should come very high in the entry, and so we prefer AACR in this respect. Considerable space is devoted to Notes in general, with, it seems, a fairly casual intermixing of retrieval information and bibliographic information. Subsequent sub-sections on Relief models, Globes, and Atlases are very similar to, and obviously the source of, similar topics in AACR.

AACR

Chapter 11: Maps, Relief Models, Globes and Atlases (British text, p 210-214).

As we know, AACR caters for an integrated catalogue of all stock, whatever its physical form. Some specialists may consider this a weakness—the code does not revolve around maps, or even special materials in general. For our own part, this seems an advantage, as it may help to integrate use of all physical forms, even if only from the author/title and description point of view.

HEADING

The Introductory note establishes that 'most libraries' have area as main entry, but this code deals with author/title entries. It is reassuring that AACR reminds us in effect that there can be an overlap of heading (inferred area/subject) and notes.

R 210 reminds us, essentially, of the principle of intellectual responsibility. No query so far; but we find the next statement rather enigmatic: 'If the subject aspect is the principle feature, the rules of entry for books and book-like materials are applied (Chapter 1): if the geographic aspect is the principle feature, Rule 211 is applied'. In fact Chapter 1 consists of over fifty pages, containing thirty-three rules, often with divisions and sub-divisions, reaffirming in effect the basic two commandments of AACR's heading rules: (a) Enter under the chief author intellectually responsible for a work; and (b) When you reach the point of being driven up the wall in deciding on (a), fall back on title entry. We fail to see the relevance of all this to whether a map is primarily of 'geographic' or 'subject' interest. However, having quietly slid over this problem, the rest is plain sailing. R 211A allows us to accept any individual or body 'excluding a commercial firm other than a map publisher'(!) as, in effect, the main author heading. Added entries are allowed for those who did not come first in the assessment of 'explicit primary responsibility'. R 211B deals with the 'not explicit' situation, resulting in the following order of preference: (1) Surveyor; (2) Cartographer; (3) Engraver 'if known to be also the cartographer'; (4) 'Corporate body, including a map publisher', that prepared the maps. The examples show that that shunned category, the trade publisher, may actually be admitted to the honoured ranks of first choice author heading; (5) Title—apparently as a last resort. Yet, an example under (4), *Everyman's encyclopaedia's world atlas,* receives its main entry under John Bartholomew & Son, with added entry under Bartholomew—virtually the same entry word, with no specific reminder of possible added entry under title. For this we must invoke R 33P: which goes to show that the map cataloguer must know AACR well, that is, if he is using it as an authority and wishes to employ it fully. One of the two alternatives under (4) gives more strength to title entry, actually allowing the Times Atlas to be entered under TIMES rather than John Bartholomew & Son.

DESCRIPTION (R 212)

The content and order of the parts of the Description are as follows:

(1) Title, preference in any choice being for the title within the borders
(2) Author, etc statement
(3) Scale, preference being for ratio form of expression
(4) Edition
(5) Imprint
(6) Collation
(7) Series
(8) Notes, with considerable detail given, and 13 items being listed
(9) Two or more maps on one sheet
(10) Analytical entries

Parts of item 9 and 10, in fact, cover added (analytical) entries as well as description.

Further rules deal with 'Relief models' ('a three-dimensional map other than a globe') (R 213; Globes R 214); and Atlases (R 215).

R 143 D.1.b includes maps as part of collation for monographs: map, or maps, is given in alphabetical order with other illustrative materials.

Readings

Checklist of works cited in or relevant to this chapter. General works in the checklist with the first chapter of this book (p 28-29) also include information on the topics covered by this chapter. Full bibliographic citations are given in the consolidated Bibliography, p 304-312. A list of abbreviations is given on p 7. The titles of periodical articles are given within quotation marks.

AA 1908

AACR 1967

ALA 1949

ALONSO 'Feasibility study on computer-produced map catalogue'

AMERICAN GEOGRAPHICAL SOCIETY *see* DRAZNIOWSKY

BM

BOGGS *The classification and cataloging of maps and atlases*

CRONE 'Notes on the classification, arrangement and cataloguing of a large map collection' (Royal Geographical Society)

CUTTER

DRAZNIOWSKY ' Cataloging and filing rules in the [American Geographical] Society's collection '

DRAZNIOWSKY ' The need for map cataloging '

EASTON 'Automating the Illinois State University Map Library '

FINK 'A comparison of map cataloging systems '

FRIEDMAN *Cataloguing and classification in British university libraries*

GREAT BRITAIN. *War Office. Manual of map classification and cataloguing see* PARSONS

HAGEN 'An information retrieval system for maps '

LC *Map Division*

LC *Maps: a* MARC *format*

LCRDC

LEE *English county maps . . .*

MURPHY ' Map collection prepares to automate . . .'

PARSONS *Manual of map classification and cataloguing . . . Directorate of Military Survey . . .*

RISTOW ' The Library of Congress: computerised map cataloging project '

RISTOW ' What about maps?'

ROYAL GEOGRAPHICAL SOCIETY *Storage and preservation of maps*

US *Office of Strategic Services . . . Cataloger's manual*

WOODS ' Map cataloging . . .'

CHAPTER FIVE

Serials

BASICALLY, by ' serials ', we are thinking of printed, mainly letterpress, documents: (a) with a reasonably permanent title of some sort; (b) appearing at regular—but not necessarily frequent—intervals; (c) whose contents are usually different from issue to issue; and (d) with no planned end to the sequence after a certain number of issues. Categories which we have in mind in this definition are mainly: (a) newspapers, usually daily, part-weekly, or weekly; (b) periodicals, usually weekly, monthly, two-monthly, quarterly, or six-monthly; (c) annuals, or ' multi-annuals ', usually two-yearly or five-yearly.

Newspapers appear to overlap periodicals in that both can appear weekly. Usually the physical format of each is a distinguishing factor: we can recognise the (London) *Observer* as a weekly newspaper, but the *New statesman* as a weekly periodical. A further distinguishing factor is the type of content of each, the predominating factor in the former being mainly news, while in the latter it is usually comment, opinion and reviews. Format need not matter much in cataloguing, except that: (a) a catalogue has to name locations, usually via call numbers, which must take account of various oversize and similar special sequences; and (b)—less importantly if the location is clearly indicated—the description should, in theory at least, give the physical size of a work in its collation as a warning to the reader of what he may have to contend with.

Works of the ' newsletter ' type may be issued by some professional and social organisations. These are often like newspapers in format, though sometimes smaller. They may be issued irregularly, yet we safely put them under ' serials ' as they conform in other respects. Their main disadvantage in libraries is not to cataloguers, but to acquisition staff, as the latter have no clear guide as to when to call up non-arrivals. As long as they are numbered, they do not present citation problems.

We have to include 'part-weekly' under newspapers since some newspapers may be issued, say, twice a week. One example stocked by many libraries is the *London gazette*. Some may say this particular example could also be an entry problem, because its author may be considered to be the British Government.

Some newspapers have supplements, either regularly such as the 'magazine' colour supplements of some weeklies, or irregularly: to take a random example—the *West Australian* early in 1972 had a special long insert dealing with the north-west of the State and which may prove of information value in the future.

Some daily newspapers may have a regular weekly, usually Sunday, counterpart or alter ego. These may be connected by title, as with the *Australian* and the (late) *Sunday Australian*. As to whether cataloguers should, or need to, take such a connection into account is a nebulous and controversial problem, since it may imply passing political judgement.

Periodicals are more expensive to produce, and to distribute in some cases. Hence their producers seem less likely to indulge in vagaries like impromptu supplements, for special occasions, of the newspaper type, since this might affect their frequency and weight and thus distribution timing and costs. 'Supplements', such as the *Autocar*'s London Motor Show, are usually an integral part of the periodical, as indicated by their pagination. Whether such supplements require special indexing, however, may be another matter. Some periodicals have what might be called supplements in the form of separate publications derived from the content of the regular issues; the *Gramophone*'s *LP catalogue*, issued quarterly, is an example. Some periodicals produce an allied annual, possibly under its own title, but perhaps with a derived title. Again, some periodicals—and occasionally newspapers—publish their own indexes, under their own authorship and imprint. However, there may be indexes produced by outside, or apparently outside, individuals. An example of the latter is Procktor's index to the *Engineer;* a well-known past example was Palmer's index to the *Times*. It may be decided to enter such works either independently or as subsidiaries of the parent work: another entry problem. An example of an index reaching the status of a positive work in its own right is the Subject index to the printed books in the British Museum. Presumably this started as an index to the BM author catalogue, although even in its early days it was known as 'Fortescue' after its compiler. A further complication arises here: it started as a monographic 'continuation' type work, but according to our definition it evolved into a serial.

We are now in the realms of annuals and multi-annual publications. There are, possibly, five types of annual or similar publications. (a) There is the yearbook of a subject which presents a symposium of articles outlining and documenting advances in the subject during the period, *eg Yearbook of education,* and in the past the *Year's work in librarianship.* The complete contents change from year to year. (b) There is the directory-type of work, whose contents are updated from year to year, *eg Statesman's yearbook* and *Whitaker's almanack.* However, some such works are not restricted wholly or mainly to directory-type information, as an examination of runs of the above two works will show. Examples giving even less directory-type information are the *Commonwealth yearbook of Australia* and the *Official yearbook of Great Britain.* We could call the succeeding issues of such works revised editions just as we have revised editions of monographic works. (c) There are special types of annual or multi-annual works which consist solely of cumulations of other works which strictly are periodicals. Such examples are *British national bibliography* and *British technology index.* Some are issued under regular, but different, titles, *eg* the lists of publications given in the weekly *Bookseller* appear quarterly, then annually, as the *Cumulative book list.* We have to distinguish such a work from *British books in print,* compiled, apparently independently, from publishers' catalogues, but by the same corporate author in the form of a commercial publisher: Whitaker. (d) There is the annual suplement to a large monographic work, *eg Britannica book of the year* as a means of updating *Encyclopaedia Britannica.* Such supplements may not be annual, or even published at predetermined intervals, as has been demonstrated in the past by *Chambers's world survey* as a supplement to *Chambers's encyclopaedia.* (e) Finally, there is the maverick serial so superbly exemplified by the *Libraries, museums and art galleries yearbook.* This satisfies all of our requirements for annuals, as a part of serials—except that it does not come out every year. Works like this are like other directories and similar quick-reference books but the latter do not imply in their titles that they are serials. This situation can lead to highly artificial decisions being made as to whether such works are entered in the serials catalogue or in the monographs catalogue, assuming such works are entered in separate sequences. Some even more unlikely works might qualify on grounds of periodicity as serials, *eg Encyclopaedia Britannica* itself has an approximately *annual* revised reprint, in addition to its annual supplement, while *Chambers's encyclopaedia* makes no pretence at regular, *eg* even five-yearly, isues. A rather similar problem can be posed by the new directory, or similar, which starts life apparently as a monographic-type work, but which through popularity becomes in effect a serial, *eg* an annual.

Where a library maintains separate public catalogues for serials as differentiated from ' normal ' monographic works, one can—or should—appreciate the confusion of users who find what seem to them to be similar types of works in different catalogues.

The situation can be made even more complicated in libraries which treat so-called ' continuations ' as yet a third category, however convenient this practice may be for acquisition purposes. A continuation may be defined as a series whose individual issues are numbered and can be said to stand as monographs in their own right, but which are treated as a whole for acquisition and cataloguing purposes. An example is the series of (UK) Library Association pamphlets, of which there is no predetermined end. We feel that such works should be catalogued and classified individually. At least a compromise could be made by making individual author and subject entries, most conveniently effected in a dictionary catalogue, even if the file of such a series is classified and shelved at one point in the library, *eg* at the most specific class number, and possibly in a Pamphlet sequence. The ' continuation syndrome ' can be most important in retrieval, since such indefinite series increasingly form important parts of library stocks. A noteworthy example of the past and present is HMSO's Command papers; other current examples are issued by just about all scientific research establishments and many universities, whether called ' monographs ', ' reports ', or ' occasional papers '. Their only virtue, from the cataloguer's point of view, is that each number is usually confined to one subject, however complicated it may be, as opposed to one issue of a periodical, which may well include several articles, each of which is on a different subject, and possibly also highly complex. We are led to conclude this section, then, with a mention of the ' separate ' or ' reprint ': an article from a periodical separately printed and therefore capable of being stored as a physical unit on its own in addition to being catalogued or indexed as a separate source of information.

With many newspapers and periodicals, a second type of special cataloguing can often come in, that is when such works are represented in a library's stock as either full-size or micro copies. Increasingly, we may find that some serial bibliographies are issued primarily in this form. An example is *Books in English,* which is further complicated by being an example of so-called PCMI (Photochromic Micro Image), virtually a micro-micro form requiring a special reader.

We must now try to describe what can be meant by the cataloguing of serials; we are thinking here particularly of newspapers and periodicals. The bibliographic organisation of such documents can apply to: (a) the recording of runs of works as a whole; or (b) the analytical indexing of the contents of such works. Also of possible relevance is the organisation of cuttings from newspapers and, sometimes, periodicals. We shall be concerned mainly with the cataloguing of runs, although detailed attention to such a problem may not seem very relevant to those librarians with very small serials collections.

However, some libraries, whether, say, comparatively small special libraries, or large research libraries, may have long runs of a great number of serial titles. The accurate and satisfactory recording of such holdings is of importance to local users, and staff of course, of such libraries. It is also important to external potential users, because the library will almost certainly contribute entries to one or more union catalogues. An in-between situation is that a library may possibly issue checklists of all or some of its serial holdings, for either local or external use. It is evident that it would be very convenient if all libraries serving directly or indirectly a particular clientele could be consistent in their form of entry of runs of serials, either following a published code, such as AACR, or following rules agreed among themselves. Discussion with, and articles by, editors of union catalogues of serials demonstrate the labour and frustration caused by inconsistent contribution from various libraries to centrally-produced union catalogues. Apart from entry terms, in union catalogues and similar lists consistency is desirable in citation of holdings. Relevant here is the method of stating holdings, and the detail given about holdings. It is necessary to differentiate between brief checklists as a starting point, and detailed statements of holdings used by librarians, or users, in requesting a loan or facsimile copy of an article in a particular issue.

Checklists may give not merely a ' main entry ' but go even further back in the retrieval process and attempt a form of subject approach. An increasingly used method is the keyword approach, especially when a computer can be used to manipulate entries and print out lists with serials' titles entered, according to a multiple entry principle, under each word in the title which states or infers one aspect or another of the subject represented in the title of a serial. The National Lending Library for Science and Technology in Britain has established itself as a library manifesting this type of list. Some examples are mentioned on p 249.

Of course, criticism can be made of the keyword (in titles) approach to the subject matter of serials. However, it must be admitted that many of the serials included in such lists do have titles which explain, reasonably adequately at least, the subject coverage of such serials. The subject approach to serials, mainly periodicals, in general is commented upon next, including that of complete works and of the subject analysis of articles, etc in periodicals.

A matter of relevance to the cataloguing of some serials is that shelving may be in a sequence other than by subject. Depending possibly on cataloguing policies, newspapers and periodicals may be shelved alphabetically according to either title in all cases, or by title or issuing corporate body in other cases. General classification schemes provide for serials in their standard subdivisions, auxiliaries or common facets—what they are called depends on the scheme. Reflecting classification, a library with a classified catalogue may give entries on the appropriate places for periodicals of a subject, and for general periodicals, *ie* those with no definable subject. Similarly, a dictionary catalogue may have subject-form entries in appropriate places, *eg* SCIENCE-PERIODICALS for *Nature*. However, as inferred above, the subject arrangement on the shelves may not be considered useful.

Entry to articles in periodicals is almost always through separate indexes, whether: (a) published with the periodicals themselves; or (b) separately published ones, usually in broad fields such as technology, analysing many works; or (c) compiled by libraries. Therefore it may be considered most convenient: (a) to bring together periodicals in a 'form' section of their own rather than scatter them according to subject as primary characteristic; and (b) within this form section to arrange them in some form of alphabetical sequence. The latter may usually follow the catalogue main author/title heading. So, if the catalogue uses 'consecutive' entry for a work with various titles, sequences on the shelves would also be 'split'. The latter system, recommended by AACR, facilitates direct referral from indexes to shelved items, since indexes, and other sources, usually cite works as they were at the time the indexed articles appeared in them. As far as catalogues and check-lists are concerned, it is necessary to represent exact locations clearly in all entries for runs of periodicals, even though, in a classified catalogue if used, a class number will appear in entries and will govern the arrangement of entries in the classified file.

With annuals of the data or directory type, the shelving may follow a form-subject citation order, to gather together reference works in a sequence of their own, probably intershelved with monographic reference works. A flexible classification scheme like UDC facilitates such an arrangement by having reversible compound numbers with the colon as a joining device. Less flexible schemes may be used, with a prefix, say R, indicating primary arrangement. UDC allows for primary arrangement by various types of work if required, *eg* indexes, abstracts, dictionaries, directories, and so on. It is vital that such locations should be clearly indicated in a library's catalogues, also that all the approaches are catered for in the various form/subject approaches effected by the catalogue, whether classified or alphabetical. For example, in the alphabetical-subject catalogue there should be entries under verbal headings for department location (if necessary), forms, and subjects, all pointing to the exact department and shelf location. Shelf location as shown by dictionary catalogues can be made clear with little difficulty, since the only location shown on entries is the shelf location. In classified catalogues, the problem may be complicated by the various added entries and their respective classification notations. We suggest that just underlining the operative (primary characteristic) part of a long notation is not clear enough, although some libraries practise this commonly. So, we suggest that the actual shelf location symbol should be given in a consistent place in an entry, possibly to the top right in a card catalogue. The filing number for the entry itself can logically be in the top left corner to facilitate filing, and finding of entries, usually after use of the subject index. This practice may entail having two near-identical notations on the main entry.

The number and types of catalogues to be maintained for serials warrants some investigation. A basic problem is whether periodicals should be recorded in a separate periodicals catalogue or whether entries for periodicals should be given in a library's ' general ' catalogue, usually it being inferred that such records are available for public use. However, viewed academically, the problem can become more complicated. One complication is that there may be some confusion over the extent to which a catalogue records full and exact holdings for public use. An attitude often encountered is that users do not need minute details of holdings, since searches are pretty well always made by staff, who have access to non-public records in the form of some sort of periodicals register used by acquisitions staff to mark off issues as received. This is a satisfactory situation as long as there are always enough qualified staff on duty to deal with enquiries as they arise, and as long as there is enough monitoring of users' use of catalogues to ensure that enquirers are not frustrated by incomplete information in public catalogues. It must be remembered that potential use of individual articles in periodicals arises from two main sources: (a) a subject search, usually by staff, at the request of a user; but also (b) a document search for actual articles cited in other sources, *eg* monographic works commonly used by students, academics, research workers and others including 'ordinary' members of the public. In the latter case, and especially if a user has received instruction in the use of catalogues, indexes and bibliographies, the user may prefer to follow through his own need from bibliographic citation to location of the required article in an open access sequence, which he can then, say, take to a documentary reproduction centre or machine in the library for copying, or use for the making of notes. If a user expects, or is expected, to complete such searches himself, evidently he must know exact holdings of a run of periodicals in stock. The staff would take over only when a particular issue was not in local stock, and had to be located, via union catalogues, in other libraries. In the latter case, it would save staff time if the user could fill in a request card giving an accurate and full citation in a generally accepted form; possibly there is a need here for further instruction of users by staff. As already mentioned, we come back to the need for qualified staff on duty at all times when a library is open. If a library is open for long hours for just 'study' and not research, this restriction should be made clear to users. On the other hand, some form of periodicals catalogue may be needed for the general information of users, *eg* to inform a user that a particular work is currently stocked and displayed, and so is available for browsing, usually current issues being in the most hot demand. For such a use, a brief checklist may be sufficient. It is particularly convenient if printed lists can be made available for people to take away. Computer-printing may be considered here. The list can be compiled from, say, computer acquisition records; detail not required, *eg* supplier, renewal times for subscription, etc can be suppressed by a special program written for the purpose. This form of 'stripped' record should ideally be catered for in the original computer programming. A further advantage of using a computer is that title, or even enriched title, records can be manipulated to produce a form of permuted entry system. Such lists, *eg* on a KWIC (KeyWord In Context), or a KWOC (KeyWord Out of Context) basis, can give a quasi-subject approach, as already mentioned. Also included should be the location of works cited, including where current issues are displayed as well as where past issues are filed if in a different location.

A further problem to be settled is the inclusion of periodicals, and other serials if necessary, in any union catalogues maintained by a library. If a library is subject departmentalised, it may be that there is a union catalogue in the general service area, usually near the main entrance and service area of the library. A subsidiary but related problem is that of approach via subject as well as author/title. If a union catalogue by subject is maintained—and we suggest that with the current inevitable inter-disciplinary nature of subject approach for many topics this is needed—then periodicals should be included in a subject approach as much as is any other category of library material.

Union catalogues may be maintained for stocks of several libraries, whether by author/title, or possibly by subject as inferred above. Union catalogues restricted to serials alone may be maintained, especially by a library acting as a bibliographic centre for a region or area. Union catalogues of serials may be 'one-off', often on cards, or multiple-copy, usually in book form. Most advanced countries have these, the *British union catalogue of periodicals* in bound form, and *Scientific serials in Australian libraries*, in loose-leaf form, being examples. Usually, these are author/title only. The latter indeed causes enough difficulties in reconciling conflicting entries from a variety of sources, without complications over subject approach. If a subject approach is maintained, however, it can serve two useful purposes: (a) it can be a fairly direct source of information in an area which has a subject specialisation scheme; and (b) it can serve as a check list for libraries overhauling their stocks of periodicals.

Data under each entry should include three main elements: (a) entry, whether author or title, plus any additional information to identify a work and its various manifestations; (b) libraries holding a run; with (c) exact details, within reason, of details of holdings for each library. Cooperating libraries are usually represented by symbols, either arbitrary numbers or some form of literal mnemonics, *eg* NLW for National Library of Wales or NLA for National Library of Australia. Where nearness to requiring library is important, symbols can incorporate prefixes indicating locality, as well as name of library. Some of the problems and possibilities in compiling union catalogues of serials are given, among other information, in QUIGG's 'How to make a union catalogue', in *Catalogue and index*. More discussion on the citation and codification of serials is given later in this chapter.

At this point, we should acknowledge that there is some opinion at least that union catalogues would not be so necessary, with all their complications in reconciling contributions from many libraries, if there could be a grand central repository for periodicals for each country. A centre apparently tending towards this is the National Lending Library for Science and Technology in England. Its Director, D J Urquhart, famous, or infamous, as being a non-catalogue non-librarian, has pointed out that merely finding a location in a union catalogue does not guarantee the supply of a document (*eg* URQUHART, *LA record*). However, even if this were the case, the central repository would need a foolproof system of recording its serial holdings, allowing for slightly inaccurately cited documents, which can happen even with qualified librarians occasionally.

The NLL attempts to overcome its own lack of cross-checking and searching by the issue of sectional KWIC lists, *eg* of *English language abstracting and indexing publications*, and its *List of scientific and technical periodicals received from China*. The first of these is an example of a (very modestly) 'enriched' list, *eg* the entry for *Ibis* is followed by (Ornithology), and *G.P.—Chicago* by (Medicine). Such lists do not make searching unnecessary; they merely, quietly, push the searching back to the supplicant library. So there is still a need for some degree of verification even though the burden is partly alleviated by such lists which enter works under all significant words in their titles. Local libraries are then made responsible for ensuring that they stock such lists before they can safely make a request to a central repository. We feel, then, that the traditional union catalogue of serials has not yet been seriously threatened. If the time comes when a central repository has stocks of virtually all serials likely to be needed, presumably in microform or ultra-microform, and with its own foolproof searching mechanism, then we may feel that union catalogues will have been superceded. It is not our place here to indulge our ready fancies on how the type of repository will operate. But the least it will need will consist of: (a) on-line facilities; (b) instantaneous full-size reprinting; and/or (c) telefacsimile machinery. The time may come then, when local libraries do not need to maintain runs of serials at all, but can obtain facsimile copies of articles required, after a screen scan, at the press of a button.

In the meantime however, perhaps for a generation, we must still pay attention to the compilation of union and checklists in hard copy form. Also, it is salutary to bear in mind that American cataloguers of serials are paid salaries of $US 10,000 upwards a year. Evidently, it will pay library administrators to take into account the professional labour of cataloguing serials, apart from all the other costs involved such as duplicating and filing entries. This should, we suggest, take full account of catalogue data from central sources, especially that from MARC, whether BNB or LC.

We propose now to revert to the problem which always seems to arise with any form of special materials: whether there should be a separate catalogue for serials or whether serial entries should be filed into the library's general catalogue. As will have been seen above, various separate listings may be found most useful, and of course there is no doubt that a union list of serials as such, covering several libraries, is separate by its very nature and purpose.

Within a library, whether or not we are thinking of a union catalogue or a catalogue of one service point or department, it seems safe to say that many librarians tend to prefer a separate serials sequence for stock control purposes. Having established this, there is little doubt that a small catalogue is easier to search than a big one.

However, there are two possible arguments against this attitude in general: (a) there is, we feel, an increasing tendency for users to want to do their own searching to some extent; and (b) even to librarians, who deal with library materials every day, there seems to be an increasing tendency for confusion to arise over whether certain documents qualify as serials or not.

The first condition may arise because of increasing specialisation on the part of research workers particularly, until we reach the point that a user may be the only person who can most effectively utilise his materials. Another contributory factor is the need for increased use of libraries because of the rapidly increasing output of library materials, until we reach the point that it is impossible for professional library staff alone to cope with all enquiries. Admittedly, to try to cope with one aspect of this situation there has come into being the hybrid known as the information scientist: the subject expert with also special skills in information work. (Actually, by way of a tilt at this windmill, we venture to suggest that this type of librarian has existed as long as special librarians have existed, especially those working in libraries with a particularly narrow subject scope.) Large special libraries, especially those with a broad coverage, may employ teams of research workers whose specific job it is to act directly as middlemen between the more difficult stock and enquirers, whether in dealing with specific enquiries or compiling bulletins which include annotated lists and abstracts. Where such facilities are not possible, hence where laymen from the library point of view are using catalogues, and indexes to serials, without professional help, we suggest that there is a case for incorporating serials, and in fact as many other forms of material as possible, into a single catalogue. From participation in catalogue use studies, from discussions with students (who early on in their professional education may be regarded as intelligent and motivated laymen), and from our own use of unfamiliar catalogues, we suggest that users want as few sequences as possible. In fact, if at all possible, they would seem to prefer only one sequence to satisfy all their needs. Ultimately, their needs are information itself, irrespective of what names librarians and catalogue code compilers use to categorise the various means of imparting that information. This factor could be used in building up a case for the 'pure' dictionary catalogue, but at the moment we propose to confine ourselves to the suggestion that entries for serials should be incorporated into the 'general' catalogue, for the reasons given. The concept of the multi-media catalogue is developed in the last chapter of this book.

The second argument revolves around the increasing difficulty, in many cases, which librarians themselves have in distinguishing clearly between serials and monographic materials. It might be said, in favour of the integrated catalogue, that there is no need to try to distinguish between serials and monographic works. However, in fairness, it must be stated that there is a need, but mainly from the acquisitions, and not the retrieval point of view. This has two main aspects, One is that when a library takes out a subscription to, say, a newspaper or a periodical, it is committing future funds for an indefinite period, because of the inherent, indefinitely continuing nature of serials. Therefore special financial monitoring of serials is essential for budget-planning purposes. The other aspect is that of recording receipt of issues, and therefore having a ready means of identifying and calling up non-arrivals. For these two reasons it is not only convenient but virtually necessary for library staff to maintain separate acquisition records for such serials as newspapers and periodicals. It may be convenient to maintain yet another sequence of annuals and 'multiannuals', for which standing orders may be placed. The relevance of all this background to cataloguing is that, we suggest, some librarians may unconsciously carry over this ' separatist ' attitude to public catalogues, the ultimate purpose of which is different from that of acquisition records. Admittedly, records of serials for acquisition purposes can serve as a basis for lists of serials intended for public use, either by users of the local library, or for external use by other staffs and possibly for users of other libraries. This facility exists particularly when the acquisition records of a library's serials are mechanised. As we have already said, if detailed records of serials are computerised, these records can be printed out in a ' stripped down ' form to produce checklists giving just author/title headings, approximate holdings, and locations. Arising from this, there may well be a tendency to regard all public serial catalogue records as being necessarily separate. However, notwithstanding all this, and as we have, we hope, already substantiated, users may well find a single-sequence catalogue preferable. In any case, if a library has a computer stored and printed general catalogue, it should not be beyond the possibilities of programming to merge serial entries with those of other materials and to print out a complete catalogue.

To return to our original point, as far as the retrieval value of a catalogue is concerned, a librarian can obviate heart-searching over whether a work is technically a serial or not by going along with the user whose goal is the document and the information in it, and not an academic discussion over its nature from the acquisition point of view. From the retrieval point of view, a document may be a once-for-all symposium on a subject, or it may be an annual of the 'Advances in . . .', ' Year's work in . . .', or ' Yearbook of . . .' type. The irrelevance of the provenance of a set of published conference or seminar proceedings is brought home by the fact that a professional or similar organisation may have an ad hoc conference in a topical subject area, or it may make the same area a focal point of its regular, annual or two-yearly conference. From the acquisitions point of view the ad hoc meeting's published proceedings may be viewed as a continuation, or it may be ordered individually, while the regular conference may be a serial on standing order. As we have suggested, such detail is of no interest to the user, as long as the item is in stock when he wants it. Therefore, we suggest that the most competent retrieval—the ultimate and basic objective of a library—is best achieved by ignoring such detail, and interfiling entries for all such works in one catalogue sequence.

Wherever, and however, records are kept it will still be necessary to be able to cite an article, both accurately and as concisely as possible. Issues of most periodicals include such information as: (a) full title, plus issuing body where relevant; (b) volume number; (c) issue number; and (d) date of issue. Preceding this information, for a particular article, one needs author(s) and title of article. Following the details of the journal itself is needed a statement of the inclusive page numbers of the article in the relevant issue. We suggest that AACR practice be followed in cases of multiple or diffuse authorship for the periodical itself and for individual articles. Concerning the latter, some periodical articles suffer from diffuse authorship—many authors with apparently no one predominating as to principle contribution or typographical presentation—as do many reports.

A feasible form used by many librarians is that demonstrated by the following:

PAUTZSCH, Richard O. 'The year's work in cataloguing—1969': *Library resources and technical services* 14 (2), Spring 1970, 174-188. If such a form could be accepted there would be no need to include words like 'volume' 'number' and 'pages'. The italicising of the periodical's title could be omitted in lists of citations, as its main purpose is to make a title stand out as such when incorporated into narrative text. ('Citation and codification' of serial titles as such is dealt with on p 279-284.)

A related matter to some extent may be whether or not a serial is given monographic treatment in the catalogue or whether it is given an 'open' entry—implying continuity of receipt. It may be decided to treat annuals and special issues of periodicals as monographic works, including also subject entries as they apply to the particular issue alone, since it may deal with a component, or more specialised aspect, of the broader subject, which is the nearest we could probably get to the run of the serial as a whole. A further possibility of value to the retrievalist librarian, as differentiated from the bibliographic librarian, is the subject analysis of the papers or other individual contributions in such works. At this point, we may remind the reader again that in some cases it is difficult, from the bibliographic point of view, to differentiate between a monographic work, revised editions of which are issued occasionally, and the similar-seeming work which, almost by accident, happens to be a serial. Examples at various stages include: (British) *Who's who*, a regular annual; *Who's who in Australia*, a publication which we may expect to continue indefinitely but which strictly speaking is irregular; *Who was who*, a regular but ten-yearly publication; and, say, *Who's who in librarianship,* later issued as *Who's who in librarianship and information science.* Examples like these point up the near impossibility of treating some works as serials and others as monographic works, and the ridicule and confusion to which users of the library are liable, if such works are treated differently, to the point of dividing these works between ' general ' and serials catalogues.

MAIN ENTRY

On top of all the problems dealt with, the decision has to be made as to what is the author/title main entry. Such a decision is particularly important with serials because of: (a) the checklist which gives only one entry per item, not usually supported by added entries and/or references; and (b) the submission of entries for incorporation into union catalogues. The importance of the latter, particularly, should not need dwelling upon, especially since the union catalogue may be published, *ie* appear in multiple copies, for immediate and practical use by subscribers.

One very important cause for differences in form of entry is that associated with change of title of a serial. This can arise for various reasons. (a) There may be a change in title of work caused by a difference in the attitude or terminology of the subscribers (although the publication itself continues substantially as in the past). This can be exemplified in the change from *Library assistant* to *Assistant librarian.* A somewhat similar situation applied when the *Library world* became the *New library world,* when the periodical changed ownership and reappeared in a ' revamped ' form under a different editor. (b) There may be a change in title caused by a change in the coverage of the work (though possibly gradual), as shown by that from *Library science abstracts* to *Library and information science abstracts,* issued by the Library Association. (c) There may be a change caused by a splitting of a work into two or more separate works. An example of this phenomenon was the birth of the *Times higher education supplement* from the *Times educational supplement.* In fact the three works, *Times literary supplement, Times educational supplement* and now the *Times higher education supplement* are, strictly speaking, offshoots of the (London) *Times,* although each has reached the point of being regarded as a work in its own right. An older division is that of *Science abtsracts* into *Physics abstracts* and *Electrical and electronic abstracts,* the latter itself representing an expansion from *Electrical engineering abstracts.* (d) Finally is the case of one work being wholly absorbed by another. This seems to apply a lot to newspapers. So, the (British) *Daily sketch* became absorbed by the *Daily mail*. It was interesting to note, during the transition, the increase in the 'Mail' part of the mast head compared with the 'Sketch' part. A recent Australian example was the absorption of the *Sunday Australian* by the *Sunday telegraph*. It is worth remembering that many newspapers, whether national or local, incorporate in their titles newspapers which they have absorbed or amalgamated with; and that the earlier titles may be used in citations of articles or features of the past, and issued at the time under one of the original, and now subsidiary, titles.

There seems little point in making full added entries to cater for all or most of the types of title changes mentioned. References both ways should be sufficient. However, they should be explanatory in nature; merely '*see*' or '*see also*' do not usually give sufficient detail. So under *Library world* we may have some such construction as

For this work from 1971 *see* NEW library world

and under the (previous) entry for the Library Association *Subject index to periodicals,* we might have

For continuations of this work *see* BRITISH humanities index and BRITISH technology index.

A somewhat associated problem is that of a supplement or similar extension of a regular periodical, etc. Such works can for the most part be divided into two types: (a) those which are issued with, often in, the parent work, and in many instances with dependent titles; and (b) those which are issued separately, possibly at different frequencies, and which may have independent titles. However, there is an intermediate stage: (c) those which are issued with the parent work, but with an apparently independent title. An example of (a) was the AACOBS *supplement* issued with the *Australian library journal*. An example with a partly dependent title, but bound in the parent work, is the *School library journal* in the *Library journal*. This supplement, to add to its complexity, has two sets of pagination: its own, separately; and that of the parent work, *eg* the issue of 15 January 1972, v 97, no 2, consists of p 129-344. Of these *SLJ* takes up p 223-344, but with in addition its own pagination consisting of 2 unnumbered preliminaries and then p 1-120; *SLJ* numbering is at the top right of the page. *SLJ* has its own Index to advertisers for the 'School library journal section'. An example of (b) is the *LP record catalogue* issued as an offshoot of the *Gramophone,* and consolidating lists of records reviewed in it. A similar example is *Whitaker's cumulative book list,* which consolidates lists of new British books first appearing in the *Bookseller*. An example of (c) is *Liaison,* issued with, and now stapled into, the *Library Association record.*

There may be works with apparently dependent titles but which have assumed an independent existence of their own: the *Times* supplements have already been mentioned. These best belong to type (b). Irrespective of what is said below, we feel, probably in common with many librarians, that such works should be treated as wholly independent works, without need for references or added entries.

The cataloguing treatment of each of these categories will depend primarily on the type of library, hence clientele served, and the time available for what some practising cataloguers may regard as niceties.

Concerning works in category (a), a decision may be made by the retrieval staff as to whether such items are to be shelved or filed in a physically separate sequence. If this is the case, they warrant separate treatment in the catalogue, under their own titles, and even if the latter are 'dependent' in that they may include the word 'supplement' or similar. *See also* or explanatory references can be given from the parent work to the offspring work. There would be a note in the entries for the the offspring mentioning its connection with the parent. If the offspring is left in or with the parent, there should be a reference from the entry, usually title, from the offspring to the parent work's entries. The parent's entries would need notes explaining that it includes the offspring in its runs.

Category (b) warrants separate entry, with explanatory or simple *see also* references both ways. It should be noted that this category can, strictly, be different from such works as the *Times literary supplement,* because some at least of the actual contents of one work may be transferred and reassembled in the other work. Therefore, in a catalogue compiled on intellectual responsibility or content principles, some connection between the two should be shown. However, as in so many other cataloguing conditions, the pragmatist may maintain that those who need to know of such connections between works are told in their training or that they acquire the knowledge through experience.

Category (c), we suggest, can usually most conveniently be covered by leaving the supplementary work with the parent work physically, and merely including an explanatory or simple *see* reference in the catalogue:

eg LIAISON
see LIBRARY Association record

or LIAISON

This work is issued with the LIBRARY Association record, in the centre of each issue, and is bound with it; grey paper.

A complementary note is then needed at the main entry for the containing work:

eg under LIBRARY Association record

includes Liaison, bound with each issue.

We suggest that a somewhat similar once-for-all reference would reasonably adequately serve the *School library journal,* especially since the latter is integrally bound with, and forms a major part of, the issues of *Library journal* with which it is issued.

Despite these recommendations, we do not in general favour a generic or collective approach to serials which are connected with each other. In particular, as we have demonstrated with changed and 'divided' works, we favour the consecutive or 'several' approach emerging from the International Conference on Cataloguing Principles and as codified in AACR. We emphasise that a 'supplementary' work of a serial which is normally sought and used as an independent work should receive its own entry, irrespective of where it is actually shelved. MESH (MEdical Subject Headings) is usually the first issue of the year of *Index medicus,* yet it is used enough as a work in its own right to warrant separate entry, with notes or explantory references connecting it with the main work.

Indexes to serials, usually periodicals, consist of three types: (a) those to individual periodicals, issued by their publishers; (b) as (a), but issued independently; and (c) those to many different periodicals, issued by an independent organisation, *eg* a commercial or other publisher.

Category (a) calls for little comment. Such works are definitely dependent in intellectual purpose and usually in title and authorship. They would therefore be entered under the main work, and there is doubt about whether added entries are needed under their compilers, even if named. Category (b) would be entered under the main work, as being intellectually dependent, and almost certainly dependently titled. Occasionally the compilers would be sought enough to warrant an added entry, an outstanding example being Palmer's index to the *Times,* as already mentioned; however, 'if in doubt leave it out' would be our maxim here. Works in category (c) are still dependent intellectually, having no value other than in relation to the works analysed. However, even viewed as dependent works they would be highly diffuse in authorship. They would usually be entered under title, and we would recommend ' consecutive ' entry with explanatory references both ways for changes in titles, and mergings and splittings. It may be useful to give added entries for editors, if their names are prominent enough on title pages, and for publishers if they are likely to be used as approaches. No doubt an assiduous critic will now find an index best entered under its editor, such as that compiled by Frederick Poole, which later became established as the *Reader's guide*. In which case, we agree. Although ' Fortescue ' is an index to just one catalogue, or collection (BM), this of course is a parallel case.

A type of document associated with serials, but not yet dealt with, is the anthology or similar collection culled from a run of a newspaper or periodical. An example of the former is a selection of fourth leaders from the *Times*. Another is *Panorama 1842-1865*, edited by Leonard de Vries, and selected from the *Illustrated London news*. A third is a selection from the past features of Paul Jennings—*Oddly enough*—from the (London) *Observer*. Each of these examples demonstrates the variety of problems and of possible solutions as to choice of main entry. The first indicates entry under the parent work, since the personal authors of leaders or editorials in newspapers are not normally identified or associated with their products—not even *Times* fourth leaders, perhaps without justice as these contributions to humorous journalism are unique in their own way. The second type constitutes a collocation of contributions from a great variety of authors, but chosen for a particular purpose—in this case social history of the Victorian period of British history—as selected and presented by an editor. The indication here is towards main entry under editor, with appropriate added entries. The third type exemplifies a collection of humorous essays by a single named author which, we may dare to say, merely happen to have appeared in a particular journal. Choice of entry here appears to be on the side of the individual author concerned. In general, then, the main entry decision for selections from serials seems best indicated by the principle of intellectual responsibility, irrespective of the fact that the original type of document concerned happens to be a serial. Subject approach would be appropriate to such works as products in their own right.

Rather more generally encountered is the overall problem of conflict between: (a) title; (b) corporate author; and sometimes (c) personal editor, or even author as with the eighteenth century *Spectator*. Corporate author may involve, more specifically, names of government departments, and possibly names of commercial publishers. Individual codes, dealt with later, have varied in their emphasis on one or other aspect. (See also the later subsection on citation and codification of serials, p 279-284.) Some libraries' practices can be relevantly cited here, however, a tendency being towards purely title entry under first word, and ignoring either issuing body, or significance of words other than the first, and trying to ignore variations in first word of titles. A significant example of first word of title entry is the practice of the (British) National Lending Library for Science and Technology, whose Director literally boasts of not needing catalogues, in the conventional sense, let alone cataloguing rules. A past example from the NLL is its *Current serials received by the NLL*, 1967 (reprint 1969). In accordance with its 'rule-less' entry, all works are entered under first words, however unsought or generic these may be. A consequence is that some 400 entries are given under the word 'Proceedings . . .', from p 242 to p 249. Some entries are given in a structured form, *eg Proceedings—Australian Association of Neurologists;* others are in direct phrase form, *eg Proceedings of the Annual Micro-electronics Symposium.* In fact, it becomes difficult sometimes to see what subarrangement is used under the entry word, even allowing for the apparent (unguided) rule of — (dash) before continuing phrase, *eg Proceedings—Zoology Society UAR* comes before *Proceedings of the AEI Summer School in Electrical Engineering*. Further, it would appear that non-distinctive words, like 'of' and 'the', are ignored in arrangement — despite the choice of a non-distinctive word like 'proceedings' itself as an entry word—although the suppression of these words for arrangement purposes is not indicated typographically. The work appears to be computer-compiled and printed, and it is noteworthy that insignificant words can be suppressed for arrangement purposes while still not 'stopping' them in the actual printout. But it seems unfortunate that such words could not be given within parentheses, since computers are capable of this, as exemplified by the alphabetical subject index element of the catalogue of the Atomic Weapons Research Establishment, Aldermaston. Incidentally, it would be interesting to know how the NLL itself would catalogue (if it had a catalogue) its own *Current serials . . .;* its title page can be transcribed as: Department of Education and Science/

National Lending Library for Science and Technology/CURRENT SERIALS RECEIVED BY THE NLL . . .

In contrast with the NLL checklist, David Woodworth's *Guide to current British journals* (Library Association, 1970) uses a purely word by word arrangement, *eg* we find in order: (a) *Proceedings & transactions of the Croydon Natural History & Scientific Society;* (b) *Proceedings of the Bristol Naturalists' Society;* and (c) *Proceedings of the Cotteswold Naturalists' Field Club.* However, there are no great accumulations at the entry word 'Proceedings' since the list is arranged primarily by a classification scheme—UDC. On the other hand the alphabetical title index runs into the same problem as the NLL list. This suppresses what are apparently regarded as non-distinctive words, *eg* 'the', 'and', and 'of'—but again with no typographical indication. The notes at the beginning of the Index state that title page titles are followed; 'no inversions are employed' (p 246).

In contrast, as is shown in the later treatment of codes, it will be seen that a different principle is employed by some cataloguers, at least. Criteria which emerge are: (a) intellectual responsibility; and (b) soughtness, *ie* significance of various words in titles, both of which may conflict with that already exemplified, *ie* entry under first word of title.

The intellectual responsibility element may be invoked when, it is claimed, a serial represents the deliberations or pronouncements of the body in an official capacity, *eg* such business proceedings as an annual meeting of the body. Such a work may include rules of conduct, admission, etc relating to its members and a crystallisation of a body's attitude towards professional affairs, *eg* a library association or library board may make clear its stand over whether or not charges should be made for the loan of documents of various sorts to members of the public. The other extreme is when an organisation issues a journal (periodical, bulletin, etc) as a publisher, but does not necessarily agree with the views expressed in articles included in such a journal. These may possibly directly oppose the official policy of the body sponsoring the journal. This fact, possibly in conjunction with independence, or soughtness, of title of the journal, may result in the journal's being entered under first word of title. The title may include, or infer, the name of the sponsoring corporate body, *eg Library Association record*, or it may be independent, *eg* the Library Association of Australia's *Australian library journal,* a midway point being exemplified by the Association of Assistant Librarians' *Assistant librarian.*

On the other hand we have a title such as *North Western newsletter*, the journal of the North West Branch of the (UK) Library Association. We suggest that soughtness comes in here, and so there is a case for corporate entry. This, however, may well be rather cumbersome, we admit.

eg LIBRARY ASSOCIATION. *North West Branch*
North Western newsletter

On the other hand, the newsletter of the Western Australian Division of the Public Libraries Section of the Library Association of Australia would be catalogued as LIBRANTICS, simply because it has a distinctive title. We suggest that concessions like this to soughtness should receive consideration, even though logically they may be inconsistent. As we have suggested, both intellectual responsibility and soughtness should be taken into account, and reconciled, in choice of main entry. Whatever choice is made, in a full catalogue, references will be needed from the rejected form of entry. Perhaps we can confound the confusion even further by suggesting that the proceedings of the Northern Ireland Branch of the (UK) Library Association should be entered as NORTHERN Ireland libraries, even though on the face of it, this title starts with an orientation point, like the *North Western newsletter* mentioned above. The reason is that 'Northern Ireland' is an acknowledged name of an area while 'North Western (England)' is not. We admit that—taking another subject area—consistency can be stretched rather; *eg* we would have BRITISH medical journal, *ie* title entry; but we would have also IRISH MEDICAL ASSOCIATION. Journal, *ie* corporate author entry.

As will be gathered, we suggest that the fact that a corporate body issues a journal should not necessarily mean that the journal is, or is not, entered under title as main entry. The significance of the title, even though this is an artificial or accidental criterion, should reasonably be taken into account. Indeterminate titles, such as annual and similar reports, can feasibly receive corporate authorship on both intellectual responsibility and soughtness criteria. If there is a run of annual reports, some of which happen to have been given significant titles, we suggest nevertheless that consistent entry should be achieved, through corporate authorship entry, and the (inserted if necessary) numbering of the reports.

Publisher, in particular as quasi-corporate author, can further assume an importance, especially as a sought tag even though not conventionally of intellectual responsibility. The (UK) Library Association was once freely acknowledged as an approach to the one-time *LA subject index to periodicals*. Even now, it is associated with the two offspring of this work, *British technology index* and *British humanities index*. Possibly a more significant and lasting example is that of H W Wilson, of New York. This firm issues many serial indexes to periodicals commonly known as 'Wilson's [etc] index'. It seems churlish not to allow such a name as an approach because it is (merely?) a commercial publisher. The US firm of Bowker is in a similar position with its annual bibliographies such as *Books in print*. Another example is the British firm of Whitaker. At least references may be considered, from the name of such publishers of bibliographic and similar works, to actual titles. The use of commercial publishers' names as approaches seems to be frowned upon by current official codes. This attitude (if indeed our feelings are well founded) can be unfortunate, as the catalogue should cater for all likely approach terms occurring to users. A parallel example is that AACR specifically excludes added entries for series whose titles start with the name of a commercial publisher. It seems incongruous that certain sponsors are denied entry in the catalogue because they happen to be avowedly commercial. Yet such a work as *Science abstracts* may receive an added entry (or reference, depending on the structure of the catalogue) for the Institution of Electrical Engineers—or, say, the American Physical Society as one of several collaborating (non-commercial) organisations.

Governments are another approach to some serials, and increasingly perhaps as more socialisation of, or at least government intervention in, research and information services takes place as part of the necessary coordination and focusing of such services in the interests of economy and rapid productivity. As one example, we have the *London gazette*, issued by the British Government and published by HMSO. It is just possible that an occasional research worker may be interested in all official serials sponsored by a government, especially since they are likely to be under the control of a government, and may well be considered as purveying pronouncements of official government policy. A more frequently-cited example may be *Hansard*, in Britain or Australia. We acknowledge that a research worker may be expected to think of such a publication from his own knowledge, and if a library's staff knows this is the case with *all* its users, it is justified in not making added entries (or references) for an approach under name of government. On the other hand, we are repeatedly reminded of occasions when tyro researchers do not know of all likely sources: perhaps some librarians assume that users of libraries have their own knowledge of sources, but without factual foundation. On the other hand, it may claim that the state acts merely as publisher, *eg* HMSO publishes the *London gazette*. However, another example, the *Employment and productivity gazette*, as it is now called, previously existed for some fifty years as the *Ministry of Labour gazette*, and there is therefore a case for thinking of it still as being sought under the name of a government department. We are not pleading for what might transpire to be very cumbersome indirect corporate authorship main entry, especially since this might result, in libraries shelving periodicals by main entry heading, in a great pile up of works under the name of a country according to current codes. But we do suggest that added entries or references should be given in some form. These could take the form of separate checklists, so that such information can be conveniently available to users needing it without bulking the main catalogue itself. Very relevant here is the availability of catalogue substitutes.

Codes

BM

What we now call serials are dealt with in this code's Rules 16 and 17. R 16 is headed 'Publications of societies', and R 17 'Special headings for certain classes of books'. Both rules cater also for monographic works where relevant under the headings given, *eg* R 17 (a) deals with the Bible; while, as is evident, R 16 approaches some serials through their being issued by certain corporate authors. This slightly piecemeal approach contrasts with, say, AACR (dealt with later) which has a special rule, R 6, for 'Serials'. Interestingly, though, to some extent BM intuitively brings conditions and types of authorship in, while AACR, avowedly a 'conditions' code, seems content to deal with serials as a 'case' or category of document. This point is expanded on in the subsection dealing with AACR.

R 16 caters for official reports, proceedings, bulletins, periodicals, lists of members, 'and any other works of which a society may be regarded as the author (*eg* official histories or records of the society)'. All of these are entered under the society, *ie* they receive corporate author entry, and not, say, title entry or form entry as periodicals where applicable. The tendency towards corporate entry is reinforced by the explicit statement that, in effect, most works of which a 'learned body' is merely the publisher are entered under the organisation. At this point, a reminder may be necessary that such bodies are usually entered under place: town in the case of most, and country in the case of those of a 'definitely national character' (R 5). However, an organisation called the Proportional Representation Society apparently is not of a national character, since it is entered under London in R 16. Further, this code's classificatory tendency in parts results in the following example:

LONDON—III *Proportional Representation Society.*
Representation. The journal of the Proportional Representation Society.

A further factor contributing towards possible corporate authorship is the application of BM's tendency towards title page cataloguing. Thus a sponsoring society may get the main entry if 'its name is given special prominence on the title page . . .'.

It may further be necessary to remind the reader that international organisations receive direct entry under their names. So serials by, say, the League of Nations or the International Musical Society, or even by Freemasons, Franciscans, or Wesleyan Methodists (R 5) would receive a form of direct corporate authorship entry, and not indirect entry via any place in or from which such an organisation may operate.

Serials, among other publications, emanating from international congresses and conferences receive indirect entry via the form heading CONGRESSES followed by the name of the congress or conference. Those emanating from other congresses and conferences usually receive indirect entry via place, either country or town—the differentiation is not very clear—followed by the name of the congress or conference. An exception, which is almost not an exception in the event, is that of the so-called 'definite' organisation, entered according to the rules for corporate entry of non-government organisations. So a British nationwide organisation receives the entry word ENGLAND for its conferences, etc.

R 17 (c) deals with reviews, magazines, newspapers, journals, gazettes, annuals and similar works. This, then, is the basic rule for serials. These receive form entry under PERIODICAL PUBLICATIONS, which omnibus heading is further subdivided by place of publication, and only after this comes the title of the work. There are two important exceptions, however: (a) corporate bodies' serials; and (b) almanacs and non-perpetual calendars (an interesting infiltration of a distinction between serial and non-serial works). The title of the work appears to be the earliest form, following the precedent for change of personal name, R 11, although the basic example in the code itself is of a periodical which has not changed its name, *ie*

PERIODICAL PUBLICATIONS—London. The Quarterly Review.

Other examples are of the exceptions already mentioned, which may receive as entry term either name of town or name of country, or, directly, name of issuing body as decided by the rules for corporate authorship already outlined. It is noteworthy that no periodical receives direct entry under title, at least according to the code, although one has received the impression that the BM itself may be tending towards relaxing this rule in its current day-to-day cataloguing. In the code, the most indirect example cited is

ENGLAND—ARMY—Infantry—*Royal Warwickshire Regiment.* The Antelope. A monthly journal of the Royal Warwickshire Regiment.

However, much as one respects both corporate authorship and collocation, surely it is difficult to justify such a tortuous maze through which the catalogue user must thread his way before eventually lighting upon the title of his desired work. We are not here criticising any BM cataloguing staff, past or present. The BM code was the first codification of cataloguing practice of any note in the English-speaking world. However, emphasis in retrieval has changed a great deal, and one may hope that the new British Library when it comes along will take note of such changes.

Form entry is used for almanacs and non-perpetual calendars, under the (Latin!) heading EPHEMERIDES. Poor Old Moore! There is also a form heading for DIRECTORIES, there being no distinction made between serial and non-serial categories. The latter is understandable; as we have said already, the user may understandably not be expected to think to himself 'is my quarry a serial or a monograph?'. However, as is evident, nowadays at least, a library user is more likely to be seeking a specific directory, under its title or possibly compiler, or the range of directories relating to a particular subject area or activity, and such omnibus headings are not likely to be helpful in either case, both being more specific than the very broad heading used.

In conclusion on BM in relation to serials, we cannot but state that it is not awfully helpful for either specific work requests or for generic searches according to criteria normally used nowadays. However, since the British Museum itself is such a valuable source of materials, BM rules must be known if full use is to be made of its bibliographic records pending computerisation according to AACR/MARC format, for headings at least.

CUTTER

As we might expect, CUTTER defined the term ' serial ', being possibly among the first to attempt to crystallise the characteristics of this type of work. He included in his definition the three essential characteristics: ' a publication issued in successive parts, usually at regular intervals, and continued indefinitely ' (p 22). This definition should rule out undue confusion with ' continuation ', but he then defines this as ' any part after the first of a publication issued in parts at different times, *whether a serial* [our italics], an irregular publication, or a book ' (p 18). This definition seems to be broader than his ' serial ' then. However, the rule for cataloguing continuations (R 16) infers that such a work is what AACR would call a dependent work, *eg* similar to an index to an existing publication. We feel therefore that we need not pursue ' continuations ' in the CUTTER sense in the present context. CUTTER defines ' periodical ' as ' a work issued at intervals which are usually regular; it is generally written by many contributors ' (p 21). A much more detailed definition appears at R 133 Periodicals, where we are warned not to ' confound periodicals with serials ' (p 59), though in fact the enlarged definition does, we suggest, overlap largely with ' serial ' as defined in CUTTER p 22. We recommend the detailed discussion, with examples, on p 59 for reading by students wishing to investigate the topic further. We agree with CUTTER of course in his differentiation between, say, *Encyclopaedia Britannica* and a normal periodical publication. However, in pursuance of his criterion that a periodical is [only] *generally* (our italics) written by many contributors, we do not see that, say, *Brownson's quarterly review* does not therefore qualify. CUTTER seems to feel that such a work should be excluded because it does not conveniently fit his ruling for title entry. This is an interesting case of working back from the emergent criteria of a work, resulting in an assumption that the type of work must necessarily be of diffuse authorship, and then having to back down in the face of a small handful of isolated examples. CUTTER's tentative allowance that a periodical by one author may be entered as though a monograph, if followed, is not very helpful in bibliographic control, as in an acquisitions department. What CUTTER seems unable to acknowledge is that a publication which is technically a serial, and in particular a periodical, can be a work of single authorship. Such examples have existed in fact for a long time, as is shown by the eighteenth-century *Spectator* by authors such as Joseph Addison and Richard Steele.

R 133 is the main rule for entry of periodicals. It states simply that periodicals are to be treated as anonymous and entered under the first word, not an article or serial number. Almanacs and other annuals receive the same treatment. CUTTER does not specifically include multi-annual works, but it would appear reasonable, from the definition given, to treat these similarly: we cannot imagine CUTTER differentiating between say, the *Year's work in librarianship* and *Five years' work in librarianship*. Similarly, too, it seems likely that *British librarianship and information science 1966-1970*, edited by H A Whatley, would go under title and not editor, especially since, in another context, the code says that a reference should be made from the editor when the periodical is commonly called by his name, *ie* even in such cases, title entry is prescribed.

CUTTER, then, demonstrates a marked contrast from BM, by definitely preferring not only title entry, but first word of title. BM uses the latter only as a last resort for anonymous works, while, as we have seen, direct title entry does not even get into the race for periodicals. In this respect CUTTER sets a precedent which all later English-language codes have followed to some extent.

A substantial variation is given for periodicals (and serials in CUTTER's terminology) issued by 'societies', which are entered under the societies (R 60), where it states that 'Societies are authors of their journals, memoirs, proceedings, transactions, and other publications'. It is not apposite in this context to embark on the treatment of corporate authors in CUTTER, but we would remind the reader that the code tends to prefer, according to our interpretation, colloquial and direct entry rather than official and indirect entry, so the Bodleian Library is entered as such, and not via Oxford University, and certainly not University of Oxford.

In addition to title or author entry, periodicals receive a form entry, either all under PERIODICALS or according to language, as ENGLISH PERIODICALS, FRENCH PERIODICALS, *etc* (R 192). Almanacs too receive form entry under ALMANACS, also subject entry as apposite (R 176). Extracts from periodicals apparently receive entry under title of periodical only if the title of the periodical is given in the title of the work. Examples show inverted headings such as PUNCH, A BOWL OF (R 134). The inference seems to be that other works are entered under their own titles, as anonymous works; a reference is prescribed from the periodical. (It must be remembered that CUTTER commonly uses references where today an added entry would be given, as the code originated under the assumption of a conventionally printed catalogue.) This apparent inference may seem in part to contradict R 102 which asserts that periodicals are best known by their titles. However, this attitude is further contradicted by an additional note to R 134 inferring that a single author's work republished from a periodical goes under the author, with not even a reference from the periodical itself.

Periodical directories are entered under first word of title, unlike non-periodical directories which go under editor. This ruling may be inconvenient for those users who could not care less if a directory is technically a serial or a monograph. However, it may please the librarian if his chief interest in document records is bibliographic control.

True to form, dear old CUTTER could not make up his mind dogmatically over change of title. R 133 gives a choice between original title, mentioned first and possibly therefore preferred, and what we now call consecutive entry with explanatory references under all headings. The first may have been inspired by the fact that the code was compiled for a printed catalogue, which makes recataloguing difficult; we might note that latest title is not considered, this obviously being the most difficult in a conventionally printed catalogue.

AA 1908

This code usefully gives definitions of 'serial' and 'periodical'. Generally, these definitions are still acceptable in that 'serial' is taken to include 'periodical'. However, newspapers are not mentioned under 'serial' and are specifically excluded—justifiably—under 'periodical'; the term is not defined in its own right. Yet, the rule for cataloguing newspapers is grouped with the rules for other serials and it seems reasonable to assume that they therefore belong to serials in the emergent attitude of the code. A further point worth noting is that journals of societies are also excluded from ' periodical ' and yet are not cited under ' serial ' along with ' memoirs, proceedings, and transactions of societies '. Nevertheless, ' a regular periodical issued by a society or an institution ' is dealt with under the general rule for periodicals. There may be some nice distinction between ' journal ' and ' periodical ' which has escaped us.

The basic rule for Periodicals is R 121, which covers both heading and a brief outline of essential description detail. (It will be remembered that this code covers both headings and description.) The basic decision for heading is first word of earliest title not an article, with what are called ' brief entries ' under later forms. If the brief entries include notes of changes of title and holdings the earliest title entry need not be inconvenient to the user, but it might cause extra work for cataloguers compared with consecutive entry. Added entries are required for editors. Analytical entries are required for monograph supplements: it seems to be assumed, then, that these go under the parent work, with which we do not necessarily agree, as can be inferred from our preliminary comments on serials. Normally corporate bodies' periodicals also go under title, especially if this is distinctive. Exceptions are: (a) when the work is issued at long intervals, and (b) when the work consists only of transactions, etc of the organisation, in which cases corporate entry is prescribed. We do not agree with (a), since an infrequent work can still have a distinctive title. The critical point emerging seems generally, however, to revolve around distinctiveness of title, with which we agree.

Noteworthily, we have in this rule one of the few American exceptions in the code, preference being for latest title when there has been a change. We suspect that the American exception arose because of the likelihood of a later title becoming better known, judged retrospectively from ALA 1949. As with the British rule, brief entries are usually prescribed for other titles, though references are regarded as sufficient for slight changes. This latter seems sensible.

Even more noteworthy is a footnote which foreshadows consecutive entry, for a ' continuation ' with new numbering, with notes referring to earlier and later entries. (We assume that ' continuation ' here does not carry the modern interpretation of, say, a continuous series of monographic-type works with no envisaged conclusion.)

There follows a useful account of LC practice, mainly dealing with a degree of descriptive detail which most librarians would regard as necessary, at least for stock record purposes. LC, following—or more likely leading—the ALA, has main entry under latest title.

R 122 deals with extracts from periodicals. Such works go under the parent title if it is given in the title of the work in hand, with relevant added entries. If the periodical is not named, entry is under collector, or title if there is no author-equivalent given. We certainly agree with the inference that collected contributions by a single author go under that author. Examples given in support of R 122 seem to indicate, in general, preference for title of collection, while we tend to prefer, in certain cases at least, entry under title of parent periodical. This topic is exemplified in detail under AACR.

R 123 deals with almanacs, year-books, etc, which go under title. No quarrel here, as long as we accept the case-orientation of the code.

R 124 advises that newspapers, like periodicals, are entered under first word of title not an article. Presumably earliest form applies (following the precedent of R 121), so that the newspaper commonly known now as the *Yorkshire post* would be entered as *Leeds intelligencer*. Variant editions such as Sunday or evening papers are entered consecutively with connecting added entries or references, with which we agree. The examples show rather differing titles, such as the *Evening times* as compared with the *Times, Washington.*

The final relevant rule in this code is that for Directories (R 125). Here, we feel that an unnecessary distinction is made between periodically issued directories—usually title entry, and non-periodically issued directories—under compiler if named on title page, otherwise under title. We have already dealt with this problem, and we suggest that it is confusing for the user to distinguish academically between 'serial' and 'non-serial' for such works, especially since, at first publication, it may not be obvious whether a work is going to be technically a serial or a non-serial. A case which comes to mind here is Richard Slessor's *History: a guide to first degree courses in United Kingdom universities* (Careers Research and Advisory Centre, 1966), a monograph-looking work, but which was intended to be revised annually.

ALA 1949

As we know, this code, dealing with headings, is complemented by LCRDC. Rather interestingly, it starts off, in its treatment of serials, as more of a conditions code than AACR 1967, which has a specific rule for serials as a case. R 5 Collections and serials embraces ' material in which the responsibility for the intellectual content is so divided that no one of the contributors can be considered the chief author '. Of the many solutions possible, title entry is preferred, but only when ' it is distinctive or when it is the least variable element . . .'. *Pace* AACR and Lubetzky (and under pressure from various thoughtful students!) we cannot help admitting the pragmatic commonsense of such an answer.

Despite its apparent conditions-based introduction, ALA quickly lapses into case-type categories of work, of which such examples as Festschriften and encyclopaedias and dictionaries may not detain us except to note their somewhat common condition with serials. The main port of call is R 5C Periodicals and newspapers. The former is directly defined in the Glossary, while the latter is indirectly covered by a note at the same point. The basic rule is to enter under the latest title, with references from others. Although not specified as such, and as LCRDC infers, a better known title other than the latest may take precedence. An interesting and useful rider is that a publication with new numbering is regarded and treated as a new work—a prefiguration of consecutive entry. Title entry extends to periodicals issued by corporate bodies. Proceedings of corporate bodies are not mentioned here but under R 71; these receive corporate entry since there is no mention of what happens if they are given distinctive titles.

Added entries for editors, important index compilers and relevant corporate bodies are prescribed. Most of the examples of added entries seem justified, according to conventional code practice. There are further sub-rules which differentiate rather finickily between titles starting with the initials of corporate bodies and those of editors and publishers.

R 5C(2) is the main rule for newspapers and it largely follows that for periodicals, but with provision for references from ' catch-titles '. Each edition—Sunday, evening, morning, etc—receives independent entry, which parallels and forecasts consecutive entry for change of title. Special numbers of newspapers may be entered separately, though usually under title of main work. An over-nice distinction is drawn between a ' special number ' and ' a single monograph issued as a supplement to a periodical ', which gets author entry (R 25C), although a series of monographs forming a supplement goes ' under the name of the periodical, unless the series has a distinctive title ' (R 25D). We are reminded of R 25C-D under R 5, but out of place, since the reminder is separated from the relevant rules by an instruction to add places of publication to titles where necessary.

R 5C(4) deals with collections of extracts by various authors. We agree in general with the solution of entry under parent title, and further with the decision to enter extracts from a periodical by one author under the author. We do not necessarily concur with the alleged lack of need for an added entry under a periodical contrasted with the alleged need for one under a newspaper.

R 5D needlessly deals separately with cases like almanacs and year-books since the basic rule has already given title entry. Because of the case orientation of the code, change of title must be covered by precedent with periodicals. The same applies to 'a directory published serially' (R 5E). However, nonserial directories go under compiler if mentioned on the title page. Elsewhere we have commented upon the unhelpfulness of distinguishing between serial and nonserial directories. Case study is manifested in distinguishing between telephone directories issued by various personal compilers and those issued by corporate bodies (R 5F3-4): the fact that such works are telephone directories is immaterial. R 5F then goes on to deal with series, and so is not relevant to our present study; however, it could overlap with our interpretation of 'continuation'.

Serials are also dealt with indirectly under R 27 Indexes, in subsections C, D and F. Indexes to individual serials go under title of serial in the form The CLASSICAL journal. (*Indexes*). The examples conflict in form with those in LCRDC R 7:11, which has a page of examples in tabular form, contrasting with the narrative transcribed form of ALA. R 27 in general subscribes to a most-sought solution for entry, whether title or author, which we support.

LCRDC

A special chapter is devoted to Serials, along with one each on Maps, Music, Facsimiles, and Incunabula—a choice which incidentally helps to vindicate our choice of special materials for this book.

The first paragraph of the relevant chapter, 7, includes a useful summary of the types of bibliographic data needed in relation to serials, and as already dealt with earlier in this chapter. However, the second and third paragraphs seem to confuse the basic terms 'serial', 'series', and 'monograph' (p 51). For example, we have the statement 'Whether a serial is monographic (*ie* a series) or not does not affect its cataloguing . . .'. We need not dwell again upon terminology, as this was touched upon on p 243. It will be gathered that we do not agree with this code's interpretation of these terms and that of 'continuation'.

The outline of detail given in a serials entry, as compared with that on a monograph, may be worth consideration (p 51-52). The attitude towards holdings of a library may be regarded as ambivalent, as the code does not seem to recommend how much detail is to be given on this vital topic. In some cases we may have full information; in others, in effect, we are referred to staff-only records. How to record holdings is dealt with in more detail later in the code.

Although the code does not set out to prescribe rules for choice of heading, the inference from R 7:3 is that latest title should normally receive preference. But exceptions are allowed for earlier forms which virtually resolve the whole rule into 'best known, but latest title in case of doubt'.

Sensibly, minor variations in titles from issue to issue may be disregarded in recording the title (R 7:4). We may also omit ordinal numerals, *eg Annual report* becomes *Report;* but no immediate explanation is forthcoming that this format presumably enables a run of such a work to receive just one omnibus entry. We agree with this treatment when a library holds a complete, or near-complete, run. Details of holdings are given, usefully, immediately after title or sub-title, and before less-frequently needed data such as Imprint and Collation. More than enough information on the two latter components is catered for. The occasional example of pedantry occurs, as when both forms for a changed place name are to be given, in the form Oslo (Christiania). Notes warrant some detailed attention from librarians who wish to exercise complete bibliographic control and efficient, useful identification, as differentiated from those records which set out to be just a check list.

The code's treatment of supplements (R 7:9), special numbers (R 7:10), and indexes (R 7:11) corresponds very approximately with our own earlier recommendations. However, we do not necessarily agree that indexes to individual volumes should not be recorded. Also, noteworthily, the code does not deal with indexes to many, diverse serials such as those issued by the Wilson Company. The code finally deals with 'bound withs' and analytical entries. The former is self-evident, and in any case may not need to be invoked often in many libraries. The latter deals mainly with runs which are part of other runs, and not directly with the entry of individual articles. They may be covered by either notes or actual analyticals depending on whether titles are 'sufficiently important', a vague but valid criterion.

AACR

This code deals with both heading and description for normal printed serials; in addition it covers non-printed materials where relevant, *eg* phonorecords (R 252G).

The basic rule for entry is an unashamed example of a case. The British text includes also all monographic series, assuming apparently main entry, because it further mentions series added entries. This can well cause confusion, since we would normally expect to give monographic works in series individual entry. The North American text clearly extends the rules only to added entries for series, so it is less likely to cause confusion.

The British and North American texts diverge in emphasis over entry. The British text has a basic rule for entry under title (R 6A). Exceptions are: (a) when a serial is 'issued by or under the authority of a corporate body', other than a commercial publisher, and when the body is named in the title, in full or in an abbreviated form; or when the title consists of a generic term or phrase needing the body's name for identification purposes (R 6B); and (b) when in effect the rules for personal authorship could be applied. The North American text assumes a negative attitude towards title entry, allowing entry under title only when not issued by a corporate body or not of personal authorship (R 6A). If in doubt over conflict between corporate and title entry, corporate is preferred (R 6B2). Both texts could feasibly be interpreted to result usually in consistent decisions; perhaps too much has been made in some quarters of their differences. Where there is any doubt we prefer the British emphasis. However, the North American text is clearer and more concisely expressed than the British, although we do not favour the enumeration of certain specific cases, *eg* biographical dictionary, in R 6B1, apparently excluding cases not cited. The simple use of 'for example' or 'etc.' could have mitigated this situation, even though the basic principle is still open to question in these conditions-oriented days.

For change of title, or author where given the entry decision, consecutive entry is recommended. This is well known by now and needs no comment except for pleased approval. However, the code does not emphasise the need for explanatory references in all directions. Admittedly Chapter 5 References is there to be invoked wherever needed throughout the whole code. However, some other rules obviously calling for references spell out the need through their examples, *eg* many of those under the rules for Headings for persons. We have to wait until we get to the Notes section of Description for serials before being given the faintest of reminders, by, say, 'successor to . . .', that we may possibly then infer that explanatory references could be useful. The matter could easily have been clarified by a short rule along the lines of the alternative rule for pseudonyms, R 42B (footnote 5, p 63), resulting in, say, '*see also previous title* . . .'.

Further treatment of serials emerges from the conditions rules for related works, R 19, where special numbers of serials, collections of extracts from serials, and works produced by editorial staffs of serials are given as cases exemplifying the condition. Any of the sections of this extensive rule can be applied to serials, and the desired result of course is that serials' related works receive consistent treatment with other related works, but within the case-based rules for original entry detailed above. In brief, related works with dependent titles usually go under the original heading (R 19A), while 'other related works', in effect those with independent titles, receive their own main entry (R 19B). Usually, added entries are prescribed for the rejected heading. As it happens, there are no true serials in the examples for dependent titles, although, say, indexes to single periodicals are paralleled by the example of an index to a monographic work which was compiled by writers other than the original author. So Procktor's index to the *Engineer* would go under the latter. But we are reminded to refer to R 167B10 and R 167B12, dealing with Description of serials. Under R 19A we are not reminded of the need for added entries in certain cases, although we are in R 19B. R 33 Added entries would have to be invoked.

Several examples under R 19B crystallise the treatment of 'other related works' of serials. *Cumulative book index*, a serial supplementing the monographic *United States catalog*, receives its own main entry. A special issue with its own editor, of the *Studio*, receives entry under the editor of the special issue. A special issue with no stated editor, of the *Times*, receives main entry under its own (distinctive) title. A supplement with its own author, of the *Bulletin of the National Association of Watch and Clock Collectors*, receives main entry the author. A collection of excerpts from various issues of the *Times literary supplement* goes under its own (distinctive) title. A collection of essays edited by a named writer, from the *Atlantic monthly*, goes under the editor. A work by a personal author and the editors of *Life* (named in that order) goes under the author. Finally, a work by the editors of *Life* and a personal author (named in that order) goes under *Life*. In all cases other approaches are covered by added entries, except that in the penultimate example given above, in which entry goes under author of the work, we are not reminded to make an added entry under the title of the work itself.

It can be seen that serials are well covered by R 19B and its examples. Bearing in mind the many inconclusive arguments possible over choice of main entry—and even whether in these days the concept of main and added entries is still valid—we agree with the solutions given to the cases exemplified. Nevertheless, the student should turn to the code, note the examples, and come to his own conclusions. It may need emphasis that in these examples the code steers an even course between the Scylla and Charybdis of intellectual responsibility and title-page/soughtness cataloguing.

Chapter 7 Serials is contained in part II Description of the code and not in part III Non-book materials which covers both entry and description for special materials as far as they need additional treatment to that in parts I and II. Therefore, entry is not recapitulated in Ch 7.

The definition and categories of documents treated as serials are expanded upon and taken to include 'works published frequently or regularly in new editions (such as guide books, who's whos) of which the library holds several parts . . .' (British text, p 183). We applaud this extension of the meaning of the term. It seems to help bring together the British and North American texts (see our previous comments on the North American R 6). More importantly, it gives positive guidance in some of the problems which we outlined in the earlier part of this chapter. However, it cannot solve the basic problem of where to start searching if a library maintains separate catalogues of serials in relation to monographic works. Despite the intention of AACR and more recent advocacies of the integrated catalogue, quite a few libraries do this, as we have already stated, and this in a way is a reason for our including serials in this book, which culminates in a plea for the ultimate complete integration of all catalogue records of a library's stock.

Ch 7 also embraces monographic series which have been entered collectively, following the British text's R 6.

A useful summary of the aims of serial descriptive cataloguing is given. The first of the three aims is to describe a whole published set of a serial. Hence AACR sets out to deal with a complete bibliographic unit, irrespective of the library's holdings. It here serves a directly bibliographic purpose which may not necessarily have immediate value in a library, and so may not be strictly adhered to: for if interpreted literally the code would have a library identify and record, say, special issues and supplements as well as earlier or later runs under various titles which the library does not hold. A corrective follows in the second aim, *ie* to record a library's holdings, which is usually what an enquirer wants to know in the first instance. If requirements are not in stock, it seems reasonable then to turn to catalogue substitutes. We would not expect a library's catalogue to record the existence of editions of monographic works not in stock. The third aim is doubtless dear to all cataloguers' hearts, *ie* to minimise alterations because of changes in the publication life of serials. This aim is reflected also in the practice of consecutive entry for changed titles, etc, as already demonstrated in R 6, and so might well have been embodied at that point.

The detailed rules will not be dealt with here, as some reflect earlier rules of the code in relation to monographic works, examples being sources of information for data and conditions under which an author's name may be omitted. However, we shall name the data to be given and the order in which it is to be given, because this information provides a useful approach to comment on the code which the student may wish to pursue.

R 161 Organization of the description names the following: Title; Subtitle if required; Volumes and dates of serial as published; Place of publication; Publisher; Date if required; Collation; Series statement if any. Only then follows library's holdings, embedded within whatever (other) notes are required. It is evident that we would prefer to name local holdings higher in the entry: almost every user of a library's catalogue surely needs information before, say, such physical description as normally given in Collation.

In a retrieval oriented catalogue we would probably omit several of the items named and rearrange some of the others. We would suggest the following, which would be suitable for most libraries' purposes without seeming to cause undue difficulty with MARC format: (a) Title; (b) Subtitle if needed to distinguish between identical or similar titles; (c) Holdings include volume designation and dating; (d) Notes of relevant changes of titles and similar variations such as splittings and mergings and special issues and supplements if striking, with indexes held; (e) Location in library. AACR itself at R 6 ensures that corporate bodies are named in the heading where needed. Title may not need to be repeated where it forms the heading for title-entry works. However, we would prefer at least a separate, short title heading in such cases to facilitate filing and finding. Data such as publisher and place of publication would be needed for works with identical titles and where there had been a significant change. In such instances they might come between (b) and (c), since they are needed for actual identification of a work. Full information in AACR/MARC detail would be retained in the staff records to facilitate inter-library cooperation, compilation of union catalogues, and participation in central catalogue services. The manipulation of the full data to produce the 'minicatalogue' required for retrieval purposes would be reasonably straightforward in a computer-manipulated and printed catalogue.

Having voiced fairly radical treatment of AACR's outline, we freely admit that the code itself allows for sensible economies, *eg* long titles may be abbreviated, and minor changes ignored, while useful but long sub-titles may be relegated to the Notes. We have already mentioned another example of a useful abbreviation in obviating repetition of some corporate bodies' names in the description when they form the heading. However, we would reverse the rule and make the omission the rule and not the exception. There seems little need to bring in whether or not the corporate name precedes or follows the generic title. Actually, even the AACR rule seems to be contradicted by one of its examples:

OXFORD BIBLIOGRAPHICAL SOCIETY.
Oxford Bibliographical Society proceedings and papers.

R 163 Volume designation and dating could be invoked for our purposes outlined above, *eg* for 'closing' entries when a serial ceases publication or stops being taken by a library. R 163C Definitions and limitations has particular relevance also, since it can help clarify exact holdings. The treatment of Imprint, R 164, is reasonably brief and to the point—if one needs such information. It is doubted whether much of the Collation, R 165, is needed in many libraries at all; as with monographic works, we suggest that the collation should be the first to go when simplified cataloguing is practised, which it is commonly. R 166 Series statement covers the type of information, relating to subseries, which naturally could go with notes concerning title-splitting and merging, as already dealt with. Some of the more relevant parts of Notes, R 167, have been covered. Other relevant and useful parts include frequency—the value of which can be imagined where relevant without further comment, names of editors—though highly selective such as when well known to the (knowledgeable) cataloguer, responsible body if it helps identify a serial or infer its quality, publisher changes if these are reflected in the character of the work, and indexes. It is perhaps worth noting that indexes are tabulated under ' INDEXES ' (as mentioned in relation to LCRDC), which conflicts with AACR's treatment of indexes of monographic works (R 155) which has a dash followed by the transcribed title of the index. Finally, we favour the need for analyticals, inferred by R 168, in all types of catalogue. By way of a Parthian comment, we feel bound to mention here the need also for subject analytical entries in many cases.

A very useful commentary on AACR's treatment of serials is that by G E Hamilton in the Seminar on the Anglo-American Cataloguing Rules (detailed in the bibliography). We have not used this article in the preparation of this work, as we have tried to preserve a fresh approach. Hence, the student may find the Seminar article a useful antidote to the present author's predilections and emphases.

Citation and codification

We have dealt with what might be called conventional methods of cataloguing titles, and where relevant, corporate authors of serials, and this attitude is pursued in our study of the various codes. We have also given a brief reminder on how to cite articles from serials.

This section is included because there has grown up a need both for abbreviating serial titles themselves, arising mainly from computer manipulation of such data, and, possibly also affected by computer needs, for standardising methods of citation in union catalogues. The latter is dealt with first here.

The main problems are succinctly given in the article by KOSTER (see Bibliography), who, as Editor of the *British union catalogue of periodicals* (BUCOP) can claim to have come across most likely difficulties. As to heading, KOSTER firmly recommends entry under first word of title, however generic, *ie* where AACR would enter under corporate body. 'The implication that AACR is unsatisfactory in this area, reflecting cataloguing procedures in the old national and university libraries [presumably in Britain], is evidenced by the fact that title entry is fairly common in most union catalogues.' We must point out that the older libraries and union catalogue editors are not necessarily correct, especially since the inference is that union catalogues follow the form used by the older libraries simply because that is the form used by these major contributors to the union catalogues. And that form may have evolved before modern principles were thought of. We have to consider use of published union catalogues in conjunction with catalogues compiled according to AACR. Of course, multiple approach could be used, whether in the form of repetition of entries or through references. The Library of the Western Australian Institute of Technology's serials record is based on two separate lists, a full one by first word of title, and a second one under corporate headings where relevant. Such a solution can be conveniently implemented using computer manipulation; the WAIT Library is using MASS (MARC-based Automated Serials System), which is MARC-compatible and therefore AACR-compatible. (Full bibliographic citation is given in the Bibliography under BIRMINGHAM . . .) This may be the best solution, as satisfying in turn both convention and modern principles. A copy of both lists could be made available for public use if expected (although in fact the final WAIT printout is in one sequence of authors and titles). This would usually be in research-oriented libraries, in which one might hope that users are reasonably well acquainted with the serials and relevant organisations in their fields of interest. While on the needs of approaches to serials, we could mention that a KWIC, or, preferably, a selectively enriched KWIC, system could be used for a reasonably adequate but computerised subject approach.

KOSTER suggests that, where corporate bodies' names feature in titles, these should be incorporated, following the first word entry. First would come name of subordinate body; this would be followed by name of parent organisation. This seems feasible if title entry is to be used, since it caters, we feel, with the way serials are often cited in ordinary speech. The method can also be computerised to cater for all types of corporate author approach, provided tags are established for both parent and subordinate bodies. In BUCOP's *New periodical titles* (*eg* the 1971 issue), there is an 'Index of sponsoring bodies'. Change of title is catered for by separate entries. However, it may be noted that LC's *New serial titles* (*eg* January 1972 issue) conforms to conventional corporate authorship practice where relevant.

The quantity and order of description also warrant attention, and we suggest that reference could be made to BUCOP as an example of one of the fullest forms of entry which is likely to be conveniently available to most readers. Detail in this example corresponds nearly enough to that recommended by AACR. However, as KOSTER infers, union catalogues rarely give such detail. A BUCOP example is reproduced here from KOSTER:

ENGINEERING PRODUCT DATA
ENG. PROD. DATA.
(HEYWOOD)
LONDON I, 1964-1965 . . .
SUBS: EM & D. PRODUCT DATA.
(Holdings)

We nourish a pipe dream of the time when comprehensive national and even international union catalogues are maintained as computer storage with random access for any reasonably conceivable approach. We are pleased that this hope is shared by a practitioner, and KOSTER rightly infers that, when this happens, libraries which have already computerised their serials stocks but using a bare minimum of data will be faced with the choice of not participating fully in the system or of overhauling all their records with the attendant inevitable and considerable inconvenience and expense. KOSTER suggests that the proposed Standard Bibliographic Description could be drawn upon, as follows:

1a: Title proper—1b: Sub-title. (standard serial title abbreviation)—
2a: Volume designation (Edition statement)—
3a: Place of publication—3b: Publisher (and/or Sponsoring body where not part of title). —3c: Year of publication.—(5c: Standard Serial Number),—7: Notes. (Library Code and holdings).

The parts within parentheses are insertions. Abbreviations for serial titles would follow part 2 of the British Standards Institution BSI 4148 when issued, the latter having been internationally agreed.

Mention of title abbreviation brings us to the second basic problem to be covered here, that of title abbreviation formulae or codes; relevant also is that of location codes in union catalogues (see also again p 248). Perhaps we may be allowed to make the, apparently naïve, statement that we regret the need for such codification, but practitioners and especially computer-users have found it to be as necessary as, say, the use of classification notation for shelf or file arrangement of documents.

Title codes could take, generally, two forms: (a) literal and mnemonic; or (b) numerical and arbitrary. An example of (a) has already been demonstrated in the sample BUCOP entry reproduced above, and another example may be found in the article, in relation to MEDLARS, by CHAREN (see Bibliography); while (b) is brought into the adapted SBD, also mentioned above, in the form of a Standard Serial Number (SSN) somewhat corresponding to Standard Book Numbers (SBN). This latter concept is explained in, *eg* HORNER, p 367-369 as far as it had been developed at the time. Since then the International Standard Book Number (ISBN) has been realised, and is now commonly used in Britain and the US; it is formed by prefixing a digit representing the country, bringing the number to ten digits.

The BUCOP literal example has an obvious expressive value, so that the user is likely to be able to recognise the actual title of the serial from the information given because it gives a stem for each word: ENG can feasibly be taken to represent 'Engineering' or, say, 'Engineers'. However, a far more abbreviated form has been evolved, with a standard total length of six letters. This is CODEN, dating from 1963 and now used by a number of publishers and libraries and covering some 115,000 titles by 1970. An example is given by WALL & WILSON (see Bibliography): JACS-AT. JACS represents *Journal of the American Chemical Society*. The A is a further identifying factor for when the preceding four initials could represent more than one title. The T is a check character, corresponding to the final digit in SBN's. Despite the brevity of the notation, it still has some literal mnemonic value, and regular library users may reach the stage of readily identifying CODEN meanings, especially since CODEN is used on many serials themselves and readers will get used to associating them with the accompanying titles. It is evident that CODEN ignores cataloguing principles manifested in standard catalogue codes, such as AACR, and thus makes a strict title approach more than ever necessary. Users may even get used to the fifth, identifying character in cases where the title itself consists of more than the allowed maximum representation of four words. On the other hand, it may be maintained that the representation of the title is so abbreviated as to make it meaningless to many users. We have not come across reports of any systematic and comprehensive studies establishing user reaction to the system. A further disadvantage of CODEN is that it does not use a notation which is wholly international, however well-known roman upper case may be in countries not using the roman alphabet. Here, the arguments usually raised in relation to classification notation can be applied, *eg* the contention that people in general remember the symbols and ordinal significance of arabic numerals more readily that those of letters.

This brings us to the chief rival of CODEN—the Standard Serial Number (SSN). The SSN concept did not evolve until 1968, some five years after CODEN, by which time CODEN was well on the way to acceptance, in some areas at least. Bearing in mind the present popularity of CODEN, efforts have already been made to establish a form of switch mechanism for converting CODEN to SSN. SSN is composed basically of eight digits, the first seven being the identifying number, and the eighth being a check digit. Because of the similarity of SSN with SBN, there is the possibility of confusion between the two, especially since at least one noteworthy publisher, HMSO, has taken to using SBN's on serials (WALL). However, this need not cause a serious problem, we suggest. Where there is a danger of confusing the two, a publisher or a library could prefix the SSN with some such symbol as S, which should not result in the resulting code's being difficult to manipulate by computer.

Factors other than cataloguing must be taken into account in deciding for either CODEN or SSN. These, together with summary, and very useful, lists of advantages and disadvantages of the two systems, are given by WALL. The latter article comes out in favour of CODEN. We are not convinced of this as yet, partly because SSN is similar to SBN in terms of both its structure and internationally recognised symbols. In conclusion on this topic we certainly do agree with WALL & WILSON that, whatever system is decided upon, it should be widely publicised. Just as SBN's are now used in MARC entries, and in fact constitute the chief arbitrary tag for search purposes, so should SSN's (or CODEN if decided upon) serve a similar purpose when our hope for national, and even international, integrated machine storage of bibliographic data for serials is achieved.

The question of citing holdings of local libraries in union catalogues is rather parallel to that of title citation. As already mentioned, either literal mnemonic symbols or arbitrary digits can be used. Our preference is that—whatever coding is decided upon—it should be expressive. The reason is that a supplicant library may well have to take into account geographical location of a 'holding' library, and an expressive notation can obviate a great deal of referring back to the, essential, key list which interprets the coding used. Literal mnemonics can be useful, since, as is evident, their meanings become increasingly obvious to the user, especially if a member of a library's staff who is engaged on regular checking. On the other hand, for internationally recorded holdings, there is something to be said for numerals with a systematic expression of location, from continents to countries, and then to states or counties as relevant. We are not pressing hard for any specific method, although we favour a system derived from UDC place notation, but we do suggest firmly that agreement should be reached over a uniform system to be used in all union catalogues which are published and which have a wide circulation.

Readings

Checklist of works cited in or relevant to this chapter. General works in the checklist with the first chapter of this book (p 28-29) also include information on the topics covered by this chapter. Full bibliographical citations are given in the consolidated Bibliography, p 304-312. A list of abbreviations is given on p 7. The titles of periodical articles are given within quotation marks.

AA 1908

AACR 1967

ALA 1949

BM

BIRMINGHAM LIBRARIES CO-OPERATIVE MECHANISATION PROJECT. MASS

CHAREN 'MEDLARS abbreviations for medical journal titles'

CUTTER

DAVINSON *The periodicals collection . . .*

DEWS, J D *The institutes of education union list of periodicals processing system*

FRIEDMAN *Cataloguing and classification in British university libraries*

GRENFELL *Periodicals and serials . . .*

KOSTER ' Standard serial citation . . .'

LCRDC

NLL review, January 1972 (Notes on NLL lists of serials)

OSBORN *Serial publications . . .*

PRUSSIAN instructions (PI)

QUIGG ' How to make a union catalogue '

ROTH ' Scientific serial lists '

SEAGER ' Order of entries ' (Of serials)

SEMINAR ON THE ANGLO-AMERICAN CATALOGUING RULES (1967) (Paper 6)

STEWART *A computerized serials record system . . .*

THOMPSON ' Rules for subject headings, periodicals subject index '

URQUHART ' The regional bureaux and the NLL '

WALL ' Codification of periodical titles . . .'

WHATMORE *News information: the organisation of press cuttings...*

CHAPTER SIX

The multi-media catalogue and the computer

A BASIC problem in special cataloguing, as already stated, is whether or not to incorporate entries for various special materials in a general catalogue of a library. This issue can be considered under three main headings: (a) the compilation of a separate catalogue for each individual form, whether each is book or nonbook; (b) the compilation of a special multi-media catalogue incorporating all nonbook materials; and (c) the compilation of a single catalogue to include entries for all materials in a library, whether book or nonbook.

A precedent is set by various agencies which issue single-medium lists and catalogues. Some of these agencies are firms and other organisations which deal with a specific medium, and so, of course, these examples cannot be said to advocate separation in retrieval systems in libraries. A well known example is the *British national film catalogue,* recording the stock of one organisation. However, we should mention that the Library of Congress, which receives all materials under copyright deposit, issues separate catalogues for such forms as films and filmstrips; and phonorecords; and in the past it issued one for maps and atlases. We should also mention that BNB issues a separate publication of scores and works about music in the *British catalogue of music,* even repeating the entries for works about music as compared with BNB itself, although classified according to the BCM's own scheme.

Notwithstanding, we recommend the principle of integrating, as far as possible, entries for all forms. The chief reason for this is that information enquiries do not necessarily cite a particular form, and even if they do they may not cite yet other relevant physical forms. This may happen because of ignorance on the part of the enquirer, who may be, say, book-oriented, and may not know of other forms. Current awareness services might include, under certain subject headings, not only bookform materials but any form of presentation of a subject. Such a facility would, we suggest, be of direct value mainly in teaching institutions, at all levels. As will come up again later, it would be vital to emphasise clearly the physical form, since the use of a document, by a teacher for example, would depend on the availability of suitable apparatus for playing, screening, etc.

A further factor in favour of integrated catalogues is the increasing use of various forms in conjunction with each other. This situation is no novelty. The fact of ' accompanying material ' has been long known and catered for in codes. A very common example is that of a recording, which will perhaps be on disc, with accompanying letterpress material, such as one of Chaucer's *Canterbury tales* together with a copy of the printed text. In the past, the accompanying material has usually been regarded as subsidiary, even though in fact it may have been necessary for the full exploitation of a document, *eg* a film strip intended for instructional purposes with accompanying teacher's lecture notes, or, to take a reverse example, a programmed text accompanied by slides or records. Contrary to current emphasis on the audio-visual ' kit ' as a new phenomenon, we suggest, then, that this form has been with us for a long time. However, a new situation may arise when, in certain cases, it is difficult to decide which is the predominant medium, *eg* as to whether a sound recording ' accompanies ' a text, or the text ' accompanies ' a sound recording. For this reason, as well as to ensure that all materials are exploited as fully as possible, we suggest that a so-called multi-media catalogue is needed. However, since accompanying material is often in textual form, it seems reasonable to reach the logical conclusion of the wholly integrated catalogue principle, and to represent ' the media ' and conventional textual material in the same catalogue. For similar reasons it is theoretically justifiable to include any ' special ' textual materials such as serials in the integrated catalogue. As we have said in the last chapter on Serials, it is often difficult for the librarian, let alone the average library user, to decide what is, and what is not, a serial. We suggest very firmly, then, that all the stock of a general library should be recorded in one integrated catalogue, with the usual author, title and subject approaches.

Nevertheless, there will still exist the need for a physical form approach, mainly, we feel, for the librarian's benefit for stock record and housekeeping purposes, but also in some cases for the immediate use of the library's clientele. The latter may happen, when, say, a teacher is making up a film or record programme for general use, or when a new piece of equipment has been acquired and the teacher particularly wishes to experiment with it. The librarian's need may arise from the need for a stock record for such purposes as stock-checking, statistics, accounting, and calling up of items not received. Strictly speaking, these last are not catalogue uses, the basic object of a catalogue being the exploitation of stock by users, whether directly or indirectly. However, as we know, much of the data for housekeeping purposes is the same as that used for exploitation.

Inevitably, with the use of a basic set of data for various purposes, there arises the concept of an integrated systems approach, with the use of a computer for selecting from a comprehensive store, and manipulating the data to specific ends. From the user's or librarian's housekeeping point of view, entries for documents in a particular form could be selected, manipulated and printed out in whatever order was required for the purpose. An essential need is to be able to list all materials in a particular form, *eg* filmstrip. In turn, this means that each physical form must not only be represented, as in standard, *eg* AACR, cataloguing practice, but also it must be a field on its own, and with a tag to facilitate its use as an access term.

Nowadays AACR is justifiably regarded as a working basis for much full bibliographic cataloguing, and its structure is usually assumed in MARC formats, whether for book or for nonbook materials. AACR does include provision for spelling out some physical forms as potential tags. Particular examples emerge in Ch 14 Phonorecords, which caters for an italicised qualifier following a uniform title, one such being:

> BACH, Johann Sebastian
> [Sonatas and partitas, violin, S.1001, G minor] *Phonodisc*

Phonodisc could reasonably be made a field, with its own tag. Similar provisions apply for other physical forms starting with the stem 'phono . . .', such as *phonotape* and *phonowire*. It should be possible to enable a search to be made on the stem 'phono' to facilitate retrieval of all sound recordings, whatever their physical form. Incidentally, in the example given above, the full stop (period) has been omitted at the end of the author heading, and following '*Phonodisc*', despite its being, inconsistently, included in the code. However, by accident, the code may have provided a means whereby nonbook, as differentiated from book, forms of material might be retrieved by computer, the full stop acting as a searching and retrieval device for most 'special' materials as opposed to conventional materials.

According to AACR, other special forms are not so conveniently indicated by a potential field attached to a uniform title. To take Ch 15 Pictures [etc] as an example, in some samples an indication of physical form of presentation is spelt out, while in others it is not:

eg PRINCE, George
The International Meridian Conference, Washington, 1884 . . . (*Photoprint by Prince*)

and LATROBE, Benjamin Harry
[Proposed arsenal at Pittsburgh. Rendering, elevations, plans] . . .

In the first example it might be feasible to ask a computer to search on an italicised term following the title, viz *Photoprint* . . . But in the second example, the physical form is incorporated into the uniform title, and, short of a word-by-word program, it is hard to see how an intelligent selective computer search could be made except by restructuring the heading and/or title.

A similar problem exists for music scores, which are not designated as such in headings or uniform titles, although in some instances the word 'score' occurs in the collation. Yet another problem occurs even when a potential field is suggested in AACR; this is when there is a possible difference of opinion over a term to be used. This situation is exemplified in Ch 12 Motion pictures and filmstrips, when the main text of the code recommends '*Motion picture*', yet a footnote states that '*Film*' may be preferred. This would not pose much of a problem for locally generated data, but it could cause some degree of difficulty at least if locally generated entries using the 'British English' term had to be merged with, say, LC generated entries, which naturally would use 'American English'.

Similar types of problem are manifested by the many other forms of document, when it comes to computerised manipulation and retrieval of selected forms, as well as of subjects. And, as we feel we can assume, computerisation is the only feasible hope of achieving a multiple-access approach to both information as such and special forms of presentation.

We wish to sum up, at this point, that not only a multi-media catalogue may be needed, but also that a generously multi-approach catalogue is needed. There should be approaches along the lines of a principle which we feel Cutter would have approved. Potentially, in one sequence, one could approach or trace information according to, not only author-type and title headings, but also subject headings and physical form headings; subject headings could consistently be subdivided according to form of presentation. As we have said, such a complex manipulation of data and approaches can be realised only through the use of the computer.

Some libraries are already computerising, or planning to computerise, their bibliographic data on special materials. In some cases, systems are being, or have been, introduced for certain individual forms, depending on local need, *eg* the Library of the Western Australian Institute of Technology has a multiple-approach computer-printed catalogue for slides. At the time of writing (1972) other media have not been planned for in this particular instance. Despite some academics' pipe dreams of an integrated systems approach, there is a lot to be said for experiment with a single medium. Problems relating to programming, computer storage, and access can be identified and solved comparatively inexpensively. However, we suggest that such achievements should be regarded as research and development projects rather than as ends in themselves. A most important aspect of such an experimental project is actual use of the resultant catalogue or index. In a comparatively 'closed' situation, as in the library of an educational institution, potential users of such a system can be canvassed and their comments recorded and analysed. Such a catalogue use study, if carefully planned and executed, could be extremely helpful as a pointer towards the potential exploitation of a comprehensive system.

When libraries reach the point of finally appreciating that so-called 'special' materials are not so special that they may be rejected as 'normal' stock, or if actually acquired hidden away and largely avoided, it should be possible for multi-library catalogue use studies to be made. From these could emerge an idea of what library clienteles really need in relation to special materials. Judging by one experiment, in Pearl River Public Library, New York (GELLER), when a multi-media catalogue—and even stock-integration—policy is implemented, the users readily respond to such facilities: 'Users do like to find related materials on a given subject on one place'. Admittedly, as the article says, 'one situation does not connote a trend'; but we suggest that this situation is at least a symptom of the, as yet, unrealised potential of once-'special' library materials.

Just as normal monographic materials are being recorded on centrally produced computer tapes, as it happens MARC tapes, so there is more and more talk of doing the same for special materials. Also, as is commonly known, there are central computer stores, regional, national, occasionally international, of bibliographic data relating to articles, reports, etc in certain subject fields. These can be searched on demand for specific subject requests. At the moment, MARC tapes for monographic materials are sold to interested libraries to use as they think best—or apparently, at present (1972), to be merely accumulated with a view to future use. Also, as one useful by-product, MARC tapes are used centrally as a basis for the computer output microfilm (COM) production of the 'micro-microform' *Books in English* by BNB. There is not as yet a convenient facility for libraries to draw upon a national, let alone an international, central computer store for only the data which they require, either for documents which they have in stock or for searches on demand from users. However, there is a proposal, and presumably a hope, for setting up such a central, national, store, in Britain, to be tapped on demand for certain special materials. The proposal is put forward in what we suggest could become a most important report issued with the authority of the (British) National Council for Educational Technology (GILBERT).

The Gilbert Report is confined in scope to audio-visual materials used in education. However, education and modern teaching techniques are probably the main stimulant to the increase in use and acceptance of at least the large audio-visual sector of special materials likely—or even unlikely—to be encountered by most librarians. Further, the report interprets 'education' in a broad sense, and some documents which might formally be dubbed 'recreational' are likely to be embraced by its proposals. This interpretation does not affect the variety of physical forms, but it could affect the size of any central store established, and this in turn could mean that any local library's stock of nonbook materials may stand a reasonable chance of being as well comprehended by the central store as, say, a general library's book stock might be covered by MARC tapes.

The physical forms contemplated are listed as follows (p 13-15):

Sound or audio recording

Gramophone record: a recording of sound on disc.

Sound or audio tape: a recording of sound on magnetic tape carried on an open reel.

Audio cassette or cartridge: a sound tape contained in a cassette or cartridge.

Visual images: still

Slide: a small unit of transparent material containing an image, mounted in rigid format, usually 2″ × 2″, and designed for use in a slide viewer or projector.

(*Stereoscopic slide*: slides, presented in pairs, designed to produce a three-dimensional effect when used with a stereoscopic viewer or projector.)

Filmstrip: a roll of film containing a succession of images designed to be viewed one at a time.

Transparency: a sheet, or combined set of sheets, of transparent material, carrying information, designed for use with an overhead projector.

Wallchart: a large sheet of information arranged in tabular or diagrammatic order, designed for public display.

Flipchart: an integrated graphic presentation on separate sheets hinged together in easel format.

Flash card: a card having words, numerals, or pictures, designed for rapid identification, with or without an integrated sound track.

Print: a picture with accompanying text which makes the print significant for study purposes.

Art Print: a printed reproduction of a work of art—*eg* painting, drawing, sculpture, etc.

Picture or Drawing: a two dimensional drawing, painting, portrait, photograph, or a print of any of these, produced on opaque backing.

Visual images: moving

Film: film, bearing a sequence of images which create the illusion of motion when projected, and carried on an open reel.

Film loop: an endless loop of motion picture film usually contained in a cassette.

Film cartridge: a length of motion picture film contained in a cartridge.

Videotape: magnetic or other tape, carrying a series of TV images recorded magnetically, electronically or holographically. (Any of these may bear an integral sound track.)

Visual images with sound

A recording of moving visual images may carry an integral sound track (*eg* Sound Film).

A set of slides, or a filmstrip, may be accompanied by an associated sound recording on a gramophone record or, more usually, tape (commonly referred to as Tape-Slide).

Programmed materials

Carried on transparent, opaque or magnetic substrates and designed for viewing directly or by projection, or for use with a computer; may have the physical form of a book.

Artefacts and Realia

Map: a flat representation of part or all of either the earth or the heavens.
Globe: a sphere with a representation or a map of the earth or of the heavens.
Chart: a sheet of geographic or other information arranged in tabular or diagrammatic order.
Relief model: a three-dimensional geographical map other than a globe.
Model: a three-dimensional representation of an object, either exact or to scale.
Diorama: a scene reproduced in three dimensions by placing objects, figures, etc in front of a representational background.
Realia: actual objects or specimens.

Microforms

(Microreproduction: a miniature reproduction of printed or other graphic matter which cannot be utilised without magnification.)
Microfiche: a microreproduction on a flat sheet of film.
Microfilm: a microreproduction on a roll of film.
Micro-opaque: a microreproduction on opaque material.
Aperture card: a card with an opening or openings within which microreproduction on film is mounted.

Combinations

Kit: a combination of items in two or more media designed to be used as a unit.
Game: a boxed set of materials designed for educational play.

It is envisaged that any records of documents would include commercial, 'semi-commercial' (from, say, professional bodies), and even some locally produced items. Incorporated—in fact the core of such a data base—would be entries from large national collections in Britain such as the National Film Archive and the British Institute of Recorded Sound.

We might note at this point that in 1972 a proposal was made from another source (CIG : BAKEWELL) that there should be a 'British national discography' along the lines of the *British catalogue of music* and of course BNB itself; if such a work were realised its contribution to the type of data base contemplated could be substantial. Also here we might recall that the Library of Congress has a potential which has progressed beyond this stage: its catalogue coverage already embraces audio-visual materials thanks to US legal deposit, which appears to be automatically comprehensive of all physical forms of documents. We hope that the new British Library when it emerges will have copyright coverage at least equal to that of the Library of Congress.

To return to the Gilbert Report, with its attempts at cumulating such data as is at present available in Britain, we have to appreciate that, at the moment, a large variety and types of records would have to be drawn upon to realise the hope of a comprehensive collection of bibliographic data on nonbook materials. It is anticipated that such information could be reconciled, and incorporated consistently into a central store, without the central cataloguers having to sight the actual documents. This situation may, at first sight, seem to be analogous to that of compiling union catalogues of, say, books, or serials. However, in such cases, it is usually expected, or at least hoped, that entries have been compiled by professional cataloguers and, at least to some extent, according to a standard recognised code. We feel that GILBERT possibly minimises the technical difficulties in such a process. However, we feel that such a project is possible, and that bibliographic niceties so dear to some—dare we say, conservative—cataloguers *must* give way to the immediate need of producing data of use to many libraries. To digress, but with a purpose, we might recall that some BM cataloguers seem to have wanted to delay indefinitely the photo-printed BM catalogue while they indulged their penchant for bibliographic perfection on the bibliographic information needed all over the world. We had the privilege of meeting Sir Frank Francis, then BM's director, in the early 1960's, and he commented that, in effect, he had had to get his cataloguers to eschew academic bibliographic niceties and to get on with producing a catalogue for real live *use*. Librarians must have in mind not colleague-cataloguers' academic criticism, but the ultimate use of their product in document and information retrieval. In short, if any minor errors emerge—hard luck. The main concern should be use of the data to enable documents to be identified and exploited by users of libraries all over the country or even the world. In sum, then, we support the layman's proposition of integrating data from whatever source so that it can be drawn upon in real live situations. It is better to have some—however inconsistent—sort of information about nonbook materials, and soon, than wait for the millennium when all material is catalogued perfectly down to the last punctuation mark. We do not apologise for this apparent tirade: there are still far too many cataloguers who derive more satisfaction from the use of a square bracket than from the knowledge that they are serving users' needs for information *today*, not in three months' time when they finally have finished their games and pass on their toys to a vague depersonalised public whom—through unfortunate library management—they never meet.

So, then, we keenly recommend the concept of the centrally accumulated data base hoped for in GILBERT, and we further hope that people can be found to do the accumulating, assimilating, and production for use of such information.

However, to realise such a hope, two needs must be borne in mind: (a) an overall organisation; and (b) a detailed organisation for the manipulation and output of bibliographic data according to the needs of requesting centres, assumed to be libraries which receive and formulate enquiries.

(a) is worked towards by a system as reproduced from GILBERT, p 50, figure 1 (see p 296 of this book). This includes four components: (a) the actual producers of documents; (b) central cataloguing agencies; (c) a computer store; and (d) printers for producing usable hard copy as required. It is technologically possible for (c) and (d) to be parts of the same apparatus: a lot depends on the physical type of product expected in reply to an enquiry, and the type of physical presentation acceptable by users. A single enquiry might be satisfied with a 'one-off' computer printout, but a resource centre's own complete catalogue may demand a more sophisticated physical presentation.

(a) is further enhanced by the system reproduced from GILBERT, p 52, figure 2 (see p 297 of this book). The essential advances of this system on the previous diagram is that it introduces the real users of nonbook materials, and it shows how they are integrated into an information retrieval system ranging from producers, via a central store and enquiry-coordinating service, through catalogue agencies, and back to enquirers.

A major component of this system is the Central Bibliographic Service, linking libraries and similar information service centres with

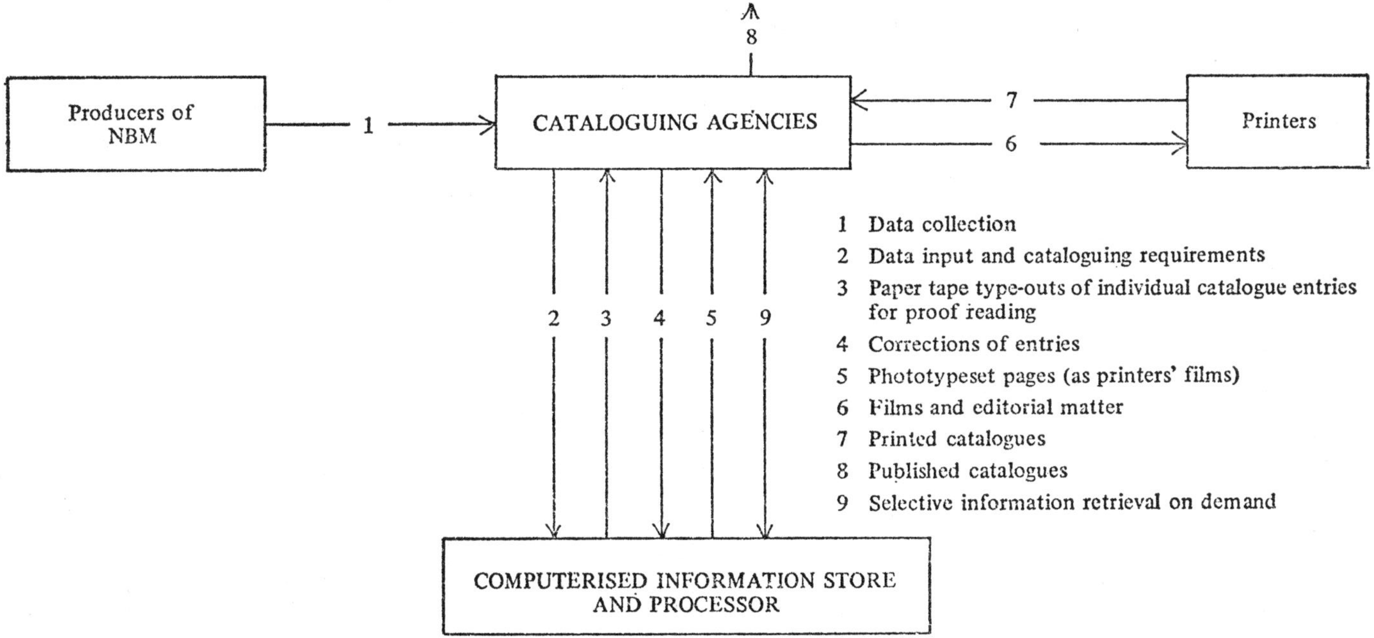

Figure 9a *Computerised cataloguing service for nonbook media* (*GILBERT, p 50*)

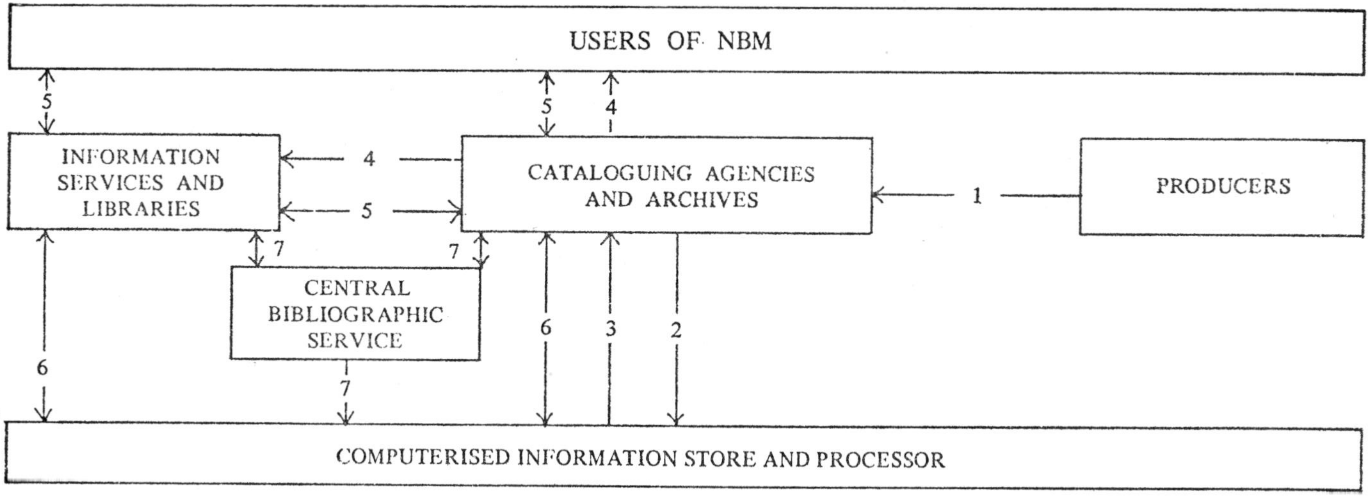

1 Data collection
2 Data input and cataloguing requirements
3 Computer-produced catalogues
4 Published catalogues
5 Enquiry service
6 Information retrieval
7 Bibliographic guidance and organisational co-ordination

Figure 9b *Overall bibliographic organisation of nonbook materials* (*GILBERT, p 52*)

L

a computer store and with cataloguing agencies, and, ultimately, with users of nonbook materials—the final objective of the exercise.

So far, we could envisage the service as providing computer-printed lists for individual enquiries. However, this concept would, in effect, put the cart before the horse. Before individual searches are initiated, it is reasonable to expect general lists to be searched, in much the same way that *Index medicus* may be searched manually before a MEDLARS (MEDical Literature Analysis and Retrieval Service) search is initiated by computer. The report, then, envisages a printed bibliographic service, which corresponds to the records of normal books covered by BNB or —in the film world—works covered by the *British national film catalogue*.

An important experiment in producing a printed bibliography of films—and noteworthily executed using a MARC-based format—has been conducted by BNB at the request of the National Council for Educational Technology. A sample of the BNB-produced catalogue of films is given in GILBERT (p 65-66) reproduced between pages 298 and 299. It will be seen that BNB-type feature headings are given to 'interpret' class numbers, *eg*

371.8 —EDUCATION. THE STUDENT

371.89— History and Geography

Sufficient information is given to identify a film technically, and to indicate (in the summary) its subject coverage and potential use.

A noteworthy quotation from GILBERT is that 'no significant problems were encountered, and that there is every reason to suppose that the MARC system can be used for the cataloguing of NBM' [nonbook materials] (p 64). The inference is that all nonbook materials could conveniently be catered for in the MARC format, and presumably entries for all forms could be integrated into one catalogue.

The sample catalogue entries would be part of a so-called HELPIS system: Higher Education Learning Programmes Information Service, as an adjunct to LERMISTOR: Learning Materials Information Store. But, confirming what we said earlier, the range of types of materials and of actual documents prepared for the system make it seem likely that the actual store of bibliographic data, and the spadework which would go into programming in the broadest sense, would encompass a lot of the work of all sorts needed to make the whole system operative.

It may be useful at this point to try to consolidate the main components of creating the type of integrated system envisaged in the report as a whole, and as demonstrated microcosmically by its sample

FIGURE 3 – SPECIMEN PAGE FROM HELPIS CATALOGUE

371.3944 – Programmed learning

The development of teaching machines and programmed learning. Bolton: Bolton Coll. of Ed. (Technical), 1968, Mr C. Hancock, Dept. of Educational Technology. TV. 1": Philips. 23mins.

Summary: Theories of programmed learning. History of programmed learning - Pressey, Crowder, Skinner. Survey of teaching machines. Recent developments. Note on use: Used with handout summarising main points.

(B71-00055)

Programmes and teaching machines in Leicestershire Junior Schools. Loughborough: Loughborough Coll. of Ed., 1965-66, Dr Leedham, Centre for Educational Technology. F. sd(mag.) col. 16mm.. 20mins.

Summary: Made in 1965/6 for Leicestershire to introduce the topic to teachers and to show some of the methods used in integrating programmes. Note on use: Useful as a commentary of development in this sphere.

(B71-00056)

What is programmed learning?. Loughborough: Loughborough Coll. of Ed., 1970, Dr Leedham, Centre for Educational Technology. TV. 1": Ampex 5103; Philips. 1/2": Shibaden; Nivico. 20mins.

Summary: This made for the APLET demonstration at NAVEX. It shows what the range is of the application of programmed learning: schools, colleges, universities, WEA, hospitals.

(B71-00057)

371.396 – Lecture method

How not to: an illustration of a short lecture containing many of the more common faults. Uxbridge: Brunel Univ., 1969, Mr R. Schofield. TV. 1": Ampex 7003. 10mins.

Summary: A lecture is given on the subject of the reliability of examinations. The intention is to provide material which will give rise to group criticism and thus to illustrate the kind of constructive discussion it is hoped to provoke by the recordings of the participants themselves.

(B71-00058)

371.4 – EDUCATION. GUIDANCE & COUNSELLING

371.42 – Educational and vocational guidance

Vocational guidance: a case study. Glasgow: Strathclyde Univ., 1970, Mr D. Willings, Dept. of Industrial Administration or Mr D. Campbell Cassidy, Audio Visual Unit. TV. 1": Ampex 7003. 60mins.

Summary: Presentation of a case based on past of a student who was wrongly advised about the subject to read at University - the implications - commentary on the process of guiding the subject to more suitable course of study.

(B71-00059)

371.46 – Social guidance

School counselling - individual - personal. Coventry: Coventry Coll. of Ed., 1969, Mr G. Kelly, Education Dept. TV. 1": Ampex 7003. 45-50mins.

Summary: Teenage girl has accidentally become involved in the theft of a car. She has not told her parents but fears they may discover the truth. The counsellor helps her to achieve the solution. Note on use: Transcript available. Sound tape in conjunction with this effective in discussion.

(B71-00060)

371.8 – EDUCATION. THE STUDENT

371.89 – History and geography

Lullingstone-69. London: Avery Hill Coll. of Ed., 1969, Avery Hill College Television Service. F. sd. (mag.) B & W. 16mm. 20mins.

Summary: Visit to a Roman villa - children at Junior School level. 1. Journey to villa.- 2. Villa interior. - 3. Classroom follow up work. Note on use: Useful also as an indication to parents of the value of this kind of visit if properly prepared in advance.

(B71-00061)

371.9 – EDUCATION. EXCEPTIONAL PUPILS

371.912 – Deaf and hard-of-hearing

Visual and audio clues. Manchester: Manchester Univ./UMIST, 1969, Director, Television Service. TV. 1": Ampex 7003. 40mins.

Summary: Mr Gordon Campbell, lecturer in parent guidance in the Department of Audiology, demonstrates various ways in which the hearing-impaired child can be helped to come to terms with the problem of communication.

(B71-00062)

372.1 – ELEMENTARY SCHOOLS

372.125 – Grouping of pupils for instruction

Brixington School. Exmouth. Rolle Coll. of Ed., 1970, Mr D. Leech. F. sd. (mag.) col. 16mm. 15 mins.

Summary: Brixington C.P. School, Exmouth was opened in 1969, purpose-built for open-plan organisation and the running of the integrated day. The film shows the children at work in the school, following their normal activities. There is no direction. The film unit always arrived without notice. The children are from 5-11 years old.

(B71-00063)

Children are people. Bromley: Stockwell College of Education, 1970, Dept. of Mass Media & Communications. F. sd. (com. opt.). col. 16mm. 42mins.

Summary: A study of vertical grouping in eleven schools in England from 5-11 years of age.

(B71-00064)

372.2 – LEVELS OF ELEMENTARY EDUCATION

372.216 – Nursery schools

The nursery school. (2 parts). Deptford: Rachel McMillan Coll. of Ed., 1968, Mrs S. Thomas. TV. 1": Ampex 7803. 60mins. each.

Summary: 1. Teacher's role in the nursery school. An hour's tape of children at play. - 2. Parents in the nursery school. A sequence of situations in which parents participate e.g. settling, medical, discussion, etc. Restrictions on use: Not for general loan. But willing to show, under supervision, in college.

(B71-00065)

372.3/8 – ELEMENTARY SCHOOL CURRICULUM

372.35 – Science

Scientific experience in the infant school. (2 parts). Cheltenham: St Mary's Coll. of Ed., 1969, Science Dept. F. st. col. standard 8. 20mins. each.

Summary: Film made on two separate locations at infant schools in Cheltenham. Practical work illustrates children's attitudes, interests, and methods of inquiry in the field of science.

(B71-00066)

372.4 – Reading

Educational technology: some aspects within the first schools. Coventry: Lancaster Poly, 1970, Mr A. Wright, Design Dept. F. sd. (mag.) B & W 16mm. 20 mins.

Summary: The film was sponsored by the Nuffield Foundation (Resources for Learning). It is about the problems of primary school children who have reading difficulties. It also concerns immigrant children who are learning English as their language. *Primary classification 37133*

i.t.a.: an introduction. Coventry: Coventry Coll. of Ed., 1970, Mr S.W. Allen, Education Dept. TV. 1": Ampex 7003,5103. 22mins.

Summary:The programme reviews the difficulties experienced by children learning to read traditional orthography and discusses ways in which Pitman's initial teaching alphabet helps to overcome these. The **i.t.a.** characters are shown, and mention is made of the availability of i.t.a. reading schemes. The programme is intended as an introduction to the subject. Note on use: There is an accompanying handout.

(B71-00067)

372.7 – Mathematics

All square. Nottingham: Nottingham Coll. of Ed., 1969, Mr A. Morley, Mathematics Dept. TV. 1": Ampex 7003. 35mins.

Summary: A study of 4 junior school children experimenting with making patterns using cardboard squares and the geometrical and arithmetical ideas that arise.

(B71-00068)

A mathematics programme for disadvantaged infant school children. Deptford: Rachel McMillan Coll. of Ed, 1970, Mr E. Choat. F. st. col. super 8. 20mins.

Summary: College/school relationships in the teaching of maths to disadvantaged infant children. The programme being formulated by the teachers. Students at work in the teacher's classes, illustrating various methods of approach. Using the environment to compensate for the lack of mathematical experiences. Restrictions on use: Not for general loan. But prepared to show, under supervision, in college.

(B71-00069)

372.72 – Arithmetic

Using Dienes apparatus. Coventry: Coventry Coll. of Ed., 1968, Mr G. Pacey, Mathematics Dept. TV. 1": Ampex 7003. 42mins.

Summary: Children at different levels use Dienes multi-base arithmetic blocks including exchanging, recording, addition and subtraction. The programme takes the form of an explanatory lecture amply illustrated by classroom situation.

(B71-00070)

Figure 10

Sample from HELPIS (Higher Education Learning Programmes Information Service) (GILBERT, *p 65-66*)

Catalogue of materials available for exchange produced in March 1971 and including a variety of audiovisual materials.

First the documents have to be made, and, as with printed monographic media, they come from a great variety of organisations, and may range from commercial materials for national or even international distribution, to perhaps items locally produced for use in just one educational institution. An example of the latter—local products—which comes to mind, though in fact Australian, is a series of videotaped lectures made in the Princess Margaret Hospital, Perth, for the education of nurses. A decision must be made somehow and somewhere as to which documents are to be recorded in the central system. A sort of parallel situation in letterpress materials might be the locally printed—or typewritten—reports on research, *eg* higher degree theses, produced by the thousand in colleges and universities. Such products may be merely academic exercises or they may transpire to embody an original contribution to their subject and therefore have value in a broader context.

We then come to the need for all such worthy documents to be catalogued, adequately and according to a generally accepted method. An obvious need is that documents on one subject but in varying physical forms and from a diversity of origins must finish up with a uniform subject heading, whether verbal or codified. This operation would call for the recognition of a uniform subject approach if it were to cater ultimately for a wholly consistent integrated record at the projected central store.

Then comes the need for items' entries to be selected and to be notified to the central store. Approaches and description need to be either consistently expressed or given fully enough in whatever form for consistent records to be brought together accurately at the catalogue compilation centre. The problem of integrating dissimilar entries for similar documents is as old as the compilation of union catalogues, and goes back to at least medieval England when a union catalogue of the manuscripts in monastery libraries was compiled. The problem is vastly intensified nowadays because of the fantastic increase in the quantity of documents, and in the present context it is inevitably exacerbated by the variety of physical forms. A J Wells has stated 'The largest single problem in system terms arises at this point since there is no unique identifier for each item which would provide a ready means of eliminating duplicate standard descriptor fields from the file. This is a major problem since the same item may be input into the data bank from any or all of the agencies' (GILBERT, p 59-60). Inevitably here we must bring up the fact of standard book numbers, and further, international standard book numbers. There is an obvious need for some form of unique identifying tag for nonbook materials, just as there has developed a system for normal books in several countries, *eg* Britain and the USA. To plan and execute such a system would involve a lot of planning, and in fact we find it hard to envisage it being carried through. Presumably a prefix for each form would be required, as well as a unique number for each document. A unique identifying system does already exist for sound recordings in disc form, even though the notation used, assigned by manufacturers (*ie* publishers), is often complex. It is conceivable that at least commercially produced documents could be subjected to the same type of routine to which publishers of books seem to have responded so well in those countries now using standard book numbers. It would appear that co-operating publishers of books have readily appreciated the value of such a system. All we can hope for at the moment is that publishers of nonbook materials would respond to the appeal and convenience of just such a system.

The next stage is the assembling and editing of bibliographic data at the relevant centre and its feeding into the store, say in computer disc form to facilitate the random access envisaged. This stage necessitates the allocation of tags and fields in a uniform way: this is why we have inferred that initial compilation of data should be made, if at all possible, according to an accepted code for author/title and description and according to a standard system for the subject approach. UDC is the most widely accepted system—whatever faults it may have at present. An advantage of UDC is that it has built-in symbols for various types of physical form, which can be represented either through the use of the colon for linking 'main' notations, or through the addition of symbols, to represent physical forms. We suggest that in a central store the use of 'main' notations would represent the type of flexibility required for access according to physical form, as well as the obvious requirement for access according to the subject of a document. Further, experiments have demonstrated that UDC—despite its occasionally awkward facet indicators—can be computerised. The inputting of bibliographic data might, we feel, be the most difficult part of the operation—possibly even more difficult than locating information in the first place. However, experiments with MARC-based formats seem to indicate that the project is viable. Input would embrace the functions of both bibliographic-oriented and retrieval-oriented catalogues, as we call them. This means that bibliographic detail in descriptions and approaches would have to be as detailed, minute, and varied as might be needed by any user of such a system. If, for example, the system were to be completely acceptable and useful, it would have to embrace ' depth indexing ' (mainly subject) as well as the more conventionally expected approaches and detail.

We now come to the ultimate objective of the system: use. It is envisaged that the data base would be drawn upon in four main ways:

(a) Machine-readable data, in the form of magnetic tape, could be obtained as required by user-libraries and resource centres, preferably using ' Standard Nonbook Numbers ' for access, but the system should cater for other approaches such as conventional author/title headings as commonly cited and as arrived at by the application of, say, AACR. We reiterate here that work is in progress on a new comprehensive nonbook code in Britain, but at the time of writing (mid-1972) this had not been produced. A decision would have to be made as to which code would be implemented, in the same way that users of MEDLARS must conform to the index language used as tags for medical subject terms. If a decision could not be reached, there would need to be additional fields to cater for tags according to the two or more codes used, either in the form of added entries or as references, to act as a sort of translation system between apparently rival headings. In fact, if a very brief unit entry method could be developed—although this would conflict with the principle of the bibliographic-oriented catalogue—it might be possible to have a multiple-entry, rather than a reference, structure, as detailed in the first chapter of this book. However the store would be structured, the resultant tapes would be used by local libraries and centres to construct catalogues for their own stocks, selecting whatever details and approaches were relevant to their needs.

(b) The central store could be used for printouts resulting from searches initiated by local libraries, etc in response to requests for comprehensive information according to any approach: subject, physical form, author, collaborator and so on. Such a function would be similar to that performed by various data banks in selected subject fields at the moment. It is envisaged that such searches would be made mainly in subject areas, with physical forms as a further basis for selection depending upon the availability of apparatus for use of the various media. But it could also be used in support of, say, experiments, or programmes for entertainment or education, using a particular medium, an obvious example being the moving film, or 'motion picture', or 'cinema' depending on the approach term used in the system.

(a) and (b) could overlap in that a local centre may acquire magnetic tapes to use in local specific subject and/or form searches.

(c) A more sophisticated application approaches the limit of accessibility to data stores usually envisaged, in that a local centre could possibly be on line to the central store. We know that mainly, according to our observation, on-line systems seem to be operated by industrial and commercial organisations. So, it is technologically feasible that a similar system could be used for objective information retrieval via a local community-oriented service. This seems a logical next stage of development leading on from the, now common, linking of libraries and information centres by teleprinters. The physical manifestation of information at the local centre—screen display, facsimile printing, or normal printout—would depend on local facilities.

(d) Finally, comes the vital factor of location of required documents. In this respect, the central store would serve as a union catalogue. A field in the store indicating local holdings would need to be established, but this could be a fairly routine matter. It could also serve as an approach for printing out of local holdings. A notation could be established to ensure that various degrees of 'local-ness' could be identified. As already mentioned in the context of subject and form approaches, UDC might be implemented here, using its 'place' numbers. Of course, union catalogues could be printed out as required.

Despite the lists produced in the US by NICEM (National Information Center for Educational Media), there is not in progress any system attempting to do all that needs to be done. I feel keenly that the time will come when either such a system has to be realised or we shall lose contact with nonbook-based information and its sources.

It is acknowledged that as yet the GILBERT proposals are confined to Britain. Today one country—tomorrow the world?

Readings

Checklist of works cited in or relevant to this chapter. Reference may also be needed to the checklist following the first chapter, on p 28-29. Documents on the computerisation of individual forms are listed in the relevant sections. Full bibliographic citations are given in the consolidated Bibliography, p 304-312. A list of abbreviations is given on p 7. The titles of periodical articles are given within quotation marks.

AACR 1967

AECT *Standards for cataloging nonprint materials*

BADTEN 'Commercial media cataloging ...'

BAKEWELL 'Cataloguing and indexing activities'

BIRMINGHAM LIBRARIES CO-OPERATIVE MECHANISATION PROJECT. MASS

BRADFORD 'New media—new methods'

BRYANT, P *The Bath mini-catalogue*

'COMMERCIAL media cataloging ...' (Library journal)

COX 'The cataloging of nonbook materials ...'

DAILY 'The selection, processing and storage of non-print materials ...'

GELLER 'A media troika and MARC ...'

GERLETTI 'Digital apoplexy ...'

GILBERT *Non-book materials: their bibliographic control ...*

HALL *Potential use of* MARC *records in three libraries ...*

ICCP

MCNALLY *A guide to the practice of non-book librarianship ...*

RIDDLE *Non-book materials: the organization of integrated collections*

RUFSVOLD 'Software: bibliographic control and the NICEM indexes'

Bibliography

At the end of each chapter, shortened references are given for works relevant to that chapter, whether or not actually cited in the text. This Bibliography cites all works in one alphabetical sequence, under headings usually according to AACR (although the purist may occasionally quarrel with our preference for personal, as opposed to corporate, headings). Where it seems necessary, an indication is added of how the work is cited in the text. There is also a separate list of abbreviations at the front of the book. In addition, the Index includes shortened entries under authors or titles of works cited substantially in the text.

This overall pattern entails some repetition, but we have decided on it to obviate searching and cross-referring as far as possible, as well as to preclude obtrusive footnotes in the text.

ALONSO, Patricia A G 'Feasibility study on computer-produced map catalogue' *Australian library journal* 21(6) July 1972 245-252.

AMERICAN GEOGRAPHICAL SOCIETY *Cataloging and filing rules for maps and atlases in the Society's collection*, by Roman Drazniowsky. Revised and expanded edition, 1969. DRAZNIOWSKY

AMERICAN LIBRARY ASSOCIATION *Division of Cataloging and Classification ALA Cataloging rules for author and title entries* (Chicago, second edition 1949). ALA 1949

ANDERSON, S 'Cataloging the contents of certain recordings' *Library resources and technical services* 9 Summer 1965 359-362.

ANGLO-AMERICAN CATALOGUING RULES British text; London: LA, 1967 (North American text; Chicago: ALA, 1967). AACR

ASHWORTH, Wilfred *Handbook of special librarianship and information work.* Third edition edited by Wilfred Ashworth (London: Aslib, 1967).

ASLIB: *Film Production Libraries Group Cataloguing Committee Film cataloguing rules* (London: Aslib, 1963). ASLIB

ASSOCIATION FOR EDUCATIONAL COMMUNICATIONS AND TECHNOLOGY *Standards for cataloging nonprint materials* (Washington, revised edition 1971).

BADTEN, Jean 'Commercial media cataloging: what's holding us up?' by Jean Badten and Nancy Motomatzu *Library journal* 93 15 November 1968 4352-3.

BAKEWELL, K G B 'Cataloguing and indexing activities' *Library Association record* 74(6) June 1972 101-102. (Includes comment on hope for the *British national film catalogue* 'to cover all types of film', and for a British national discography, at the Cataloguing and Indexing Group of the LA's seminar on the British Library.)

BARNES, C 'Classification and cataloging of spoken records in academic libraries' *College and research libraries* 28(1) January 1967 49-52.

BIRD, Richard W 'The cataloguing, classification and indexing of a collection of slides' *Catalogue & index* 4 October 1970 4.

BIRMINGHAM LIBRARIES CO-OPERATIVE MECHANISATION PROJECT. MASS (MARC-based Automated Serials System) by Birmingham Libraries Co-operative Mechanisation Project and Loughborough University of Technology Library. (Working Paper no 1, 1970.) (No publisher is 'officially' named, but enquirers are invited to contact the University of Aston in Birmingham or the University of Technology, Loughborough, for information if needed.)

BOGGS, S W *The classification and cataloging of maps and atlases,* by S W Boggs and D C Lewis (New York: Special Libraries Association, 1945). BOGGS

BOHANAN, William J 'Cataloguing A-V materials' *Eastern librarian* 4(2) 1969 132-134.

BRADFORD, Susan 'New media—new methods' *Catalogue & index* 24 Winter 1971 3-5.

BRITISH FILM INSTITUTE *Rules for use in the cataloguing department of the National Film Archive* (London, fifth revised edition 1960) BFI (See also the Institute's *Film extract catalogue* (Cover title: *Study extract catalogue*) for its examples of very full plot synopses.)

BRITISH MUSEUM *Rules for compiling the catalogue of printed books, maps and music in the British Museum* (London, revised edition 1936). BM

BROXIS, Peter F *Organising the arts* (London: Bingley, 1968—85157 051 8; Hamden, Conn: Archon Books; Melbourne: Cheshire).

BRYANT, E T *Music librarianship: a practical guide* (London: James Clarke, 1963).

BRYANT, Philip *The Bath mini-catalogue: a progress report* by Philip Bryant, Gillian M Venner and Maurice B Line (Bath, England: Bath University Library, 1972—90084 321 7). BRYANT, P

BURKETT, J *Special materials in the library: a series of 14 lectures . . .* edited by J Burkett and T S Morgan (London: LA, 1963).
CARSON, D M 'Cataloging non-book materials' *Wilson library bulletin* 39(7) March 1965 562-4.
CHAREN, Thelma 'MEDLARS abbreviations for medical journal titles' by Thelma Charen and Constantine J Gillespie *Bulletin of the Medical Library Association* 59(3) July 1971 420-429.
CHIBNALL, Bernard 'The National Film Library and its cataloguing rules' *Journal of documentation* 11 June 1955 79-82.
COATES, E J *British catalogue of music classification* (London: BNB, 1960).
COLLISON, Robert L *The treatment of special material in libraries* (London: Aslib, 1957).
'COMMERCIAL media cataloging—what's around? An SLJ survey of available services, their range of materials, cataloging policies, and marketing patterns' *Library journal* 93 November 15 1968 4345-4351.
COWLEY, J D *Bibliographical description and cataloguing* (New York: Burt Franklin, 1949). (1970 reprint.)
COX Carl T 'The cataloging of nonbook materials: basic guidelines' *Library resources and technical services* 15(4) Fall 1971 472-478.
CRONE, G R 'Notes on the classification, arrangement and cataloguing of a large map collection' (Royal Geographical Society) *Indian archives* 7 January-June 1953 8-13.
CROZET, Rene 'Cataloguing a photograph library' *Unesco bulletin for libraries* 18(3) May-June 1964 127-129.
CUMMINGS, F 'The art reference library' *College and research libraries* 27(3) May 1966 201-206.
CUNNINGHAM, V 'From Schmidt-Phiseldeck to Zanetti' *Notes* 23(3) March 1967 449-452. (On IAML vol 3, 'Code for full cataloguing'.)
CURRALL, Henry F J (*editor*) *Gramophone record libraries: their organisation and practice* (London: Crosby Lockwood, 1963); Hamden, Conn: Shoe String Press).
CUTTER, Charles A *Rules for a dictionary catalog* (Washington: Government Printing Office, fourth edition rewritten 1904). (Various reprints by LA, London.)
DAILY, Jay E 'The selection, processing, and storage of non-print materials: a critique of the Anglo-American cataloging rules as they relate to the newer media' *Library trends* 16 October 1967 283-289.
DAVINSON, D E *The periodicals collection: its purposes and uses in libraries* (London: Deutsch, 1969—233 95962 9).

DEWS, J D *The institutes of education union list of periodicals processing system,* by J D Dews and J M Smethurst (Newcastle upon Tyne, England: Oriel, 1969—85362 060 1). (Sympleglades series, no 1.)
DOVE, Jack *Music libraries;* original edition by Lionel Roy McColvin and Harold Reeves, completely rewritten, revised and extended by Jack Dove (London: Deutsch, 1965, vol 1).
DRAZNIOWSKY, Roman [Code] *see* AMERICAN GEOGRAPHICAL SOCIETY.
DRAZNIOWSKY, Roman 'The need for map cataloging' *Special libraries* 61 May-June 1970 236-237.
EASTON, William W 'Automating the Illinois State University Map Library' *Special Libraries Association bulletin* 67 1967 3-9.
FANNING, David C 'The cataloguing of film material in the National Film Archive' *Library world* 62 June 1961 280-2.
FANNING, David C 'The National Film Archive' *Library Association record* 64(2) February 1962 36-8.
FINK, Mary Ellen 'A comparison of map cataloging systems' *Special Libraries Association bulletin: Geography and Map Division* 50 December 1962 6-11.
FRIEDMAN, Joan *Cataloguing and classification in British university libraries: a survey of practices and procedures,* by Joan Friedman and Alan Jeffreys (Sheffield: University of Sheffield, Postgraduate School of Librarianship, 1967).
GAMBEE, Budd L *Non-book materials as library resources* (Chapel Hill: Student Stores, University of North Carolina, 1967).
GARRICK, A J 'A tape library index system for language laboratories' *Australian library journal* 18(1) February 1969 19-25.
GELLER, Evelyn 'A media troika and MARC: a progress report on a/v cataloging standards and services' *Library journal* 97(2) January 1972 249-253.
GERLETTI, Robert C 'Digital apoplexy: certain diagnosis, no easy cure' *Library journal* 93 15 November 1968 4354-5.
GILBERT, Leslie A *Non-book materials: their bibliographic control; a proposed computer system for the cataloguing of audio-visual materials in the United Kingdom,* by Leslie A Gilbert and Jan W Wright (London: National Council for Educational Technology, 1971—900313 21 8). GILBERT
GRAHAM, I *The cataloguing and classification of cine film at the Royal Aircraft Establishment* (Farnborough: 1959).
GREAT BRITAIN *War Office. Directorate of Military Survey. Manual of*

map classification and cataloguing, prepared for use in the Directorate of Military Survey, War Office (London: HMSO, 1947). PARSONS
GRENFELL, David 'The cataloguing of films' *Librarian and book world* 47(4) April 1958 62-4.
GRENFELL, David 'The cataloguing of newsfilm in the National Film Library' *University film journal* 8 Summer 1955 26-32.
GRENFELL, David 'Standardisation in film cataloguing' *Journal of documentation* 15(2) June 1959 81-92.
GRENFELL, David *Periodicals and serials: their treatment in special libraries* (London: Aslib, 1965).
GUNTHER, A 'Slides in documentation' *Unesco bulletin for libraries* 17(3) May-June 1963 157-62.
HAGEN, C B 'An information retrieval system for maps' *Unesco bulletin for libraries* 20(1) January-February 1966 30-35.
HALL, A R *Potential use of MARC records in three libraries: report of two surveys carried out for the Birmingham Libraries Co-operative Mechanisation Project,* by A R Hall, R M Duchesne and S W Massil (London: BNB, 1971—0 900220 32 5).
HAVARD-WILLIAMS, P 'The slide collection at Liverpool School of Architecture', by P Havard-Williams and Stella A Watson *Journal of documentation* 16(1) March 1960 11-14.
HENSEL, E 'Treatment of non-book materials' *Library trends* 2(2) October 1953 187-197.
HICKS, Warren B *The organization of nonbook materials in school libraries,* prepared by Warren B Hicks and Alma M Tillin, with Mildred M Brackett . . . (Sacramento: California State Department of Education, 1967).
HILL, T H 'Photographs: cataloguing and classification' *New Zealand libraries* 27(10) November 1964 275-283.
HORNER, John *Cataloguing* (London: Association of Assistant Librarians, 1970—900092 04 1).
INTERNATIONAL ASSOCIATION OF MUSIC LIBRARIES *Code international de catalogage de la musique* (London, New York: C F Peters, 1957-). (In progress; 3 out of 5 volumes published to date.) IAML
INTERNATIONAL CONFERENCE ON CATALOGUING PRINCIPLES *Paris, 9th-18th October 1961.* Report (London: Bingley for International Federation of Library Associations, Reprint 1969). ICCP
JOHNSON, A F *Practical cataloguing* (London: Association of Assistant Librarians, 1962).
KOSTER, C J 'Standard serial citation: bibliographical standards for

union catalogues of serials' *Catalogue & index* 21 January 1971 3-5. KOSTER

KULA, Sam *Bibliography of film librarianship* (London: LA, 1967 p 33-43).

LEE, R J *English county maps . . .* (London: LA, 1955). (LA pamphlet no 13.)

LIBRARY ASSOCIATION *Cataloguing rules: author and title entries*, compiled by committees of the Library Association and American Library Association. English edition (London, 1908). (Various reprints.) AA 1908

LIBRARY OF CONGRESS: *Descriptive Cataloging Division Rules for descriptive cataloging in the Library of Congress* (adopted by the American Library Association) (Washington, 1949). LCRDC

LIBRARY OF CONGRESS: *Information Systems Office Maps: a MARC format; specifications for magnetic tapes containing catalog records for maps* (Washington, 1970).

LIBRARY OF CONGRESS: *Processing Department Descriptive Cataloging Division Rules for descriptive cataloging in the Library of Congress: motion pictures and filmstrips*, second preliminary edition (Washington, 1958).

LIBRARY OF CONGRESS: *Processing Department Descriptive Cataloging Division Rules for descriptive cataloging in the Library of Congress: pictures, designs and other two-dimensional representations* (Washington, preliminary edition, 1959).

LIBRARY OF CONGRESS *Subject headings used in the Library of Congress* (Washington, seventh edition, 1966).

LUBETZKY, Seymour *Code of cataloging rules: author and title entry; an unfinished draft . . .*, with an explanatory commentary by Paul Dunkin (Chicago: ALA, 1960). CCR 1960

MCNALLY, Paul Terence *A guide to the practice of non-book librarianship . . .* (Toowoomba, Queensland: Darling Downs Institute of Advanced Education, 1972).

MASON, Donald *A primer of non-book materials in libraries; with an appendix on sound recordings by Jean C Cowan* (London: Association of Assistant Librarians, 1958).

MASSONNEAU, Suzanne 'Cataloging nonbook materials: mountain or molehill?' *Library resources and technical services* 16 (3), Summer 1972 294-314.

MURPHY, Mary 'Map collection prepared to automate: the US Army

Topographical Command Library' *Special libraries* April 1970 180-189.

MUSIC LIBRARY ASSOCIATION *Code for cataloging music and phonorecords; prepared by a Joint Committee of the Music Library Association and the American Library Association* . . . (Chicago: ALA, 1958). MLA

NLL *review* 2(1) January 1972. (NLL news in this issue includes notes on: Current serials received by the NLL, March 1971; and KWIC index to English language abstracting and indexing periodicals currently being received by the National Lending Library.)

NEW YORK PUBLIC LIBRARY *Music subject headings authorized for use in the catalogs of the Music Division* (Boston, Mass: Hall, 1959).

NOLAN, John L 'Audio-visual materials' *Library trends* 10 October 1961 261-272.

NOVIKOVA, Elena Andreevna 'Actual problems of contemporary music cataloging' *Notes* 23 1966/1967 103-117.

OSBORN, Andrew D *Serial publications: their place and treatment in libraries* (Chicago: ALA, 1955).

PARSONS, Edward J S *see* GREAT BRITAIN, *War Office*.

PIERCY, Esther J *Commonsense cataloging: a manual for the organization of books and other materials in school and small public libraries* (New York: 1965). (1966 reprint.)

The PRUSSIAN *instructions: rules for the alphabetical catalogues of the Prussian libraries,* translated from the second edition by Andrew Osborn (Ann Arbor, 1938). PI

QUIGG, Patrick 'How to make a union catalogue' *Catalogue & index* 13 January 1969 14-15. Pursued by a letter from D H Boolch *Catalogue & index* April 1969.

QUIGG, Patrick *Theory of cataloguing: an examination guidebook* (London: Bingley, second edition revised 1968—85157 061 5; Hamden, Conn: Archon Books).

REDFERN, Brian *Organizing music in libraries* (London: Bingley, 1966; Sydney: Bennett).

RIDDLE, Jean *Non-book materials: the organization of integrated collections* by Jean Riddle, Shirley Lewis and Janet Macdonald, in consultation with the Technical Services Committee of the Canadian School Library Association (Ottawa: Canadian Library Association, 1970). (Also later version by same authors under WEIHS).

RISTOW, Walter W 'The Library of Congress: computerized map

cataloging project' by Walter W Ristow and David K Carrington *International library review* 2 1970 391-397.
RISTOW, Walter W 'What about maps?' *Library trends* 4 October 1955 123-39.
ROGERS, Derek 'Works of art' *Catalogue & index* 5 January 1967 4-6; and 6 April 1967 10-11.
ROTH, Dana L 'Scientific serial lists' *Journal of library automation* 5(1) March 1972 51-57.
ROYAL GEOGRAPHICAL SOCIETY *Storage and conservation of maps* (London: 1955).
RUFSVOLD, Margaret I *Audio-visual school library service: a handbook for librarians* (Chicago: ALA, 1949). (1964 reprint.)
RUFSVOLD, Margaret I 'Software: bibliographic control and the NICEM indexes' by Margaret I Rufsvold and Carolyn Guss *School libraries* Winter 1971 11-20.
SCHOLZ, Dell Dubose *A manual for the cataloging of recordings in public libraries* (Louisiana Library Association, 1964).
SEAGER, Margaret 'Order of entries' [of serials] *Library Association record* 73(10) October 1971 199 (letter).
SEMINAR ON THE ANGLO-AMERICAN CATALOGUING RULES 1967 . . . *Proceedings of the seminar organised by the Cataloguing and Indexing Group of the Library Association* . . ., edited by J C Downing and N F Sharp (London: LA, 1969—85365 271 6).
SOMERVILLE, S A 'Cataloguing of gramophone records' *Librarian* 48(5) July 1959 97-99.
STEELE, Robert *The cataloging and classification of cinema literature* (Metuchen, NJ: Scarecrow, 1967).
STEWARD, Bruce Warren *A computerized serials record system for the Texas A & M University Library* (Texas: College Station, 1966).
THOMPSON, A 'Rules for subject headings, periodicals subject index, Royal Institute of British Architects' *Journal of documentation* 19(3) September 1963.
TREZISE, M 'Gramophone record libraries in Australia' *Australian library journal* 17 December 1968 377-382.
UNESCO: *Department of Mass Communication Clearing House International rules for the cataloguing of educational, scientific and cultural films and filmstrips* . . . (Paris, preliminary edition 1956).
UNESCO
US *Office of Strategic Services Research and Analysis Branch Map Division Cataloguer's manual* (Washington, revised edition 1944).

UNIVERSITY OF BRITISH COLUMBIA *Library A computer-based catalogue system for phono-disc and tape recordings* (Vancouver, BC: 1969).

URQUHART, D J 'The regional bureaux and the NLL' *Library Association record* 22(1) January 1970 11-14.

WALL, R A 'Codification of periodical titles: a note on ASTM Coden versus standard serial numbers', by R A Wall and C W J Wilson *Library Association record* 72(5) May 1970 188-190. (Includes useful short list of references.) WALL

WASSERMAN, Morton N 'A computer-prepared book catalog for engineering transparencies' *Special libraries* 57, February 1966 111-113.

WEIHS *see* RIDDLE

WHATMORE, Geoffrey *News information: the organization of press cuttings in the libraries of newspaper and broadcasting services* (London: Crosby Lockwood, 1964).

WHITE, Brenda *Slide collections: a survey of their organisation in libraries in the fields of architecture, building and planning* (Edinburgh, 1967).

WOODS, Bill M 'Map cataloging: inventory and prospect' *Library resources and technical services* 3(4) Fall 1959 257-273.

Index

Specific topics which are scattered in the text (*eg* description, individual codes) receive index entries, with appropriate qualifying terms where necessary. The Index does not, in general, collocate items which are brought together in the text of the book. When a topic is dealt with at length at a particular point in the text, these pages are cited first. '*See*' references are given from 'unused' synonyms' to 'used' terms. Occasionally, where a specific topic is inferred by more generalised treatment in the text, 'upwards' references are used, *eg* from 'novels' to 'literary works', and from 'pictures' to 'slides, etc'. Initials come at the beginning of the relevant letter, but acronyms are filed as words. References from full names and titles to initials or acronyms are given where considered necessary, but in addition a list of the most-used abbreviations is given on page 7. An illustration relating to a topic is designated by '*illus*' under a term, although examples in general are not identified as such. Bibliographic citations of works referred to in the text are indicated by '*bib cit*'.